STUDY GUIDE FOR

Lippincott Williams & Wilkins'

ADMINISTRATIVE
Medical Assisting

SECOND EDITION

Laura Southard Durham, BS, CMA

Medical Assisting Technologies Program Coordinator
Forsyth Technical Community College
Winston-Salem, North Carolina

 Wolters Kluwer | Lippincott Williams & Wilkins
Health
Philadelphia • Baltimore • New York • London
Buenos Aires • Hong Kong • Sydney • Tokyo

Executive Editor: John Goucher
Managing Editor: Jennifer Walsh
Senior Marketing Manager: Nancy Bradshaw
Design Coordinator: Stephen Druding
Production Editor: Beth Martz
Compositor: Maryland Composition

To purchase additional copies of this book, call our customer service department at (800) 638-3030 or fax orders to **(301) 223-2320**. International customers should call **(301) 223-2300.**

Visit Lippincott Williams & Wilkins on the Internet: http://www.LWW.com. Lippincott Williams & Wilkins customer service representatives are available from 8:30 am to 6:00 pm, EST.

05 06 07 08 09
1 2 3 4 5 6 7 8 9 10

Preface

Welcome to the completely revised *Study Guide* to accompany *Lippincott Williams & Wilkins' Administrative Medical Assisting, 2e*. This Study Guide is a learning resource that will help you to apply your knowledge of the information in the textbook, create Work Products that will establish a winning Portfolio, and master the skills needed to become a successful medical assistant. To help you get the most out of your studies, we've included a variety of exercises that will help reinforce the material you learned and build your critical thinking skills. This *Study Guide* is unique in a number of ways and offers features that most Medical Assisting study guides do not.

The *Study Guide* contains exercises that will reinforce your skills and knowledge of the Medical Assisting field. Each chapter includes the following:

- **Chapter Checklist**—This feature will guide you as you work through the chapter and begin to create your Portfolio.
- **Learning Objectives**—Listed at the beginning of each chapter and highlighted within the Chapter Notes.
- **Chapter Notes**—This feature includes the text headings in the left column and blank spaces for note-taking in the right column.
- **Content Review**—This feature is divided into two parts: Foundations Knowledge and Application. The Foundation section contains Key Terms, Matching Exercises, and Review Questions. The Application section features Critical

Thinking Practice questions; Patient Education questions; and Documentation Practice exercises.
- **Active Learning Exercises**—These exercises require you to become an active participant in your learning and will allow you to apply your recently acquired knowledge and skills to the medical assisting profession. Active Learning exercises will help you retain new information, build confidence, and show you how to gather information and learn from sources other than the textbook.
- **Professional Journal Page(s)**—Each chapter will include a Journal page that will encourage you to Reflect, Ponder, Solve, and Experience.
- **Skill Practice**—These exercises include Skill Practice Activities, Forms, Work Products, and Competency Evaluation Forms.
- **Chapter Self-Assessment Quiz**—These quizzes are comprised of multiple-choice questions consistent with the certification exam format.
- **Skill Sheets**—These are included for every procedure in the textbook. Each form has a place for students to complete a self-evaluation, partners to evaluate them, and, finally, for the instructor's evaluation.

This *Study Guide* has been developed in response to numerous requests from students and instructors for a concise, understandable, and interactive resource that covers the skills necessary to become successful in the Medical Assisting field.

Reviewers

Lippincott Williams & Wilkins gratefully acknowledges the contributions of the following reviewers for their valuable comments and suggestions:

Gerry Brasin, CMA, AS, CPC
Education Coordinator
Premier Education Group
Springfield, MA

Sherry Brewer, CMA-AC, BS
Preceptor
Medical Assisting Department
Cuyahoga Community College
Cleveland, OH

Patricia Donahue, MS
Associate Professor
Office and Computer Programs Department
Monroe Community College
Rochester, NY

Sharon Harris-Pelliccia, BS, RPAC
Department Chair, Medical Studies
Mildred Elley
Latham, NY

Joyce Minton, MA
Program Director
Medical Assisting Department
Wilkes Community College
Wilkesboro, NC

Brigitte Niedzwiecki, RN, BSN, MSN
Medical Assistant Program Director
Chippewa Valley Technical College
Eau Claire, WI

Marianne Van Deursen, BS
Medical/Dental Assisting Director
Continuing Ed
Warren County Community College
Washington, NJ

Contents

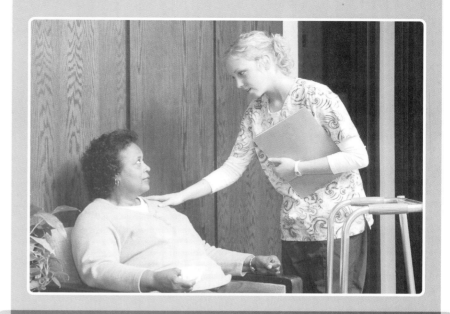

PART

I

Introduction to Medical Assisting

Understanding the Profession

CHAPTER 1

Medicine and Medical Assisting

Chapter Checklist

- ☐ Read textbook chapter and take notes within the Chapter Notes outline. Answer the Learning Objectives as you reach them in the content, and then check them off.
- ☐ Work the Content Review questions—both Foundational Knowledge and Application.
- ☐ Perform the Active Learning exercise(s).

- ☐ Complete Professional Journal entries.
- ☐ Complete Skill Practice Activity(s) using Competency Evaluation Forms and Work Products, when appropriate.
- ☐ Take the Chapter Self-Assessment Quiz.
- ☐ Insert all appropriate pages into your Portfolio.

Learning Objectives

1. Spell and define the key terms.
2. Summarize a brief history of medicine.
3. Identify the key founders of medical science.
4. Explain the system of health care in the United States.
5. Discuss the typical medical office.
6. List medical specialties a medical assistant may encounter.
7. List settings in which medical assistants may be employed.
8. List the duties of a medical assistant.
9. Describe the desired characteristics of a medical assistant.
10. Identify members of the health care team.
11. Explain the pathways of education for medical assistants.
12. Discuss the importance of program accreditation.
13. Name and describe the two nationally recognized accrediting agencies for medical assisting education programs.
14. Explain the benefits and avenues of certification for the medical assistant.
15. List the benefits of membership in a professional organization.

Chapter Notes

Note: Bold-faced headings are the major headings in the text chapter; headings in regular font are lower-level headings (i.e., the content is subordinate to, or falls "under," the major headings). Make sure you understand the key terms used in the chapter, as well as the concepts presented as Key Points.

TEXT SUBHEADINGS   **NOTES**

Introduction _____

_____

> **Key Term:** multiskilled health professional
> **Key Point:**
> • You have selected a fascinating and challenging career,
>   one of the fastest growing specialties in the medical field.

☐ **LEARNING OBJECTIVE 1:** Spell and define the key terms.

History of Medicine _____

_____

Ancient Medical History _____

_____

> **Key Term:** caduceus
> **Key Point:**
> • Some of these early medications played a key role in the
>   development of our modern pharmacology.

☐ **LEARNING OBJECTIVE 2:** Summarize a brief history of medicine.

Modern Medical History _____

_____

> **Key Point:**
> • Great minds collaborated to advance medical and scientific
>   theories and perform experiments that led to discoveries of
>   enormous benefit in the fight against disease.

☐ **LEARNING OBJECTIVE 3:** Identify the key founders of medical science.

Strides in the Prevention of Disease Transmission _____

_____

_____

Possibilities in Surgery _____

_____

_____

Women in Medicine _____

_____

Important Discoveries

Recent Medical History

Key Term: medical assistant
Key Points:
- Throughout the next three decades, public health protection improved and advancements continued. Government legislation mandated clean water, and citizens reaped the benefits of preventive medicine and education about health issues.
- New discoveries will continue to expand the parameters of medicine as further research in recombinant DNA, transplantation, immunizations, diagnostic procedures, and so forth push back the boundaries of health care and make today's therapies seem as primitive as those we have just covered.

The American Health Care System

Key Term: outpatient
Key Point:
- The allied health care arena has grown quickly. New professions have been added to the health care team, and each one is an important part of a patient's total care.

☐ **LEARNING OBJECTIVE 4:** Explain the system of health care in the United States.

The Medical Office

Key Point:
- The patient's health care encounter can be pleasant or unpleasant, depending on the skills and the attitude of the team.

☐ **LEARNING OBJECTIVE 5:** Discuss the typical medical office.

Medical Specialties

Key Term: specialty

☐ **LEARNING OBJECTIVE 6:** List medical specialties a medical assistant may encounter.

The Medical Assisting Profession _____

_____

_____

What Is a Medical Assistant? _____

_____

Key Terms: clinical; administrative

☐ **LEARNING OBJECTIVE 7:** List settings in which medical assistants may be employed.

Duties of a Medical Assistant _____

_____

Key Term: laboratory

Administrative Duties _____

_____

Clinical Duties _____

_____

_____

Laboratory Duties _____

_____

☐ **LEARNING OBJECTIVE 8:** List the duties of a medical assistant.

Characteristics of a Professional Medical Assistant _____

_____

Key Point:
• Medical assistants play a key role in creating and maintaining a professional image for their employers.

☐ **LEARNING OBJECTIVE 9:** Describe the desired characteristics of a medical assistant.

Members of the Health Care Team _____

Key Term: multidisciplinary
Key Point:
• A multidisciplinary team is a group of specialized professionals who are brought together to meet the needs of the patient.

☐ **LEARNING OBJECTIVE 10:** Identify members of the health care team.

Health Care Providers _____

Physicians _____

Physicians Assistants _____

Key Point:
• Their scope of practice corresponds to the supervising physician's practice.

Nurse Practitioners _____

The Nursing Profession _____

Key Term: inpatient
Key Point:
• Nurses work with physicians and implement various patient care needs in the **inpatient** or hospital setting.

Allied Health Professionals _____

The History of Medical Assisting _____

Key Point:
• The need for a highly trained professional with a background in administrative and clinical skills led to the formation of an alternative field of allied health care.

Medical Assisting Education _____

Key Term: externship
Key Point:
• After you finish school, your education should not stop.

☐ **LEARNING OBJECTIVE 11:** Explain the pathways of education for medical assistants.

Medical Assisting Program Accreditation _____

Key Term: accreditation

☐ **LEARNING OBJECTIVE 12:** Discuss the importance of program accreditation.

The Commission of Accreditation of Allied Health Education Programs _____

The Accrediting Bureau of Health Education Schools _____

Key Term: certification

☐ **LEARNING OBJECTIVE 13:** Name and describe the two nationally recognized accrediting agencies for medical assisting education programs.

Medical Assisting Certification _____

☐ **LEARNING OBJECTIVE 14:** Explain the benefits and avenues of certification for the medical assistant.

Certified Medical Assistant _____

_____

Key Terms: recertification; continuing education unit

Registered Medical Assistant _____

_____

Medical Assisting and Related Allied Health Associations _____

_____

Association Membership _____

_____

☐ **LEARNING OBJECTIVE 15:** List the benefits of membership in a professional organization.

American Association of Medical Assistants _____

_____

Key Point:
• The purpose of the AAMA is to promote the professional identity and stature of its members and the medical assisting profession through education and credentialing.

American Medical Technologists _____

_____

Key Point:
• The AMT and its governing body are set up similarly to the AMAA, with local, state, and national affiliations, opportunities for continuing education, professional benefits, and a professional journal.

Professional Coder Associations _____

_____

The American Health Information Management Association _____

_____

Employment Opportunities _____

_____

Key Point:
• Because of the flexible, multiskilled nature of their education, medical assistants can work in a variety of health care settings.

Content Review

FOUNDATIONAL KNOWLEDGE

1. A Brief History

Place the following list of events in the correct order in the table, with 1 being the oldest event, and 6 being the most recent.

a. Moses is appointed the first public health officer.

b. Hippocrates turns medicine into a science.

c. Egyptians perform the first skull surgeries.

d. The bubonic plague sweeps Europe and Asia and kills millions.

e. The Greek physician Galen is the first to document a patient's pulse.

f. The Renaissance fosters great strides in medicine.

1.	**2.**	**3.**
4.	**5.**	**6.**

2. Great Thinkers

Modern history is filled with notable individuals who made great breakthroughs in the field of medicine. Without their efforts, many of us wouldn't be alive today! In the chart below, draw a line to match the scientist with his or her contribution to medicine.

Scientist	Contribution to Medicine
1. Andreas Vesalius	**a.** Founder of modern nursing
2. Edward Jenner	**b.** Discovered x-rays
3. Louis Pasteur	**c.** Discovered the smallpox vaccine
4. Florence Nightingale	**d.** "Father of Modern Anatomy"; wrote the first relatively correct anatomy book
5. Wilhelm Konrad Roentgen	**e.** Invented pasteurization, which eliminated bacterial transmission

3. My Country, My Health Care

What is the purpose of the Centers for Medicare and Medicaid Services?

_____

_____

4. The following are three specialists who may employ medical assistants. Describe what each does.

a. allergist: _____

b. internist: _____

c. gynecologist: _____

5. Name That Task

As a medical assistant, you must be "multiskilled," or skilled at completing many different tasks. Almost all the tasks you will complete fall into one of two categories: administrative and clinical. But what's the difference between administrative and clinical tasks? Read each selection below and determine whether the task requires your clinical or administrative skills, then place a check in the appropriate column.

Task	Administrative	Clinical
a. preparing patients for examinations		
b. maintaining medical records		
c. ensuring good public relations		
d. obtaining medical histories		
e. preparing and sterilizing instruments		
f. screening sales representatives		

6. You've Got Character
Read the following scenario and answer the question below.

Mrs. Esposito approaches Jan, a medical assistant, at the front desk. Jan has recently treated Mrs. Esposito's son, Manuel, for a foot injury. Mrs. Esposito asks Jan if she may have her son's medical records to show Manuel's soccer coach that he will be unable to play for the rest of the season. Jan explains to Mrs. Esposito that because her son is 18 and legally an adult, she must have his permission to release his medical records. Mrs. Esposito is furious, but Jan calmly explains that the physician would be happy to write a note for Manuel to give to his soccer coach explaining his injuries. Mrs. Esposito thanks her for this information and apologizes for becoming angry.

From the list below, circle the **two** characteristics of a professional medical assistant that Jan exhibited in the above scenario.

Accuracy	Good interpersonal skills
Ability to respect patient confidentiality	Ability to work as a team player
Honesty	Initiative and responsibility

7. Name That Person

I am generally regarded as the team leader. I am responsible for diagnosing and treating the patient. Who am I?

_____

_____

8. Review the list of job titles below. Circle those that are considered allied health professionals.

Dentist	Electrocardiograph Technician	Nurse
Health Information Technologist	Medical Assistant	Physician Assistant
Nuclear Medical Technician	Nutritionist	Physical Therapist
Nurse Practitioner	Pharmacist	Risk Manager

9. What Came Next. . . ?

Medical assisting has been practiced as a profession for less than 100 years, so the profession has grown rapidly to meet the needs of patients. Read the following events in the left column and place them in the correct order in the right column, with 1 being the oldest event and 5 being the most recent.

a. The American Association of Medical Assistants (AAMA) was founded.	**1.**
b. The Board of Trustees of the AAMA approved the current definition of medical assisting.	**2.**
c. A certification examination for CMA was conducted and set the standards for medical assistant education.	**3.**
d. Dr. M. Mandl opened the first school for medical assistants.	**4.**
e. Illinois recognized the AAMA as a not-for-profit educational organization.	**5.**

10. Julia is a student in her last year of a medical assisting program. What must she complete before graduating?

    a. Certification

    b. An associate's degree

    c. An externship

    d. Curriculum

11. Who is eligible to take the RMA examination? Circle all that apply.

    a. Medical assistants who have been employed as medical instructors for a minimum of five years

    b. Medical assistants who have been employed in the profession for a minimum of five years

    c. Graduates from ABHES-accredited medical assisting programs

    d. Graduates from CAAHEP-accredited medical assisting programs

12. Sign Me Up!

As a medical assistant wishing to learn more about the medical field, you may decide to join a national organization, such as the American Association of Medical Assistants. Can you name three of the six benefits of association membership?

    1. _____

    2. _____

    3. _____

13. Employment

Complete the following sentence with the correct word from the word bank.

Medical assistants work under the direct supervision of a licensed _____ .

nurse	medical assisting instructor
health care provider	medical office manager

14. Jamie would like to become a medical assistant and asks for your advice. Describe his educational options and suggest what program might be best for him.

_____

_____

15. You feel strongly about attending a program that has accreditation. Your friend also wants to attend school to become a medical assistant and doesn't understand why accreditation is important. What would you tell him?

_____

_____

16. Name the two nationally recognized accrediting agencies.

    1. _____

    2. _____

17. The AAMA and AMT have developed certification examinations that test the knowledge of a graduate and indicate entry-level competency. Review the information about the interested applicants in the chart below and indicate if they are eligible for the CMA or RMA exam or both.

Interested Applicants	Eligible for the CMA Exam	Eligible for the RMA Exam
1. Jorge graduated from an ABHES-accredited medical assisting program.		
2. Carla graduated from a CAAHEP-accredited medical assisting program.		
3. Jason has been working as a medical assistant for almost six years.		

18. List three settings in which a medical assistant may be employed.

a. _____

b. _____

c. _____

19. Match the following key terms to their definitions.

Key Terms

a. caduceus _____

b. medical assistant _____

c. outpatient _____

d. specialty _____

e. clinical _____

f. administrative _____

g. laboratory _____

h. multidisciplinary _____

i. inpatient _____

j. externship _____

k. accreditation _____

l. certification _____

m. recertification _____

Definitions

1. completed by a CMA every 5 years by either taking the examination again or by acquiring 60 CEU's

2. describing a medical facility where patients receive care but are not admitted overnight

3. a subcategory of medicine that a physician chooses to practice upon graduation from medical school

4. referring to a team of specialized professionals who are brought together to meet the needs of the patient

5. regarding a medical facility that treats patients and keeps them overnight, often accompanied by surgery or other procedure

6. a medical symbol showing a wand or staff with two serpents coiled around it

7. voluntary process that involves a testing procedure to prove an individual's baseline competency in a particular area

8. regarding tasks that involve direct patient care

9. an educational course during which the student works in the field gaining hands-on experience

10. a multiskilled health care professional who performs a variety of tasks in a medical setting

11. a nongovernmental professional peer review process that provides technical assistance and evaluates educational programs for quality based on pre-established academic and administrative standards

12. regarding tasks that involve scientific testing

13. regarding tasks that focus on office procedures

20. True or False? Determine whether the following statements are true or false. If false, explain why.

a. The Hippocratic Oath is still a part of medical school graduation ceremonies.

b. The makeup of the medical team is the same for every office.

c. Recertification can only be obtained by taking the examination again.

d. The purpose of the AAMA is to promote the professional identity and stature of its members and the medical assisting profession through education and credentialing.

APPLICATION

Critical Thinking Practice

1. Why is the ability to respect patient confidentiality essential to the role of the medical assistant?

_____

_____

2. The medical office in which you work treats a variety of patients, from all ages and backgrounds. Why should you work with a multidisciplinary health care team? What are the benefits to the patients?

_____

_____

Patient Education

1. You are preparing a patient for her examination, but the physician is running behind schedule. The patient is becoming anxious and asks you to perform the examination, instead of the physician. You tell her that you will go check how much longer the physician will be. But she responds, "Can't you just perform the exam? Aren't you like a nurse?" How should you respond?

_____

_____

Documentation

1. The patient who asked you to perform the examination now refuses to wait for the physician. Even though she has a serious heart condition requiring monthly check-ups, she leaves without being treated by the physician. You need to write a note that will be included in her chart and in an incident report. What would you say?

_____

_____

Active Learning

1. Many of the Roman and Greek gods and goddesses were symbols of health and medicine. Research on the Internet for information about caduceus. Write a paragraph explaining when and why modern Western culture adopted this symbol. Then, draw your own symbol for medical assisting and explain what each part represents.

2. Talk with a grandparent or another older adult, and ask him or her to tell you about a medical discovery that he or she remembers well. Create a "before and after" chart, explaining what life was like before the discovery, and the changes and benefits that came about after the discovery.

3. Review the list of specialists who employ medical assistants in textbook Table 1-2. Choose one specialist that interests you the most. Perform research on what kinds of procedures the specialist performs. Then consider what kinds of tasks a medical assistant employed by this specialist might perform. Write a letter to this specialist explaining why you would want to work in this kind of office. Be sure to include specific references to the tasks and procedures that interest you based on your research.

Professional Journal

REFLECT

(Prompts and Ideas: Are you concerned about meeting the patient needs and the standards of day-to-day operations in a medical office? Are you concerned about your ability to complete clinical and administrative tasks? Think about the medical office that you visit as a patient. In what ways does the medical assistant keep the office running smoothly? What changes would you like to see?)

_____

_____

_____

_____

_____

PONDER AND SOLVE

1. Scope of practice for medical assistants can vary from state to state. In some states, certified medical assistants are not allowed to perform invasive procedures, such as injections or laboratory testing. Why is it important to understand your scope of practice before beginning work in a new medical office?

_____

_____

2. What are the ways in which an externship prepares you for your career as a medical assistant?

_____

_____

_____

_____

_____

_____

_____

_____

Chapter Self-Assessment Quiz

1. The earliest recorded evidence of medical history dates to the early:
   a. Greeks.
   b. Romans.
   c. Egyptians.
   d. Christians.
   e. Chinese.

2. Which of the following is true of the Middle Ages?
   a. Medicine focused on comforting patients rather than finding cures for disease.
   b. The establishment of universities helped spread the practice of medicine.
   c. Vesalius wrote the first relatively correct anatomy textbook.
   d. Advances in sanitation promoted good personal hygiene practices.
   e. Anton von Leeuwenhoek invented the microscope.

3. Marie and Pierre Curie revolutionized the principles of:

 a. nursing.

 b. disease.

 c. infection.

 d. physics.

 e. radioactivity.

4. The medical assistant's role will expand over time because of:

 a. a growing population.

 b. the risk of disease and infection.

 c. advances in medicine and technology.

 d. a financial boom.

 e. more effective training programs.

5. What drives the management practices of the outpatient medical facility?

 a. The desire to compete with other medical facilities

 b. The need to adhere to government rules and regulations

 c. The attempt to fit into mainstream medical opinion

 d. The effort to retain medical employees

 e. The focus on hiring specialized health care workers

6. Which of the following tasks is the administrative team responsible for in the medical office?

 a. Physical examinations

 b. Financial aspects of the practice

 c. Laboratory test processing

 d. Minor office surgery

 e. Drawing blood

7. Which of the following is a clinical duty?

 a. Scheduling appointments

 b. Obtaining medical histories

 c. Handling telephone calls

 d. Filing insurance forms

 e. Implementing ICD-9 and CPT coding for insurance claims

8. Empathy is the ability to:

 a. care deeply for the health and welfare of patients.

 b. keep your temper in check.

 c. show all patients good manners.

 d. remain calm in an emergency.

 e. feel pity for sick patients.

9. If a patient refers to you as a "nurse," you should:

 a. call the physician.

 b. ignore the mistake.

 c. politely correct him.

 d. send him home.

 e. ask the nurse to come into the room.

10. A group of specialized people who are brought together to meet the needs of the patient is called:

 a. multiskilled.

 b. multifaceted.

 c. multitasked.

 d. multidisciplinary.

 e. multitrained.

11. A medical assistant falls into the category of:

 a. nurse.

 b. physician assistant.

 c. medical office manager.

 d. allied health professional.

 e. office manager.

12. The discovery of which vaccine opened the door to an emphasis on preventing disease rather than simply trying to cure preventable illnesses?

 a. Smallpox

 b. Cowpox

 c. Puerperal fever

 d. Typhoid

 e. Influenza

13. In 1991, which group approved the current definition of medical assisting?

 a. The U.S. Department of Health and Education

 b. The Health Management Organization

 c. The American Medical Technologists

 d. The American Association of Medical Assistants

 e. The State Department of Health

14. All accredited programs must include a(n):

 a. medical terminology course.

 b. computer course.

 c. externship.

 d. certification examination.

 e. multidisciplinary program.

15. What is the requirement for admission to the CMA examination?

   a. Successful completion of 60 CEUs

   b. Successful completion of an externship

   c. Graduation from high school

   d. Graduation from an accredited medical assisting program

   e. Successful completion of a GED program

16. An oncologist diagnoses and treats:

   a. disorders of the musculoskeletal system.

   b. disorders of the ear, nose, and throat.

   c. pregnant women.

   d. the aging population.

   e. benign and malignant tumors.

17. A CMA is required to recertify every:

   a. 1 year.

   b. 2 years.

   c. 5 years.

   d. 10 years.

   e. 15 years.

18. Which organization offers the RMA examination?

   a. American Medical Technologists

   b. American Association of Medical Assistants

   c. American Academy of Professional Coders

   d. American Health Information Management Association

   e. American Board of Medical Specialties

19. Which of the following is a benefit of association membership?

   a. Time off from work

   b. Networking opportunities

   c. Hotel expenses

   d. Free health insurance

   e. Externship placement

20. Which specialist diagnoses and treats disorders of the stomach and intestine?

   a. Endocrinologist

   b. Gastroenterologist

   c. Gerontologist

   d. Podiatrist

   e. Internist

2

Law and Ethics

☐ Read textbook chapter and take notes within the Chapter Notes outline. Answer the Learning Objectives as you reach them in the content, and then check them off.

☐ Work the Content Review questions—both Foundational Knowledge and Application.

☐ Perform the Active Learning exercise(s).

☐ Complete Professional Journal entries.

☐ Complete Skill Practice Activity(s) using Competency Evaluation Forms and Work Products, when appropriate.

☐ Take the Chapter Self-Assessment Quiz.

☐ Insert all appropriate pages into your Portfolio.

1. Spell and define the key terms.
2. Identify the two branches of the American legal system.
3. List the elements and types of contractual agreements and describe the difference in implied and express contracts.
4. List four items that must be included in a contract termination or withdrawal letter.
5. List six items that must be included in an informed consent form and explain who may sign consent forms.
6. List five legally required disclosures that must be reported to specified authorities.
7. Describe the four elements that must be proven in a medical legal suit.
8. Describe four possible defenses against litigation for the medical professional.
9. Explain the theory of respondeat superior, or law of agency, and how it applies to the medical assistant.

10. List ways that a medical assistant can assist in the prevention of a medical malpractice suit.
11. Outline the laws regarding employment and safety issues in the medical office.
12. List the requirements of the Americans with Disabilities Act relating to the medical office.
13. Differentiate between legal issues and ethical issues.
14. List the seven American Medical Association principles of ethics.
15. List the five ethical principles of ethical and moral conduct outlined by the American Association of Medical Assistants.
16. Describe the purpose of the Self-Determination Act.
17. List 10 opinions of the American Medical Association's Council pertaining to administrative office procedures.

Note: Bold-faced headings are the major headings in the text chapter; headings in regular font are lower-level headings (i.e., the content is subordinate to, or falls "under," the major headings). Make sure you understand the key terms used in the chapter, as well as the concepts presented as Key Points.

TEXT SUBHEADINGS	NOTES
Introduction _____	

Key Term: fraud

☐ **LEARNING OBJECTIVE 1:** Spell and define the key terms.

The American Legal System _____

Key Term: litigation
Key Point:
• Our legal system is in place to ensure the rights of all citizens.

Sources of Law _____

Key Terms: common law; stare decisis; precedents
Key Point:
• The foundation of our legal system is our rights outlined in the Constitution and the laws established by our Founding Fathers.

Branches of the Law _____

Key Term: civil law

☐ **LEARNING OBJECTIVE 2:** Identify the two main branches of the American legal system.

Public Law _____

Private or Civil Law _____

Key Terms: tort; breach

The Rise in Medical Legal Cases _____

_____

Key Term: malpractice

Physician-Patient Relationship _____

_____

_____

Rights and Responsibilities of the Patient and Physician _____

_____

Key Point:
• In any contractual relationship, both parties have certain rights and responsibilities.

Contracts _____

_____

Key Term: contract
Key Point:
• A contract is not valid unless all three elements are present.

Implied Contracts _____

_____

Key Term: implied contracts

Expressed Contracts _____

_____

Key Term: expressed contracts

☐ **LEARNING OBJECTIVE 3:** List the elements and types of contractual agreements and describe the difference in implied and expressed contracts.

Termination or Withdrawal of the Contract _____

_____

Key Terms: protocol; locum tenens
Key Point:
• Clear documentation is essential.

☐ **LEARNING OBJECTIVE 4:** List four items that must be included in a contract termination or withdrawal letter.

Consent _____

_____

Key Terms: consent; durable power of attorney
Key Point:
• The law requires that patients must **consent** or agree to being touched, examined, or treated by the physician or agents of the physician involved in the contractual agreement.

Implied Consent _____

_____

Key Term: implied consent

Informed or Expressed Consent _____

_____

Key Terms: informed consent; expressed consent; emancipated minor
Key Point:
• Never coerce (force or compel against his or her wishes) a patient into signing a consent form.

☐ **LEARNING OBJECTIVE 5:** List six items that must be included in an informed consent form and explain who may sign consent forms.

Refusal of Consent _____

_____

Key Point:
• Patients may refuse treatment for any reason.

Releasing Medical Information _____

_____

Key Point:
• Although the medical record itself belongs to the physician, the information belongs to the patient.

Legally Required Disclosures _____

_____

Key Term: legally required disclosures

_____

Vital Statistics _____

_____

_____

Medical Examiner's Reports _____

_____

_____

Infectious or Communicable Diseases _____

_____

_____

National Childhood Vaccine Injury Act of 1986 _____

_____

_____

Abuse, Neglect, or Maltreatment _____

_____

Key Point:
- Health care workers, teachers, and social workers who report suspected abuse are not identified to the parents and are protected against liability.

Violent Injuries _____

_____

Key Point:
- Health care providers have the legal duty to report suspected criminal acts. Injuries resulting from weapons, assault, attempted suicide, and rape must be reported to local authorities.

Other Reports _____

_____

☐ **LEARNING OBJECTIVE 6:** List five legally required disclosures that must be reported to specified authorities.

Specific Laws and Statutes that Apply to Health Professionals _____

_____

Medical Practice Acts _____

_____

Key Terms: licensure; fee splitting
Key Point:
• As a medical assistant, it is your responsibility to report illegal or unethical behavior or signs of incompetence in the
medical office.

Licensure, Certification, and Registration _____

_____

Key Terms: registered; certification
Key Point:
• The physician-employer has the sole responsibility of set-
ting any limits on the duties of a medical assistant.

Controlled Substances Act _____

_____

_____

Good Samaritan Act _____

_____

_____

Basis of Medical Law _____

_____

_____

Tort Law _____

_____

Key Terms: plaintiff; defendant

Negligence and Malpractice (Unintentional Torts) _____

_____

Key Terms: negligence; expert witness; res ipsa loquitur
Key Point:
• In a legal situation, the standard of care determines what a
reasonable professional would have done.

Duty _____

_____

Dereliction of Duty _____

_____

_____

Direct Cause _____

_____

_____

Damage _____

_____

Key Term: damages

Jury Awards _____

_____

_____

☐ **LEARNING OBJECTIVE 7:** Describe the four elements that must be proven in a medical legal suit.

Intentional Torts _____

_____

Key Term: intentional tort

Assault and Battery _____

_____

Key Terms: assault; battery
Key Point:
• By law, a conscious adult has the right to refuse medical care.

Duress _____

_____

Key Term: duress

Invasion of Privacy _____

_____

_____

Defamation of Character _____

_____

Key Terms: defamation of character; libel; slander

Fraud _____

_____

_____

Tort of Outrage _____

_____

_____

Undue Influence _____

_____

_____

The Litigation Process _____

_____

Key Terms: depositions; bench trial; appeal

_____

Defenses to Professional Liability Suits _____

_____

Key Point:
• The objective of all court proceedings is to uncover the truth.

_____

Medical Records _____

_____

Key Point:
• The best and most solid defense the caregiver has is the medical record.

_____

Statute of Limitations _____

_____

Key Term: statute of limitations

_____

Assumption of Risk _____

_____

Key Point:
• A signed consent form indicating that the patient was informed of all of the risks of a procedure proves this point.

Res Judicata _____

Key Term: res judicata

Contributory Negligence _____

Key Terms: contributory negligence; comparative negligence

Comparative Negligence _____

☐ **LEARNING OBJECTIVE 8:** Describe four possible defenses against litigation for the medical professional.

Defense for the Medical Assistant _____

Respondeat Superior or Law of Agency _____

Key Term: respondeat superior
Key Points:
- The physician is responsible for your actions as a medical assistant as long as your actions are within your scope of practice.
- Never hesitate to seek clarification from a physician. If you are not sure about something, such as a medication order, ask!

☐ **LEARNING OBJECTIVE 9:** Explain the theory of respondeat superior, or law of agency, and how it applies to the medical assistant.

☐ **LEARNING OBJECTIVE 10:** List ways that a medical assistant can assist in the prevention of a medical malpractice suit.

Employment and Safety Laws _____

Civil Rights Act of 1964, Title VII _____

Sexual Harassment _____

_____

Key Point:
• In the medical office setting, the office manager must be alert for signs of harassment and should have in place a policy for handling complaints.

Americans with Disabilities Act _____

_____

Key Point:
• The law is designed to protect employees, not to require unreasonable accommodations.

Occupational Safety and Health Act _____

_____

Key Term: blood-borne pathogens
Key Point:
• Universal or standard precautions are designed to protect health care workers from blood and body fluids contaminated with HIV, hepatitis, or any contagious "bugs" by requiring that those in direct contact with patients use protective equipment (e.g., gloves, gowns, face mask).

Other Legal Considerations _____

_____

☐ **LEARNING OBJECTIVE 11:** Outline the laws regarding employment and safety issues in the medical office.

☐ **LEARNING OBJECTIVE 12:** List the requirements of the Americans with Disabilities Act to the medical office.

Medical Ethics _____

_____

Key Terms: ethics; bioethics

☐ **LEARNING OBJECTIVE 13:** Differentiate between legal issues and ethical issues.

American Medical Association (AMA) Code of Ethics _____

_____

☐ **LEARNING OBJECTIVE 14:** List the seven American Medical Association principles of ethics.

Medical Assistant's Role in Ethics —————————————————————

Key Point:
• The care you give patients must be objective, and personal opinions about options must not be shared.

Patient Advocacy ——————————————————————————

Key Point:
• Your primary responsibility as a medical assistant is to be a patient advocate at all times.

Patient Confidentiality ——————————————————————

Key Term: confidentiality
Key Point:
• Whatever you say to, hear from, or do to a patient is confidential.

Honesty ————————————————————————————————

Key Point:
• Treating the patient with dignity, respect, and honesty in all interactions will build trust in you and your professional abilities.

American Association of Medical Assistants (AAMA) Code of Ethics ———————

Principles ————————————————————————————————

☐ **LEARNING OBJECTIVE 15:** List the five ethical principles of ethical and moral conduct outlined by the American Association of Medical Assistants.

Bioethics ———————————————————————————————

Key Term: bioethics

American Medical Association (AMA) Council on Ethical and Judicial Affairs _____

_____

Social Policy Issues _____

_____

Allocation of Resources _____

_____

Clinical Investigations and Research _____

_____

Obstetric Dilemmas _____

_____

Stem Cell Research _____

_____

Organ Transplantation _____

_____

Withholding or Withdrawing Treatment _____

_____

Key Term: advance directive
Key Point:
• Today, everyone is encouraged to participate in his or her own end-of-life decisions.

☐ **LEARNING OBJECTIVE 16:** Describe the purpose of the Self-Determination Act.

Professional and Ethical Conduct and Behavior _____

Key Point:
• No health care professional should engage in any act that he or she feels is ethically or morally wrong.

Ethical Issues in Office Management _____

_____

☐ **LEARNING OBJECTIVE 17:** List 10 opinions of the American Medical Association's Council pertaining to administrative office procedures.

Content Review

FOUNDATIONAL KNOWLEDGE

1. The Branches of Law

Supply the appropriate branch of law below.

a. Branch of Law: _____

Focuses on issues between the government and its citizens

b. Branch of Law: _____

Focuses on issues between private citizens

2. All About Public Law

Public law is divided into four subgroups. In the chart below, decide which type of law is represented and place a check mark in the appropriate box.

Types of Laws	Criminal Law	Constitutional Law	Administrative Law	International Law
a. civil rights laws				
b. Internal Revenue Service				
c. trade agreements				
d. rape				
e. murder				
f. abortion				
g. extradition				
h. Food and Drug Administration				
i. burglary				
j. Board of Medical Examiners				

Physician-Patient Contract

3. Dr. Read places the following ad in a local newspaper on July 14:

Notice: From September 1, Dr. Michael Read will no longer be treating patients on Fridays at Lucas Surgery, 114 Chestnut Street, Northeast, MD. Queries should be directed to (443) 380-9900.

One of Dr. Read's patients, Mrs. Jones, calls the office the following day and tells them that because Dr. Read will not be in his office on Fridays, he will have to come and treat her at home instead. Who is legally correct? Explain your answer.

4. Mr. De Souza calls the physician's office to request an appointment with Dr. Phillips. The receptionist tells him that there is an available slot next Tuesday at 4 PM and asks him if he would like to take it. At this point in the conversation, which part of the physician-patient contract has Mr. De Souza already completed?

    a. Offer and acceptance

    b. Offer

    c. Offer, acceptance, and consideration

5. Dr. Duke has decided to terminate patient Mrs. Akon. The office manager drafted the following letter to Mrs. Akon. However, when you review the letter, you find that there are errors. Read the letter below and then explain the three problems with this letter in the space below.

Dear Mrs. Akon,

Because you have consistently refused to follow the dietary restrictions and to take the medication necessary to control your high blood pressure, I feel I am no longer able to provide your medical care. This termination is effectively immediately.

Because you do not seem to take your medical condition seriously, I'm not sure that any other physician would want to treat you either. I will hold on to your medical records for 30 days and then they will be destroyed.

                              Sincerely,
                              Anthony Duke, MD

    a. _____

    b. _____

    c. _____

I Consent

6. Which of the following must be included in a patient consent form? Circle all that apply.

    a. Name of the physician performing the procedure

    b. Alternatives to the procedure and their risks

    c. Date the procedure will take place

    d. Probable effect on the patient's condition if the procedure is not performed

    e. Potential risks from the procedure

    f. Patient's next of kin

    g. Any exclusions that the patient requests

    h. Success rate of the procedure

7. Some situations require a report to be filed with the Department of Health with or without the patient's consent. Read the scenarios in the chart below and decide which ones are legally required disclosures.

Scenario	Legally Required Disclosure	No Action Needed
a. A 35-year-old woman gives birth to a healthy baby girl.		
b. A physician diagnoses a patient with meningococcal meningitis.		
c. A 43-year-old man falls off a ladder and breaks his leg. He spends three weeks in the hospital.		
d. A teenager is involved in a hit-and-run accident. He is rushed to the hospital, but dies the next day.		
e. A 2-year-old girl is diagnosed with measles.		
f. A man is diagnosed with a sexually transmitted disease and asks the physician to keep the information confidential.		
g. A woman visits the physician's office and tells him she has mumps, but when he examines her, he discovers it is influenza.		

8. Lawsuits

Mrs. Stevens visits Dr. Johnson's office with neck pain. Dr. Johnson examines her and recommends that she see a specialist. Several months later, Mrs. Stevens sues Dr. Johnson for malpractice, claiming that when he examined her, he made her neck pain worse. In court, she provides pictures of her neck that show severe bruising. A specialist confirms that muscle damage has restricted Mrs. Stevens from going about her daily life. Which of the four elements needed in a medical lawsuit has Mrs. Stevens failed to prove? Circle all that apply.

a. Duty

b. Dereliction of duty

c. Direct cause

d. Damage

9. Mr. Saunders visits Dr. Finnegan with chronic insomnia and tells him that the over-the-counter medication he is using is not working. Dr. Finnegan prescribes Mr. Saunders a stronger sedative and warns him of the possible side effects. The interaction is documented in Mr. Saunders' medical record. Nine months later, Mr. Saunders files a malpractice suit against Dr. Finnegan, claiming that he has become dependent on the sleep medication. List two possible defenses Dr. Finnegan could use in court and explain what they mean.

_____

_____

10. You are a medical assistant in a busy office, and the physician has been called away on an emergency. Some of the patients have been waiting for over 2 hours, and one of them urgently needs a physical check-up for a job application. Although you are not officially qualified, you feel confident that you are able to carry out the examination by yourself. Six months later, the patient files a malpractice suit because you failed to notice a lump in her throat that turned out to be cancerous. Describe the law of agency and explain whether it would help you in the lawsuit.

_____

_____

11. List five ways that medical assistants can help to avoid a medical malpractice suit.

a. _____

b. _____

c. _____

d. _____

e. _____

Laws to Protect

12. Which of these laws protects you from exposure to blood-borne pathogens and other body fluids in the workplace?

a. Civil Rights Act of 1964

b. Self-Determination Act of 1991

c. Occupational Safety and Health Act

d. Americans with Disabilities Act

13. The Americans with Disabilities Act (ADA) prohibits discrimination against people with disabilities in employment practice. Take a look at the scenarios in this chart and assess whether or not the ADA is being followed correctly. Place a check mark in the appropriate box.

Scenario	ADA correctly followed	ADA incorrectly followed
a. A physician's office extends an offer of employment to a man in a wheelchair, but says that due to a shortage of parking, the office cannot offer him a parking space in the garage.		
b. A 46-year-old woman is refused a position on the basis that she is HIV positive.		
c. A mentally ill man with a history of violence is refused a job in a busy office.		
d. A small office with ten employees chooses a healthy woman over a disabled woman because the office cannot afford to adapt the facilities in the workplace.		
e. An office manager at physician's office sends letters to hearing-impaired patients because she is unable to contact them by telephone.		
f. A job applicant with a severe speech impediment is rejected for a position as an emergency room receptionist.		

A Matter of Ethics

14. What is the difference between medical ethics and medical laws?

_____

_____

15. Fill in the missing terms from the AMA Code of Ethics with the words from the list below.

The physician shall:

a. Practice _____ medical care with compassion while respecting human dignity.

b. Remain honest in dealings with patients and colleagues; expose colleagues with _____ _____ or who are incompetent or who engage in _____ and _____.

c. Adhere to all _____ and when needed, be a voice to _____ in the best interest of patient care.

d. Respect the rights of patients and other health care professionals; safeguard patient _____ except within the provisions of the law.

e. Continue appropriate education to remain current; request _____ and obtain the knowledge and skills of other health professionals when needed.

f. Be free to select whom to treat, where to establish a _____, and whom to associate with except in _____ _____.

g. Participate in activities to enhance the _____.

Missing Words

character deficiencies	community	fraud	confidentiality	practice
emergency situations	deception	competent	laws	consultation	lawmakers

16. List three principles of the American Association of Medical Assistants Code of Ethics.

a. _____

b. _____

c. _____

17. When a patient is hospitalized, the patient has the right to decide when to terminate treatment. What is the name of the act that allows hospitalized patients to make this decision?

_____

_____

18. As a medical assistant, you will be involved in some administrative issues. Read the following scenarios and assess whether the American Medical Association standards for office management are being met. Place a check mark in the appropriate box.

Scenario	Standards Met	Standards Not Met
a. Dr. Benson tells his medical assistant to cancel Mrs. Burke's tests because she recently lost her job and will be unable to pay for them.		
b. Mr. Grant canceled his appointment with less than 24 hours' notice. He was charged a fee as noted in a sign by the receptionist's desk.		
c. Mrs. O'Malley asks Dr. Gokool to help her fill out an insurance form. The form is a four-page document that takes Dr. Gokool an hour to fill out. Dr. Gokool charges Mrs. O'Malley $15 for filling out the form.		
d. Dr. Harris dies suddenly, and his staff tell patients that the office will close and that copies of their medical records will be transferred to another physician.		
e. Mr. Davies owes the physician's office several thousand dollars. He is moving and asks the office to transfer his medical records to his new physician. The office refuses on the grounds that Mr. Davies has not paid his bill.		
f. Mrs. Jones comes into the office for a vaccination. The physician tells the medical assistant to charge her $10 less than other patients because she is elderly and cannot afford the standard charges.		

19. Match the following key terms to their definitions.

Key Terms

a. abandonment _____

b. slander _____

c. assault _____

d. battery _____

e. bioethics _____

f. tort _____

g. civil law _____

h. common law _____

i. defamation of character _____

j. defendant _____

k. deposition _____

l. durable power of attorney _____

m. emancipated minor _____

n. fee splitting _____

o. fraud _____

p. libel _____

q. litigation _____

r. locum tenens _____

s. malpractice _____

Definitions

1. a deceitful act with the intention to conceal the truth

2. process of filing or contesting a lawsuit

3. traditional laws outlined in the Constitution

4. a theory meaning that the previous decision stands

5. a person under the age of majority but married or self-supporting

6. previous court decisions

7. a branch of law that focuses on issues between private citizens

8. the righting of wrongs suffered as a result of another person's wrongdoing

9. a substitute physician

10. an arrangement that gives the patient's representative the ability to make health care decisions for the patient

11. sharing fees for the referral of patients to certain colleagues

12. the accuser in a lawsuit

13. failure to take reasonable precautions to prevent harm to a patient

14. the accused party in a lawsuit

15. a doctrine meaning ''the thing speaks for itself''

16. the unauthorized attempt to threaten or touch another person without consent

17. the physical touching of a patient without consent

18. malicious or false statements about a person's character or reputation

19. written statements that damage a person's character or reputation

t. negligence _____

u. plaintiff _____

v. precedents _____

w. res ipsa loquitur _____

x. res judicata _____

y. respondeat superior _____

z. stare decisis _____

20. a process in which one party questions another party under oath

21. an action by a professional health care worker that harms a patient

22. a doctrine meaning "the thing has been decided"

23. a doctrine meaning "let the master answer," also known as the law of agency

24. moral issues that affect a patient's life

25. withdrawal by a physician from a contractual relationship with a patient without proper notification

26. oral statements that damage a person's character or reputation

20. True or False? Determine whether the following statements are true or false. If false, explain why.

a. If a patient is in a life-threatening situation, it is important to obtain the patient's consent before beginning treatment.

_____

_____

b. A minor cannot sign a consent form unless he or she is in the armed services.

_____

_____

c. A bench trial does not involve a jury.

_____

_____

d. In court, the burden of proof is on the defendant.

_____

_____

APPLICATION

Critical Thinking Practice

1. A family member calls to inquire about a patient's condition. You know that the patient has not given written consent for information to be passed on, but you recognize the person's voice and remember that she came in with the patient the previous day. Explain what you would say and why.

_____

_____

2. You are running late and have several tasks that need to be done immediately. You are dealing with a patient who needs to sign a consent form for a surgical procedure. The patient does not speak English very well, and you are not entirely sure that the patient understands what he is signing. List three things you should do, and explain why they are important.

_____

_____

Patient Education

1. You have a patient who has just been diagnosed with a sexually transmitted disease. After the physician leaves the office, the patient turns to you and begs you to keep the information confidential. It is obvious that the patient is worried and embarrassed. Explain how you would inform the patient about legally required disclosures and what you would say.

_____

_____

Documentation

1. Dr. Mason tells you that he needs to terminate a relationship with Mr. Stevens because he has not been keeping his appointments. He asks you to draft the letter. Write a letter to Mr. Stevens, including the correct legal information required to terminate successfully a physician-patient relationship without fear of litigation.

Active Learning

1. Research two recent medical malpractice cases on the Internet. Write a brief outline of each case and make a record of whether the tort was intentional or unintentional, and what the outcome of the case was. Compare the cases to see if there is a common theme, and draw a chart to show your findings.

2. Visit a physician's office and make a list of steps that have been taken to comply with the law. For example, if the physician charges for canceling appointments without notice, there is probably a sign by the reception desk to warn patients of the fee. How many other legal requirements can you find? Are there any that are missing?

3. As technology develops, new laws have to be written to protect the rights of patients who use it. Stem cell research is a particularly gray area, and has raised many interesting ethical dilemmas. Research some recent legal cases regarding stem cell research, and write a report on some of the ethical issues the cases have raised.

Professional Journal

REFLECT

(Prompts and Ideas: Have you or a loved one ever been mistreated by a medical professional? Have you ever been unsure of what you were signing, or not had a procedure properly explained to you? Do you have any personal beliefs that you would find difficult to keep to yourself as a medical professional?)

_____

_____

PONDER AND SOLVE

1. One of your friends is also training to be a medical assistant and has applied for a job at the physician's office where you work. You know that your friend attends anti-abortion rallies and is vehemently opposed to abortion. The physician's office you work in carries out the procedure on a regular basis. What do you do?

_____

_____

_____

2. A 50-year-old patient has just been told that his cancer has returned for the third time. He tells you that he can't face any more treatment and just wants to die peacefully. His 23-year-old daughter is devastated by her father's decision and begs you to make him change his mind. What do you do?

_____

_____

_____

_____

_____

_____

_____

EXPERIENCE

Skills related to this chapter include:

1. Monitoring Federal and State Regulations, Changes, and Updates (Procedure 2-1).

Record any common mistakes, lessons learned, and/or tips you discovered during your experience of practicing and demonstrating these skills:

_____

_____

_____

_____

_____

_____

_____

_____

Skill Practice

PERFORMANCE OBJECTIVE:

1. Monitor federal and state health care legislation (Procedure 2-1).

Name_____ Date_____ Time_____

Procedure 2-1:	MONITORING FEDERAL AND STATE REGULATIONS, CHANGES, AND UPDATES

EQUIPMENT: Computer, Internet connection, search engine or website list

KEY: 4 = Satisfactory 0 = Unsatisfactory NA = This step is not counted

PROCEDURE STEPS	SELF	PARTNER	INSTRUCTOR
1. Using a search engine, go to the homepage for your state government (Example: www.nc.gov) and/or other related sites such as: Centers for Disease Control and Prevention (CDC), Occupational Safety and Health Act (OSHA), your state medical society, and the American Medical Association (AMA).	☐	☐	☐
2. Input keywords such as: Health care finances, allied health professionals, outpatient medical care, Medicare, etc.	☐	☐	☐
3. Create and enforce a policy for timely dissemination of information received by fax or e-mail from outside agencies.	☐	☐	☐
4. Circulate information gathered to all appropriate employees with an avenue for sharing information. Any information obtained should be shared.	☐	☐	☐
5. Post changes in policies and procedures in a designated area of the office.	☐	☐	☐

CALCULATION

Total Possible Points: _____
Total Points Earned: _____ Multiplied by 100 = _____ Divided by Total Possible Points = _____ %

Pass **Fail**
☐ ☐ Comments:

Student's signature _____ Date _____
Partner's signature _____ Date _____
Instructor's signature _____ Date _____

Work Product

Document Appropriately.

Britney Smith is a 16-year-old patient who comes for her routine gynecological exam with her mother. Her mother waits in the reception area while Britney has her appointment. You are directed to collect a urine sample from Britney Smith. She refuses to give a sample. If you are currently working in a medical office, use a blank paper patient chart from the office. If this is not available to you, use the space below to write a note recording her refusal of the urine test.

_____

_____

_____

Chapter Self-Assessment Quiz

1. The branch of law concerned with issues of citizen welfare and safety is:

   a. private law.

   b. criminal law.

   c. constitutional law.

   d. administrative law.

   e. civil law.

2. Which branch of law covers injuries suffered because of another person's wrongdoings resulting from a breach of legal duty?

   a. Tort law

   b. Contract law

   c. Property law

   d. Commercial law

   e. Administrative law

3. Scientific advances are among the causes of the rise in malpractice claims because:

   a. complications and risks for new procedures have escalated.

   b. patients complain more often for receiving outdated treatments.

   c. the high costs for new technology are unaffordable for most patients.

   d. the medical community is too specialized and does not share information.

   e. physicians are able to cure more patients than in the past.

4. The Health Insurance Portability and Accountability Act of 1996 deals with the patient's right to:

   a. privacy.

   b. choose a physician.

   c. get information prior to a treatment.

   d. interrupt a treatment considered disadvantageous.

   e. refuse treatment.

5. Which of the following can lead a patient to file a suit for abandonment against a physician?

   a. The physician verbally asks to end the relationship with the patient.

   b. A suitable substitute is not available for care after termination of the contract.

   c. The patient disagrees with the reasons given by the physician for the termination.

   d. Termination happens 35 days after the physician's withdrawal letter is received.

   e. The physician transfers the patient's medical records to another physician of the patient's choice.

Scenario: A man is found lying unconscious outside the physician's office. You alert several colleagues, who go outside to assess the man's condition. It is clear that he will be unable to sign a consent form for treatment.

6. How should the physician handle the unconscious man?

   a. Implied consent should be used until the man can give informed consent.

   b. A health care surrogate should be solicited to provide informed consent.

   c. The hospital administration should evaluate the situation and give consent.

   d. The physician should proceed with no-risk procedures until informed consent is given.

   e. The physician should wait for a friend or family member to give consent on the patient's behalf.

7. Once the man wakes up and gives his expressed consent to a treatment, this implies that he:

   a. no longer needs assistance.

   b. verbally agrees in front of witnesses on an emergency treatment.

   c. authorizes the physician to exchange patients' information with other physicians.

   d. trusts the physician with emergency procedures that can be deemed necessary at a later time.

   e. is now familiar with the possible risks of the procedure.

End Scenario

8. A diagnosis of cancer must be reported to the DHHS to:

   a. alert the closest family members.

   b. protect the patient's right to treatment.

   c. investigate possible carcinogens in the environment.

   d. check coverage options with the insurance company.

   e. provide research for a national study.

9. What is the difference between licensure and certification?

   a. Licensure is accessible to medical assistants.

   b. Certification standards are recognized nationally.

   c. Licensure indicates education requirements are met.

   d. Certification limits the scope of activity of a physician.

   e. Licensure allows a professional to practice in any state.

10. The Good Samaritan Act covers:

   a. emergency care provided by a medical assistant.

   b. compensated emergency care outside the formal practice.

   c. sensible emergency practice administered outside the office.

   d. emergency practice administered in the hospital to uninsured patients.

   e. emergency care administered in the physician's office before the patient is registered.

11. The term *malfeasance* refers to:

   a. failure to administer treatment in time.

   b. administration of inappropriate treatment.

   c. administration of treatment performed incorrectly.

   d. failure to administer treatment in the best possible conditions.

   e. the physical touching of a patient without consent.

12. Which tort pertains to care administered without the patient's consent?

   a. Duress

   b. Assault

   c. Tort of outrage

   d. Undue influence

   e. Invasion of privacy

13. The statute of limitation indicates:

   a. the privacy rights of a minor receiving care.

   b. the risks that are presented to a patient before treatment.

   c. the responsibilities of a physician toward his or her patients.

   d. the right of a physician to have another physician care for his patients while out of the office.

   e. the time span during which a patient can file a suit against a caregiver.

14. The court may assess contributory negligence when a(n):

   a. team of physicians incorrectly diagnoses the patient.

   b. physician's malpractice is aggravated by the patient.

   c. patient does not follow the physician's prescribed treatment properly.

   d. patient gives inaccurate information that leads to wrong treatment.

   e. physician is entirely responsible for the patient's injury.

15. Which of these best describes the principle of patient advocacy?

   a. A medical assistant must adhere to his or her own code of conduct.

   b. A medical assistant must act first and foremost in the interest of the patient.

   c. A medical assistant must make sure the patient's information remains confidential.

   d. A medical assistant must make sure to act as a mediator between the physician and the patient.

   e. A medical assistant should only perform procedures that agree with his personal ethics.

16. Which of these is the basic principle of bioethics?

    a. All patients are entitled to the best possible treatment.

    b. Moral issues must be evaluated according to the patient's specific circumstances.

    c. Members of the medical community should never compromise their religious beliefs.

    d. The medical community must agree on a code of moral standards to apply to controversial cases.

    e. Moral issues are guidelines that the medical community is legally bound to follow.

17. What is AMA's regulation on artificial insemination?

    a. Both husband and wife must agree to the procedure.

    b. The donor has the right to contact the couple after the child is born.

    c. The procedure can only be performed legally in certain states.

    c. A donor can be selected only after the husband has tried the procedure unsuccessfully.

    d. The couple requesting the procedure has the right to gain information about possible donors.

18. What does the Self-Determination Act of 1991 establish?

    a. The physician has the last word on interruption of treatment.

    b. A person has the right to make end-of-life decisions in advance.

    c. The physician must follow advance directives from a patient verbatim.

    d. Family members cannot make decisions about terminating a patient's treatment.

    e. If a patient cannot make his own decision, a close family member can do so on his behalf.

19. Which of these patients would be unable to sign a consent form?

    a. A 17-year-old requesting information about a sexually transmitted disease

    b. A pregnant 15-year-old

    c. A 16-year-old boy who works full-time

    d. A 17-year-old girl who requires knee surgery

    e. A married 21-year-old

20. In a comparative negligence case, how are damages awarded?

    a. The plaintiff receives damages based on a percentage of their contribution to the negligence.

    b. The defendant does not have to pay the plaintiff anything.

    c. The plaintiff and defendant share 50% of the court costs and receive no damages.

    d. The plaintiff has to pay damages to the defendant for defamation of character.

    e. The plaintiff receives 100% of the damages awarded.

Communication Skills

☐ Read textbook chapter and take notes within the Chapter Notes outline. Answer the Learning Objectives as you reach them in the content, and then check them off.

☐ Work the Content Review questions—both Foundational Knowledge and Application.

☐ Perform the Active Learning exercise(s).

☐ Complete Professional Journal entries.

☐ Complete Skill Practice Activity(s) using Competency Evaluation Forms and Work Products, when appropriate.

☐ Take the Chapter Self-Assessment Quiz.

☐ Insert all appropriate pages into your Portfolio.

1. Spell and define the key terms.
2. List two major forms of communication.
3. Explain how various components of communication can affect the meaning of verbal messages.
4. Define active listening.
5. List and describe the six interviewing techniques.
6. Give an example of how cultural differences may affect communication.
7. Discuss how to handle communication problems caused by language barriers.

8. List two methods that you can use to promote communication among hearing-, sight-, and speech-impaired patients.
9. Discuss how to handle an angry or distressed patient.
10. List five actions that you can take to improve communication with a child.
11. Discuss your role in communicating with a grieving patient or family member.
12. List the five stages of grief as outlined by Elisabeth Kubler-Ross.
13. Discuss the key elements of interdisciplinary communication.

Note: Bold-faced headings are the major headings in the text chapter; headings in regular font are lower-level headings (i.e., the content is subordinate to, or falls "under," the major headings). Make sure you understand the key terms used in the chapter, as well as the concepts presented as Key Points.

TEXT SUBHEADINGS   **NOTES**

Introduction _____

_____

> **Key Term:** messages
> **Key Point:**
> • In your role, you must accurately and appropriately share information with physicians, other professional staff members, and patients.

☐ **LEARNING OBJECTIVE 1.** Spell and define the key terms.

Basic Communication Flow _____

_____

> **Key Terms:** feedback; clarification

Forms of Communication _____

_____

_____

Verbal Communication _____

_____

> **Key Terms:** paralanguage; nonlanguage
> **Key Points:**
> • You need good verbal communication skills when performing such tasks as making appointments, providing patient education, making referrals, and sharing information with the physician.
> • The ability to write clearly, concisely, and accurately is important in the health care profession.

Nonverbal Communication _____

_____

> **Key Terms:** cultures; therapeutic; demeanor
> **Key Point:**
> • A patient's face can sometimes reveal inner feelings, such as sadness, happiness, fear, or anger, that may not be mentioned explicitly during a conversation.

☐ **LEARNING OBJECTIVE 2:** List two major forms of communication.

☐ **LEARNING OBJECTIVE 3:** Explain how various components of communication can affect the meaning of verbal messages.

Active Listening _____

Key Point:
• To listen actively, you must give your full attention to the patient with whom you are speaking. Interruptions should be kept to a minimum.

☐ **LEARNING OBJECTIVE 4:** Define active listening.

Interview Techniques _____

Key Point:
• To conduct either type of interview, you must use effective techniques: listen actively, ask the appropriate questions, and record the answers.

Reflecting _____

Key Term: reflecting

Paraphrasing or Restatement _____

Key Term: paraphrasing

Asking for Examples or Clarification _____

Asking Open-Ended Questions _____

Key Point:
• The best way to obtain specific information is to ask open-ended questions that require the patient to formulate an answer and elaborate on the response.

Summarizing

Key Term: summarizing
Key Point:
• Briefly reviewing the information you have obtained, or summarizing, gives the patient another chance to clarify statements or correct misinformation.

Allowing Silences

☐ **LEARNING OBJECTIVE 5:** List and describe the six interviewing techniques.

Factors Affecting Communication

Cultural Differences

Key Points:
• The way a person perceives situations and other people is greatly influenced by cultural, social, and religious beliefs or firmly held convictions.
• To help avoid miscommunication and offending patients, you must be sensitive to these differences in all of your patient interactions.

☐ **LEARNING OBJECTIVE 6:** Give an example of how cultural differences may affect communication.

Stereotyping and Biased Opinions

Key Terms: bias; discrimination; stereotyping
Key Point:
• As a health care professional, you are expected to treat all patients impartially, to guard against discriminatory practices, remain nonjudgmental, avoid stereotypes, and have a professional demeanor.

Language Barriers

☐ **LEARNING OBJECTIVE 7:** Discuss how to handle communication problems caused by language barriers.

Special Communication Challenges _____

Key Point:
• Patients must feel that they are part of the process even if their condition requires involvement by family members or other caregivers.

Hearing-Impaired Patients _____

Key Terms: anacusis; presbyacusis

Sight-Impaired Patients _____

Key Point:
• Patients who can't see lose valuable information from non-verbal communication.

Speech Impairments _____

Key Terms: dysphasia; dysphonia

☐ **LEARNING OBJECTIVE 8:** List two methods that you can use to promote communication among hearing-, sight-, and speech-impaired patients.

Mental Health Illnesses _____

Key Point:
• Your communication should be professional, nonjudgmental, and encouraging when appropriate.

Angry or Distressed Patients _____

Key Point:
• The key to communicating with upset patients is to prevent an escalation of the problem.

☐ **LEARNING OBJECTIVE 9:** Discuss how to handle an angry or distressed patient.

Children _____

_____

_____

☐ **LEARNING OBJECTIVE 10:** List five actions that you can take to improve communication with a child.

Communicating with a Grieving Patient or Family Member _____

_____

Key Terms: grief; mourning
Key Point:
• Empathy can help you recognize a patient's fear and discomfort so you can do everything possible to provide support and reassurance.

☐ **LEARNING OBJECTIVE 11:** Discuss your role in communicating with a grieving patient or family member.

☐ **LEARNING OBJECTIVE 12:** List the five stages of grief as outlined by Elisabeth Kubler-Ross.

Establishing Positive Patient Relationships _____

_____

_____

Proper Form of Address _____

_____

Key Point:
• These terms denigrate the individual's dignity and put the interaction on a personal, not professional, level.

Professional Distance _____

_____

Key Point:
• You should not become too personally involved with patients because doing so may jeopardize your ability to be objective.

Teaching Patients _____

_____

_____

Professional Communication _____

_____

_____

Communicating with Peers _____

Key Point:
• Involvement in local community organizations and support groups is also beneficial to promoting you and your profession.

Communicating with Physicians _____

Communicating with Other Facilities _____

☐ **LEARNING OBJECTIVE 13:** Discuss the key elements of interdisciplinary communication.

Content Review

FOUNDATIONAL KNOWLEDGE

Communication Skills

1. The two main forms of communication are verbal communication and nonverbal communication. Read each form of communication below and place a check mark to indicate whether it represents verbal or nonverbal communication.

Communication	Verbal	Nonverbal
a. A patient sighs while explaining her symptoms.		
b. A patient shrugs his shoulders after being told he needs to lose weight.		
c. A patient's eyes dart around the room during an explanation of a procedure.		
d. A physician writes "take two aspirin every eight hours."		
e. A mother is given a sheet of paper describing what to expect of her baby during months 6–9.		
f. A physician puts her hand on a patient's shoulder before delivering test results.		

2. The physician has recommended that your patient Valerie schedule a mammogram because he is concerned about a lump in her breast. You explain the procedure to the patient and provide her with the information she needs to make her appointment. When you ask if she has any questions, she says no. However, you notice that there are tears in Valerie's eyes. What is the problem with this interaction, and how should you respond?

_____

_____

3. Explain what it means to listen actively.

_____

_____

Interviewing Patients

4. Physicians use the information obtained during a patient interview to help them assess the patient's health. Patients will be more willing to provide information during a professionally conducted interview. Read each of the following statements describing patient interviews. Answer *yes* if the statement describes a correct interview practice; answer *no* if it describes an incorrect interview practice. Provide an explanation on how to correct the problem for all *no* answers.

	Yes	No
a. Patient interviews can be conducted in an exam room or in the waiting room.		
b. Answering a phone call in the middle of a new patient interview is acceptable if it is a call you have been waiting for.		
c. It is important to maintain eye contact with the patient, so you do not write any patient responses down until the interview is over.		
d. You confirm which blood pressure medication and what dosage the patient is taking.		
e. There is nothing wrong with skipping questions in a patient interview that may make the patient feel uncomfortable.		
f. Introducing yourself to the patient is a nice way to start an interview.		

5. Conducting patient interviews is a major part of a medical assistant's job. It is important that you're familiar with the interview techniques. Match the name of each interview technique below with its correct description.

Interview Techniques

a. reflecting

b. paraphrasing

c. clarification

d. asking open-ended questions

e. summarizing

f. allowing silences

Descriptions

1. asking the patient to give an example of the situation being described

2. taking a moment to gather your thoughts and let the patient gather her thoughts

3. repeating what you have heard the patient say, using open-ended statements

4. asking the patient a question that begins with *what, when,* or *how*.

5. repeating what you have heard, using your own words

6. briefly reviewing the information obtained so the patient can correct any misinformation

6. Next Question, Please

When conducting patient interviews, you'll need to ask a lot of questions to learn a patient's medical history, family history, and social history, as well as information about medications and body functions. Fill in the chart below with one question in each category that you could ask a patient during an interview.

Area of Questioning	Sample Question
Past medical history	
Family history	
Body system review	
Social history	
Medications	

7. Culture Clash

Why is it important to be aware of cultural differences among people?

_____

_____

8. Explain how bias and stereotyping on the part of a medical assistant could hinder patient care.

_____

_____

9. Sharing Bad News

A young patient named Sumaja has just received news that she has breast cancer. She is becoming distressed. The medical assistant does the following things for the patient (see table below). Determine whether these were the appropriate ways to handle the situation. If it was an inappropriate action, explain why.

Action	Right	Wrong
a. Giving Sumaja information about breast cancer to read at home		
b. Providing Sumaja with phone numbers for places to call for more information		
c. When Sumaja asked if she might die, telling Sumaja that her case is not that bad and that she should be fine		
d. Giving Sumaja information on treatment options		
e. Telling Sumaja which treatment options will work best for her		

10. The Language Barrier

You are helping a new medical assistant learn how to conduct patient interviews. One of his patients is a Spanish-speaking woman who came to the office with her son and daughter. The following are some of the steps he took to get information. Write correct or incorrect after reading each statement. If you answer _incorrect_, explain what the medical assistant should have done.

a. He spoke in a normal tone and volume. _____

b. He spoke directly to the translator. _____

c. When asking a question about eyesight, he pointed to his eyes. _____

d. He used abbreviations and slang terms for medical tests. _____

e. He asked the woman's son to be the interpreter and her daughter to wait outside. _____

f. He used complex medical language to explain procedures. _____

g. He used a Spanish-English phrase book. _____

11. Keep Your Cool

A patient comes into an already crowded waiting room and asks how long her wait will be to see the doctor. When you tell her it will be approximately one hour, she starts yelling at you. She claims that you don't know how to schedule appointments correctly and that perhaps you should be replaced. You start to get angry. How should you respond?

_____

_____

12. Are You Up for the Challenge?

Your office treats some hearing-impaired patients. Place a check mark next to the suggestions that will help you to communicate with a hearing-impaired patient.

Suggestion	Yes	No
a. Gently touch the patient to get her attention.		
b. Exaggerate your facial movements.		
c. Eliminate all distractions.		
d. Enunciate clearly.		

e. Use short sentences with short words.		
f. Speak loudly.		
g. Write things down on note pads.		
h. Turn toward the light so your face is illuminated.		
i. Talk directly face-to-face with the patient, not at an angle.		

13. Mr. Webb comes into the office with his 10-year-old daughter for a checkup. He mentions that she got sunburned over the weekend, and it is blistering on her back and shoulders. Which response would be appropriate? Explain.

    a. "I will tell the doctor you are concerned about the sunburn."

    b. "Everyone with coloring like you gets sunburned. You should be more careful in the sun and use more sunscreen."

    _____

    _____

14. Children can be challenging to communicate with because their levels of comprehension vary with their ages. Read the following suggestions to help facilitate communication with children. Circle the suggestions that are most helpful.

    a. Tell children when you need to touch them and what you are going to do.

    b. Talk loudly and sternly so the child will stay focused on you and not other distractions in the office.

    c. If you think a child may be frightened, it is best to work quickly and let him or her be surprised by what you do.

    d. Rephrase questions until the child understands.

    e. Be playful to help gain a child's cooperation.

    f. When dealing with adolescents, it is always best to have a parent present.

    g. Keeping an interview professional and nonjudgmental will help keep adolescents communicating.

    h. Try to speak to children at their eye level.

15. Explain how the TDD phone system works, and list two ways in which it can be beneficial to a medical office.

    Explanation: _____

    Benefit 1: _____

    Benefit 2: _____

16. **Good Grief!**

    The five stages of grief as outlined by Elisabeth Kubler-Ross are denial, anger, bargaining, depression, and acceptance. Fill in one of the five stages of grief for each statement below.

    a. The doctor must have gotten my test results mixed up. _____

    b. I have terminal brain cancer. _____

    c. If I survive this, I will change the way I live my life for the better. _____

    d. I hate this doctor; I am going to find a new one. _____

    e. I don't care if the treatment might help me live a little longer. _____

17. A patient who you have known for five years has just been diagnosed with advanced terminal cancer. List three things you can do as a medical assistant to be supportive.

    a. _____

    b. _____

    c. _____

18. A patient calls the office with symptoms and a condition that you are not familiar with. She has used some terms that you do not understand. When you relay the message to the physician, how should you communicate the patient's problem?

_____

_____

19. Match the following key terms to their definitions.

Key Terms	Definitions
a. anacusis _____	**1.** information
b. bias _____	**2.** something that is beneficial to a patient
c. clarification _____	**3.** a group of people who share a way of life and beliefs
d. cultures _____	**4.** holding an opinion of all members of a particular culture, race, religion, or age group based on oversimplified or negative characterizations
e. demeanor _____	
f. discrimination _____	**5.** loss of hearing associated with aging
g. dysphasia _____	**6.** difficulty speaking
h. dysphonia _____	**7.** sounds that include laughing, sobbing, sighing, or grunting to convey information
i. feedback _____	**8.** the response to a message
j. grief _____	**9.** restating what a person said using your own words or phrases
k. messages _____	**10.** removal of confusion or uncertainty
l. mourning _____	**11.** formation of an opinion without foundation or reason
m. nonlanguage _____	**12.** a demonstration of the signs of grief
n. paralanguage _____	**13.** complete hearing loss
o. paraphrasing _____	**14.** briefly reviewing information discussed to determine the patient's comprehension
p. presbyacusis _____	**15.** great sadness caused by a loss
q. reflecting _____	**16.** voice tone, quality, volume, pitch, and range
r. stereotyping _____	**17.** the way a person looks, behaves, and conducts himself
s. summarizing _____	**18.** a voice impairment that is caused by a physical condition, such as oral surgery
t. therapeutic _____	**19.** the act of not treating a patient fairly or respectfully because of his cultural, social, or personal values
	20. repeating what one heard using open-ended questions

20. True or False? Determine whether the following statements are true or false. If false, explain why.

a. When the office is busy, it is okay to refer to patients by their medical condition, for example, stomach pain in room 1.

_____

_____

b. If an elderly patient does not have a ride home, a staff member in the office should offer her one.

_____

_____

c. When talking with patients, do not reveal too many personal details about your life.

_____

_____

d. It is inappropriate to carry on personal conversations with other staff members in front of a patient.

_____

_____

APPLICATION

Critical Thinking Practice

1. There is a medical assistant in your office who is easily distracted when interviewing patients. You have observed her doodling on paper and taking incomplete notes. The office manager has told her she needs to practice her active listening skills. At break time she complains to you, saying, "I don't know why this active listening is so important!" Think of a creative way to show your co-worker why active listening is a skill needed by medical assistants.

_____

_____

2. A patient's husband recently died in a car accident. She comes into the office because she needs to have a test for strep throat since she has had a fever and sore throat for two days. While there, she tells you that she is having trouble sleeping and is losing weight because she hasn't had an appetite since her husband died. You feel terrible for her, but don't know how to act or what to say. Explain why it is better to show empathy for a grieving patient rather than sympathy.

_____

_____

Patient Education

1. Mr. Rivera's wife died a year ago. Since that time, Mr. Rivera has stopped seeing friends and participating in social activities. He visits the cemetery several times a week. Mr. Rivera asks if his feelings of sadness and depression will ever go away. He wonders if he will ever feel any differently. What would you say to Mr. Rivera? How would you explain the grief process?

_____

_____

Documentation

1. You need to document the conversation that you had with Mr. Rivera in his chart. Write a narrative chart note describing your interaction with Mr. Rivera.

_____

_____

Active Learning

1. Patients who have been told they have a terminal illness will likely go through a grieving process. Their families will be grieving, too. There are resources available to patients and their families, and grief counselors can help them work through the grieving process. You have been asked to prepare a handout for patients on the benefits of grief counselors.
   - Use the Internet to research what grief counselors do and how they can help terminally ill patients.
   - Imagine yourself as a family member of the patient and create a list of questions you would ask a grief counselor.
   - Contact a grief counselor (through a local hospice program or hospital) and interview him or her.
   - Prepare a one-page handout to be given to patients and their families about the benefits of grief counselors.

2. Practice active listening with a partner. Have your partner tell you a detailed story that you have never heard before or explain a topic that you are unfamiliar with. After he or she has finished, wait silently for 2 minutes. Then try to repeat the story or steps back to your partner. Next, reverse roles and let your partner listen while you tell a story or explain a concept.

3. If you work in a pediatric office, you will certainly spend a good deal of time communicating with children. To help strengthen your communication skills with children, find a local preschool or elementary school teacher who has experience working with children. Interview this teacher about his or her communication techniques and write a list of ten tips for communicating with children.

Professional Journal

REFLECT

(Prompts and Ideas: Have you ever had trouble communicating with medical professionals for yourself or a loved one? What could you have done differently? What could they have done differently?)

_____

_____

_____

_____

_____

_____

PONDER AND SOLVE

1. You are helping a 7-year-old patient with a nebulizer for his asthma. While you are doing this, a coworker comes in the room and starts talking about her weekend. She asks why you and your girlfriend left the party early and tells you everything that went on after you left. You know this is not appropriate for a patient to hear. How would you stop your coworker, and what would you say to her later in private?

_____

_____

_____

_____

_____

_____

2. Mrs. Saltz is a very independent 70-year-old woman. She has trouble hearing, but does not acknowledge her hearing problem. The doctor has given her verbal instructions on how to take her medications, but you are not sure she completely understood him. What would you say to Mrs. Saltz? What else can you do?

_____

_____

_____

_____

_____

_____

Chapter Self-Assessment Quiz

1. Laughing, sobbing, and sighing are examples of:

  a. kinesics.

  b. proxemics.

  c. nonlanguage.

  d. paralanguage.

  e. clarification.

2. Hearing impairment that involves problems with either nerves or the cochlea is called:

  a. anacusis.

  b. conductive.

  c. presbyacusis.

  d. sensorineural.

  e. dysphasia.

3. Sally needs to obtain information from her patient about the medications he is taking. Which of the following open-ended questions is phrased in a way that will elicit the information that Sally needs?

  a. Are you taking your medications?

  b. What medications are you taking?

  c. Have you taken any medications?

  d. Did you take your medications today?

  e. Have you taken medications in the past?

4. Which of the following shows the five stages of grief in the correct sequence?

  a. Denial-anger-bargaining-depression-acceptance

  b. Acceptance-depression-bargaining-anger-denial

  c. Anger-denial-depression-acceptance-bargaining

  d. Denial-bargaining-anger-depression-acceptance

  e. Bargaining-anger-acceptance-depression-denial

5. "Those people always get head lice." This statement is an example of:

  a. culture.

  b. demeanor.

  c. discrimination.

  d. stereotyping.

  e. prejudice.

6. What can you do as a medical assistant to communicate effectively with a patient when there is a language barrier?

  a. Find an interpreter who can translate for the patient.

  b. Raise your voice so the patient can focus more on what you are saying.

  c. Give the patient the name and address of a physician who speaks the same language.

  d. Assess the patient and give the physician your best opinion about what is bothering the patient.

  e. Suggest that the patient find another physician who is better equipped to communicate with the patient.

7. When dealing with patients who present communication challenges, such as hearing-impaired or sight-impaired patients, it is best to:

  a. talk about the patient directly with a family member to find out what the problem is.

  b. conduct the interview alone with the patient because he needs to be able to take care of himself.

  c. address the patient's questions in the waiting room, where other people can try to help the patient communicate.

  d. refer the patient to a practice that specializes in working with hearing- and sight-impaired patients.

  e. make sure the patient feels like he is part of the process, even if his condition requires a family member's help.

8. A hearing-impaired patient's test results are in. It is important that the patient gets the results quickly. How should you get the results to the patient?

  a. Mail the test results Priority Mail.

  b. Call the patient on a TDD/TTY phone and type in the results.

  c. Drive to the patient's house at lunchtime to deliver the results.

  d. Call an emergency contact of the patient and ask him or her to have the patient make an appointment.

  e. Send the patient a fax containing the test results.

9. Which of the following statements about grieving is true?

    a. The grieving period is approximately 30 days.

    b. Different cultures and individuals demonstrate grief in different ways.

    c. The best way to grieve is through wailing because it lets the emotion out.

    d. The five stages of grief must be followed in that specific order for healing to begin.

    e. Everyone grieves in his own way, but all of us go through the stages at the same time.

10. Proxemics refers to the:

    a. pitch of a person's voice.

    b. facial expressions a person makes.

    c. physical proximity that people tolerate.

    d. the combination of verbal and nonverbal communication.

    e. the ability of a patient to comprehend difficult messages.

11. Which of the following situations would result in a breach of patient confidentiality?

    a. Shredding unwanted notes that contain patient information

    b. Discussing a patient's lab results with a co-worker in the hospital cafeteria

    c. Keeping the glass window between the waiting room and reception desk closed

    d. Shutting down your computer when you leave every night

    e. Paging the physician on an intercom to let him know a patient is waiting on the phone for results

12. "Those results can't be true. The doctor must have mixed me up with another patient." This statement reflects which of the following stages of grieving?

    a. Anger

    b. Denial

    c. Depression

    d. Bargaining

    e. Acceptance

13. Which of the following statements about communication is correct?

    a. Communication can be either verbal or nonverbal.

    b. Written messages can be interpreted through paralanguage.

    c. Verbal communication involves both oral communication and body language.

    d. Body language is the most important form of communication.

    e. Touch should be avoided in all forms of communication because it makes the recipient of the message uncomfortable.

14. During a patient interview, repeating what you have heard the patient say, using an open-ended statement is called:

    a. clarifying.

    b. reflecting.

    c. summarizing.

    d. paraphrasing.

    e. allowing silences.

15. What should you do during a patient interview if there is silence?

    a. Silence should not be allowed during a patient interview.

    b. Immediately start talking so the patient does not feel awkward.

    c. Fill in charts that need to be completed until the patient is ready.

    d. Wait for the physician to arrive to speak with the patient.

    e. Gather your thoughts and think of any additional questions you have.

16. The physician is behind schedule, and a patient is angry that her appointment is late. The best way to deal the patient is to:

    a. tell her anything that will calm her down.

    b. ignore her until the problem is solved.

    c. threaten that the physician will no longer treat her if she continues to complain.

    d. keep her informed of when the physician will be able to see her.

    e. ask her why it is such a big deal.

17. Why is it helpful to ask open-ended questions during a patient interview?

    a. They let the patient give yes or no answers.

    b. They let the patient develop an answer and explain it.

    c. They let the patient respond quickly using few words.

    d. They provide simple answers that are easy to note in the chart.

    e. They let the patient give his own feelings and opinions on the subject.

18. Difficulty with speech is called:

    a. dysphasia.

    b. dysphonia.

    c. nyctalopia.

    d. strabismus.

    e. myopia.

19. Adrian Makey is a 65-year-old man who recently had a mild heart attack. The medical assistant is the first person he encounters on his first visit to Dr. Liu's cardiology office. Which greeting by the medical assistant would be most professional?

    a. Hi, Adrian, how are you feeling?

    b. Hi, Gramps, how are you feeling?

    c. Hi, sweetie, how are you feeling?

    d. Hi, Mr. Makey, how are you feeling?

    e. Hi, Adrian Makey, how are you feeling?

20. The limit of personal space is generally considered to be a:

    a. 1-foot radius.

    b. 3-foot radius.

    c. 5-foot radius.

    d. 10-foot radius.

    e. 15-foot radius.

4

Patient Education

Chapter Checklist

☐ Read textbook chapter and take notes within the Chapter Notes outline. Answer the Learning Objectives as you reach them in the content, and then check them off.

☐ Work the Content Review questions—both Foundational Knowledge and Application.

☐ Perform the Active Learning exercise(s).

☐ Complete Professional Journal entries.

☐ Complete Skill Practice Activity(s) using Competency Evaluation Forms and Work Products, when appropriate.

☐ Take the Chapter Self-Assessment Quiz.

☐ Insert all appropriate pages into your Portfolio.

Learning Objectives

1. Spell and define the key terms.
2. Explain the medical assistant's role in patient education.
3. Define the five steps in the patient education process.
4. Identify five conditions that are needed for patient education to occur.
5. Explain Maslow's hierarchy of human needs.
6. List five factors that may hinder patient education and at least two methods to compensate for each of these factors.
7. Discuss five preventive medicine guidelines that you should teach your patients.

8. Explain the kinds of information that should be included in patient teaching about medication therapy.
9. Explain your role in teaching patients about alternative medicine therapies.
10. List and explain relaxation techniques that you and patients can learn to help with stress management.
11. Describe how to prepare a teaching plan.
12. List potential sources of patient education materials.
13. Locate community resources and list ways of organizing and disseminating information.

Chapter Notes

Note: Bold-faced headings are the major headings in the text chapter; headings in regular font are lower-level headings (i.e., the content is subordinate to, or falls "under," the major headings). Make sure you understand the key terms used in the chapter, as well as the concepts presented as Key Points.

TEXT SUBHEADINGS   **NOTES**

Introduction _____

_____

Key Point:
• Patient education is performed under the direction of the physician.

☐ **LEARNING OBJECTIVE 1:** Spell and define the key terms.

The Patient Education Process _____

_____

☐ **LEARNING OBJECTIVE 2:** Explain the medical assistant's role in patient education.

Assessment _____

_____

Key Term: assessment
Key Point:
• **Assessment** requires gathering information about the patient's present health care needs and abilities.

Planning _____

_____

Key Term: learning objectives
Key Point:
• Learning goals and objectives that are established with input from the patient are most meaningful.

Implementation _____

_____

Key Term: implementation
Key Point:
• **Implementation** is the process used to perform the actual teaching.

Evaluation _____

Key Term: evaluation
Key Point:
• **Evaluation** is the process that indicates how well patients are adapting or applying new information to their lives.

Documentation _____

Key Term: documentation
Key Point:
• Documentation is essential because from a legal viewpoint, procedures are only considered to have been done if they are recorded.

☐ **LEARNING OBJECTIVE 3:** Define the five steps in the patient education process.

Conditions Needed for Patient Education _____

☐ **LEARNING OBJECTIVE 4:** Identify five conditions that are needed for patient education to occur.

Maslow's Hierarchy of Needs _____

Key Points:
• Maslow arranged human needs in the form of a pyramid, with basic needs at the bottom and the higher needs at the top.
• If possible, you should involve family members or significant others in the teaching process.

☐ **LEARNING OBJECTIVE 5:** Explain Maslow's hierarchy of human needs.

Environment _____

Key Point:
• For patients to acquire knowledge, they must feel relaxed and comfortable.

Equipment _____

_____

Key Term: psychomotor
Key Point:
• Always provide written step-by-step instructions.

Knowledge _____

_____

Key Point:
• Never guess or imply that you know something that you do not know.

Resources _____

_____

Key Point:
• The more techniques that are used, the more the patient will learn and retain.

Factors That Can Hinder Education _____

_____

_____

Existing Illnesses _____

_____

_____

Communication Barriers _____

_____

Key Point:
• Any barriers to communication must be resolved before you can start teaching the patient.

Age _____

_____

Key Point:
• The age of the patient plays a very important part in the amount and type of education that you can do.

Educational Background _____

_____

_____

Physical Impairments _____

_____

_____

Other Factors _____

_____

Key Point:
- It is important that you assess the patient's readiness to learn and either try to remove or work around any obstacles that may be present.

☐ **LEARNING OBJECTIVE 6:** List five factors that may hinder patient education and at least two methods to compensate for each of these factors.

Teaching Specific Health Care Topics _____

_____

_____

Preventive Medicine _____

_____

Key Points:
- Preventing health problems is the key to living a long, healthy life.
- Fall prevention tips should be taught to all older patients or any patient who has a problem with maintaining balance or uses an ambulation device (cane, walker).

☐ **LEARNING OBJECTIVE 7:** Discuss five preventive medicine guidelines that you should teach your patients.

Lifestyle Changes _____

_____

_____

Medications _____

_____

Key Point:
- A patient's medication regimen should be reviewed at each visit to be sure the patient is taking the right medication in the right way.

☐ **LEARNING OBJECTIVE 8:** Explain the kinds of information that should be included in patient teaching about medication therapy.

Alternative Medicine _____

_____

Key Term: alternative

Acupuncture _____

_____

_____

Acupressure _____

_____

_____

Hypnosis _____

_____

_____

Yoga _____

_____

_____

Herbal Supplements _____

_____

Key Term: placebo
Key Point:
• Patients should be advised to verify the training and credentials of the practitioner they are using and to ascertain that the practitioner is appropriately licensed.

☐ **LEARNING OBJECTIVE 9:** Explain your role in teaching patients about alternative medicine therapies.

Stress Management _____

_____

Key Term: stress

Positive and Negative Stress _____

_____

_____

Psychological Defense Mechanisms _____

_____

Key Point:
- Humans employ the use of defense mechanisms to cope with the painful and difficult problems life can bring.

Relaxation Techniques _____

_____

☐ **LEARNING OBJECTIVE 10:** List and explain relaxation techniques that you and patients can learn to help with stress management.

Patient Teaching Plans _____

_____

Developing a Plan _____

Key Point:
- To ensure that teaching is done logically, always use the education process to help you formulate a plan in your mind.

☐ **LEARNING OBJECTIVE 11:** Describe how to prepare a teaching plan.

Selecting and Adapting Teaching Material _____

_____

☐ **LEARNING OBJECTIVE 12:** List potential sources of patient education materials.

Developing Your Own Material _____

_____

Locating Community Resources and Disseminating Information _____

Key Term: disseminates

☐ **LEARNING OBJECTIVE 13:** Locate community resources and list ways of organizing and disseminating information.

Content Review

FOUNDATIONAL KNOWLEDGE

Personal Ownership

1. Patients should be encouraged to take an active approach to their health and health care education. To educate patients effectively, which of the following must you do? Circle all that apply.

    a. Help patients accept their illness.

    b. Expect patients to follow your instructions without further explanation.

    c. Involve patients in the process of gaining knowledge.

    d. Provide patients with positive reinforcement.

    e. Give patients the most in-depth professional textbooks you can find.

2. Write a sentence explaining why, as a medical assistant, you must set aside your own personal feelings and life experiences when educating patients.

    _____

    _____

Educating Patients

3. Dr. Lin has created a lifestyle modification plan for her patient, Mr. Ramirez. Draw a line to match the name of each step of the patient education process on the left to the corresponding step taken by Dr. Lin and Mr. Ramirez on the right.

Name of Step	Step in Action
1. Assessment	**a.** Dr. Lin explains to Mr. Ramirez how to exercise properly and eat a healthy diet.
2. Planning	**b.** Mr. Ramirez visits with Dr. Lin to determine how his weight loss is progressing.
3. Implementation	**c.** Mr. Ramirez meets with Dr. Lin to discuss his weight problem and how it is affecting his health.
4. Evaluation	**d.** Dr. Lin records the dates and times of his appointments with Mr. Ramirez.
5. Documentation	**e.** Mr. Ramirez understands why he needs to lose weight, and together they create a weight loss schedule.

4. Suppose you want to teach a patient about the need to adopt a low-sugar diet because of diabetes, but the patient doesn't believe that diabetes is a serious health problem. If education is to be effective, then which of the following must the patient accept? Circle all that apply.

    a. Diabetes has to be managed.

    b. There is a correlation between high sugar intake and diabetes.

    c. Diabetes isn't as serious as other diseases.

    d. Diabetes management requires dietary changes.

    e. It is possible to consume large quantities of high-sugar foods, but only occasionally.

5. Ms. Jasinski is an elderly patient who has recently lost several relatives and friends. She lives alone and feels disconnected from others and, as a result, her health has begun to deteriorate. Brian, a medical assistant, gives Ms. Jasinski a friendly hug when he sees her during patient visits. He talks to her and listens to her stories. He has also encouraged her to join a senior citizens' group. Which of Maslow's hierarchy of needs has Brian helped fulfill for Ms. Jasinski?

    a. physiological

    b. safety and security

    c. affection and belonging

    d. self-actualization

6. List the five factors that can hinder patient education.

a. _____

b. _____

c. _____

d. _____

e. _____

7. Age Isn't Just a Number

Luis is an 8-year-old boy living with HIV. As a medical assistant, it is important to explain his symptoms and how the illness will be treated. You want to be honest with Luis, but you're not sure how much to explain to him. Which of the following might you do when preparing to talk with Luis? Place a check mark in the table below to answer "Yes" or "No." If your answer is "No," briefly explain why.

	Yes	No, because . . .
a. Discuss HIV with his parents; they are solely responsible for explaining his medical condition to him.		
b. Communicate with his parents; they understand Luis' developmental stage.		
c. Consider Luis' age when determining what is and isn't appropriate to say.		
d. Take Luis to a psychiatrist; he can deal with Luis' emotional reactions, and you cannot.		

8. Taking Action Against Illness

Maria is the mother of a 3-month-old baby. Though Maria's baby is healthy, you understand that infants are often susceptible to illness because their immune systems are not fully developed. Which preventive health care tip would you recommend for Maria's baby?

_____

_____

9. Speaking of Medication . . .

Read the following paragraph and fill in each blank with the appropriate word or words from the word bank below. Note: Not all of the words will be used.

I was diagnosed with heart disease, and my physician prescribed 2 mg of the (1.) _____ name drug, Coumadin™ (warfarin sodium). The medical assistant explained that this medication was (2.) _____ to me because it inhibits reactions that lead to blood clotting. She explained the (3.) _____ as one tablet every day. Possible (4.) _____ include headache and fever. She also told me to watch for bleeding or abnormal bruising, as these may be signs of an adverse (5.) _____.

Word Bank

a. side effects   d. reaction   g. brand

b. dosage   e. prescribed   h. medicated

c. route   f. activities

10. A Common Myth

Many patients believe that over-the-counter medications are 100% safe at all times. In a sentence or two, explain why this is a misconception.

_____

_____

11. Survey Says . . .

When educating patients about medications, it's important to include information regarding alternative medicines. Surveys have shown that about _____% of all Americans have used some form of unconventional medicine.

    a. 12

    b. 51

    c. 75

    d. 90

    e. 25

12. Assessing Alternatives

As a medical assistant, it is your job to assess whether a patient is using any alternative therapies. In one or two sentences, explain what information should be included in your assessment.

_____

_____

Don't Stress Out!

13. Fill in the chart below with three more possible side effects of illness and injury.

Potential Side Effects:
- Physical pain
- Stress of treatments, procedures, and possible hospitalization
- Changes in relationships with family and friends
-
-
-

14. There are two types of stress; one is good for us and the other is bad. Fill in the chart below with the differences and similarities between positive and negative stress.

Positive Stress	Both	Negative Stress

15. Which of the following is a relaxation technique that you can suggest to patients?

    a. visualization

    b. sublimation

    c. hypnosis

    d. self-actualization

    e. acupressure

A Master Plan

16. List the five elements included in every teaching plan.

    a. _____

    b. _____

c. _____

d. _____

e. _____

17. List three potential sources of patient education materials.

    a. _____

    b. _____

    c. _____

18. List three places that patients can find information about financial assistance and transportation.

    a. _____

    b. _____

    c. _____

19. Match the following key terms to their definitions.

Key Terms

    a. alternative _____

    b. assessment _____

    c. coping mechanisms _____

    d. dissemination _____

    e. documentation _____

    f. evaluation _____

    g. implementation _____

    h. learning objectives _____

    i. noncompliance _____

    j. placebo _____

    k. planning _____

    l. psychomotor _____

    m. stress _____

Definitions

1. involves using the information you have gathered to determine how you will approach the patient's learning needs

2. skill that requires the patient to physically perform a task

3. the process that indicates how well patients are adapting or applying new information to their lives

4. produced by illness or injury and may result in physiological and psychological effects

5. includes procedures or tasks that will be discussed or performed at various points in the program to help achieve the goal

6. the process of distributing information on community resources

7. includes recording of all teachings that occurred

8. the patient's inability or refusal to follow a prescribed order

9. involves gathering information about the patient's present health care needs and abilities

10. psychological defenses employed to help deal with the painful and difficult problems life can bring

11. the power of believing that something will make you better when there is no chemical reaction that warrants such improvement

12. the process used to perform the actual teaching

13. an option or substitute to the standard medical treatment, such as acupuncture

20. True or False? Determine whether the following statements are true or false. If false, explain why.

    a. Patients benefit from the use of teaching aids that they can take home and use as reference material.

_____

_____

    b. If a patient asks you a question and you're not sure of the answer, then you should give your best guess.

_____

_____

    c. A patient must have his basic needs met before self-actualization may occur.

_____

_____

d. Visualization is a relaxation technique that involves deep-breathing and physical exercise.

_____

_____

APPLICATION

Critical Thinking Practice

1. A patient wants to use alternative medicine in addition to medicine prescribed by the physician. What should you do?

_____

_____

2. A patient in your care is suffering physiologic effects from negative stress brought on by chronic back pain. What types of coping strategies would you recommend to the patient and why?

_____

_____

Patient Education

1. Julia is an 8-year-old patient who has been diagnosed with type 1 diabetes. The medical office has a preprinted teaching plan entitled "Living with Type 2 Diabetes." Should you use this plan or develop your own? Explain.

_____

_____

Documentation

1. You have completed the patient education with your 8-year-old patient Julia from the previous question. Give an example of a chart note that you might write following your discussion with her about diabetes.

_____

_____

Active Learning

1. Juggling school with other commitments may occasionally cause negative stress in your life. Make a list of how you experience stress in your daily life. Then, choose one of the three relaxation techniques discussed in this chapter. Practice that technique and then write a paragraph describing the "pros" and "cons" of the chosen technique.

2. Develop a teaching plan for a family member or friend. For example, if your mother has asthma, then do research on the Internet to find information and resources about asthma. Remember to include all of the elements of a teaching plan. Practice your teaching techniques by educating a family member or friend about a particular illness or disease.

3. Choose a health concern that may require external support. For example, a patient fighting cancer may wish to join a support group or other organization for help. Search the Internet for local, state, and national agencies that provide information, support, and services to patients with your chosen need. Then, compile this information in an informative and creative brochure, pamphlet, or other learning tool.

Professional Journal

REFLECT

(Prompts and Ideas: Are you concerned about your ability to educate patients effectively? What challenges do you foresee, and how do you plan to deal with those challenges? Think about the most effective teachers you have had. What made them so good?)

_____

_____

_____

_____

_____

_____

_____

PONDER AND SOLVE

1. The evaluation phase of the patient education process will indicate how well the patient is adapting new information to her life. If a patient has been compliant, but the teaching still hasn't worked, what might you do next to improve the results?

_____

_____

_____

_____

_____

_____

2. How can understanding Maslow's hierarchy of needs help you provide better care to patients?

_____

_____

_____

_____

_____

_____

_____

EXPERIENCE

Skills related to this chapter include:

1. Instructing a Hearing-Impaired Patient (Procedure 4-1).

2. Locating Community Resources and Disseminating Information (Procedure 4-2).

Record any common mistakes, lessons learned, and/or tips you discovered during your experience of practicing and demonstrating these skills:

_____

_____

_____

_____

_____

_____

_____

Skill Practice

PERFORMANCE OBJECTIVES:

1. Instruct individuals according to their needs (Procedure 4-1).
2. Locate community resources (Procedure 4-2).

Name _____ Date _____ Time _____

Procedure 4-1:	INSTRUCTING A HEARING-IMPAIRED PATIENT

EQUIPMENT/SUPPLIES: Patient's chart, Internet, printer, paper

STANDARDS: Given the needed equipment and a place to work, the student will perform this skill with _____% accuracy in a total of _____ minutes. (*Your instructor will tell you what the percentage and time limits will be before you begin.*)

KEY: 4 = Satisfactory   0 = Unsatisfactory   NA = This step is not counted

PROCEDURE STEPS	SELF	PARTNER	INSTRUCTOR
1. Use the patient's chart to identify the patient's communication barrier and assess the tools needed.	☐	☐	☐
2. Used an online map service and print a map of the specific route.	☐	☐	☐
3. Use the suggestions listed in Chapter 3 for communicating with the hearing-impaired to explain the appointment and directions to the patient.	☐	☐	☐
4. Speak clearly in a low tone facing the patient.	☐	☐	☐
5. Make sure the patient understood.	☐	☐	☐

CALCULATION

Total Possible Points: _____
Total Points Earned: _____ Multiplied by 100 = _____ Divided by Total Possible Points = _____%

Pass   **Fail**
☐   ☐   Comments:

Student's signature _____ Date _____
Partner's signature _____ Date _____
Instructor's signature _____ Date _____

Name _____ Date _____ Time _____

Procedure 4-2:	**LOCATING COMMUNITY RESOURCES AND DISSEMINATING INFORMATION**

EQUIPMENT/SUPPLIES: Phone book, Internet, newspaper

STANDARDS: Given the needed equipment and a place to work, the student will perform this skill with _____% accuracy in a total of _____ minutes. (*Your instructor will tell you what the percentage and time limits will be before you begin.*)

KEY: 4 = Satisfactory   0 = Unsatisfactory   NA = This step is not counted

PROCEDURE STEPS	SELF	PARTNER	INSTRUCTOR

1. Assess the patient's needs for the following:
  a. Education
  b. Someone to talk to
  c. Financial information
  d. Support groups
  e. Home health needs
	☐	☐	☐

2. Check the local telephone book for local and state resources.	☐	☐	☐
3. Check for websites for the city and/or county in which the patient lives.	☐	☐	☐
4. Be prepared with materials already on hand.	☐	☐	☐
5. Give the patient the contact information in writing.	☐	☐	☐
6. Document actions and the information given to the patient.	☐	☐	☐
7. Instruct the patient to contact the office if he has any difficulty.	☐	☐	☐

CALCULATION

Total Possible Points: _____
Total Points Earned: _____ Multiplied by 100 = _____ Divided by Total Possible Points = _____%

Pass   **Fail**
☐   ☐   Comments:

Student's signature _____ Date _____
Partner's signature _____ Date _____
Instructor's signature _____ Date _____

Chapter Self-Assessment Quiz

1. During assessment, the most comprehensive source from which to obtain patient information is the:

    a. physician's notes.

    b. immunization record.

    c. medical record.

    d. family member.

    e. nurse.

2. If a patient is not following physician's orders, you should determine:

    a. how long the order hasn't been followed.

    b. why the order is not being followed.

    c. how to make the patient follow the order.

    d. why the patient agreed to follow the order.

    e. if the physician has another suggestion for new orders.

3. Which of the following is an example of a psychomotor skill that a patient may perform?

    a. Telling the physician about his symptoms

    b. Explaining how a part of the body is feeling

    c. Walking around with a crutch

    d. Watching television in the waiting room

    e. Listening to a physician's instructions

4. Which part of Maslow's pyramid is the point at which a patient has satisfied all basic needs and feels he has control over his life?

    a. Safety and security

    b. Esteem

    c. Self-actualization

    d. Affection

    e. Physiologic

5. Noncompliance occurs when the patient:

    a. experiences a decrease in symptoms healed.

    b. forgets to pay his bill.

    c. refuses to follow the physician's orders.

    d. requests a new medical assistant to assist the physician.

    e. agrees with the physician.

6. The power of believing that something will make you better when there is no chemical reaction that warrants such improvement is:

    a. self-relaxation.

    b. positive stress.

    c. acupuncture.

    d. placebo.

    e. visualization.

7. Patient education should consist of multiple techniques or approaches so:

    a. the patient can apply her new knowledge to real-life events.

    b. the patient will learn and retain more.

    c. the patient will understand that there are many ways to look at an issue.

    d. the patient will know where you stand on her health care options.

    e. the patient will have a wider choice of treatments.

8. One mental health illness that can hinder patient education is:

    a. diabetes.

    b. Lyme disease.

    c. obstructive pulmonary disease.

    d. Alzheimer disease.

    e. anemia.

9. Health assessment forms that assess a patient's education level may also help you determine a patient's ability to:

    a. read.

    b. listen.

    c. communicate.

    d. respond.

    e. evaluate.

10. Before developing a medication schedule, you should evaluate the patient's:

    a. prescribed medication.

    b. side effects.

    c. changes in bodily functions.

    d. daily routine.

    e. bowel movements.

11. Which is an example of a recommended preventive procedure?

    a. Regular teeth whitening

    b. Childhood immunizations

    c. Daily exercise

    d. Yearly lung cancer evaluations

    e. Occasional antibiotics

12. Which of the following is true of herbal supplements?

    a. A medical assistant can recommend that a patient start taking herbal supplements without the physician's approval.

    b. A health store clerk is a good source of information on supplements.

    c. Products that claim to detoxify the whole body are generally effective.

    d. Supplements will not interfere with blood sugar levels because they are not medication.

    e. Patients should be advised that because a product is natural does not mean it is safe.

13. One example of a physiologic response to negative stress is:

    a. elevated mood.

    b. hunger pangs.

    c. headache.

    d. profuse bleeding.

    e. energy boost.

14. In Maslow's hierarchy of needs, air, water, food, and rest are considered:

    a. affection needs.

    b. safety and security needs.

    c. esteem needs.

    d. self-actualization needs.

    e. physiologic needs.

15. Breathing exercises can be done:

    a. at the gym.

    b. in the medical office.

    c. at home.

    d. anywhere.

    e. at work.

16. Humans use defense mechanisms to:

    a. cope with painful problems.

    b. increase their sense of accomplishment.

    c. decrease effects of chronic physical pain.

    d. learn to get along well with others.

    e. explain complicated emotions to medical staff.

17. Support groups give patients the opportunity to:

    a. exchange and compare medical records.

    b. meet and share ideas with others who are experiencing the same issues.

    c. spread the good word about the medical office.

    d. obtain their basic physiologic needs.

    e. learn more about malpractice suits.

18. When selecting teaching material, you should first:

    a. choose preprinted material.

    b. create your own material.

    c. assess your patient's general level of understanding.

    d. let the patient find a book from the clinic library.

    e. ask the patient to create a list of specific questions.

19. Acupressure is different from acupuncture because:

    a. it does not use needles.

    b. it is not an alternative medicine.

    c. it cannot be used with cancer patients.

    d. it does not require any licensure.

    e. it is less effective.

20. If your community doesn't have a central agency for information and resources, then you should create a(n):

    a. hierarchy of needs.

    b. teaching plan.

    c. telephone directory.

    d. information sheet.

    e. flowchart.

PART

II

The Administrative Medical Assistant

Chapter Checklist

- ☐ Read textbook chapter and take notes within the Chapter Notes outline. Answer the Learning Objectives as you reach them in the content, and then check them off.
- ☐ Work the Content Review questions—both Foundational Knowledge and Application.
- ☐ Perform the Active Learning exercise(s).
- ☐ Complete Professional Journal entries.
- ☐ Complete Skill Practice Activity(s) using Competency Evaluation Forms and Work Products, when appropriate.
- ☐ Take the Chapter Self-Assessment Quiz.
- ☐ Insert all appropriate pages into your Portfolio.

Learning Objectives

1. Spell and define the key terms.
2. Explain the importance of displaying a professional image to all patients.
3. List six duties of the medical office receptionist.
4. List four sources from which messages can be retrieved.
5. Discuss various steps that can be taken to promote good ergonomics.
6. Describe the basic guidelines for waiting room environments.
7. Describe the proper method for maintaining infection control standards in the waiting room.
8. Discuss the five basic guidelines for telephone use.
9. Describe the types of incoming telephone calls received by the medical office.
10. Discuss how to identify and handle callers with medical emergencies.
11. Describe how to triage incoming calls.
12. List the information that should be given to an emergency medical service dispatcher.
13. Describe the types of telephone services and special features.

Chapter Notes

Note: Bold-faced headings are the major headings in the text chapter; headings in regular font are lower-level headings (i.e., the content is subordinate to, or falls "under," the major headings). Make sure you understand the key terms used in the chapter, as well as the concepts presented as Key Points.

TEXT SUBHEADINGS	NOTES

Introduction _____

_____

☐ **LEARNING OBJECTIVE 1:** Spell and define the key terms.

Professional Image _____

_____

Importance of a Good Attitude _____

Key Term: attitude
Key Point:
• Ask yourself how you would feel in a similar situation, how you would want to be treated.

The Medical Assistant as a Role Model _____

Courtesy and Diplomacy in the Medical Office _____

Key Term: diplomacy
Key Point:
• Courtesy and diplomacy are fundamental to successful human relations.

First Impressions _____

Key Point:
• The patient's perception of the medical office is based in part on the impression you make.

☐ **LEARNING OBJECTIVE 2:** Explain the importance of displaying a professional image to all patients.

Reception _____

The Role of a Receptionist _____

_____

Key Term: receptionist

_____

Duties and Responsibilities of the Receptionist _____

_____

_____

Prepare the Office _____

_____

Key Point:
• The office should be left in a professional manner.

_____

Retrieve Messages _____

_____

Key Point:
• No matter how a message has been sent, however, all information must be treated confidentially and handled according to HIPAA regulations.

_____

Prepare the Charts _____

_____

_____

Welcome Patients and Visitors _____

_____

_____

Register and Orient Patients _____

_____

_____

Manage Waiting Time _____

_____

_____

☐ **LEARNING OBJECTIVE 3:** List six duties of the medical office receptionist.

☐ **LEARNING OBJECTIVE 4:** List four sources from which messages can be retrieved.

Ergonomic Concerns for the Receptionist _____

_____

Key Term: ergonomic

_____

☐ **LEARNING OBJECTIVE 5:** Discuss various steps that can be taken to promote good ergonomics.

_____

The Waiting Room Environment _____

_____

_____

General Guidelines for Waiting Rooms _____

_____

Key Term: closed captioning

_____

Guidelines for Pediatric Waiting Rooms _____

_____

_____

Americans with Disabilities Act Requirements _____

_____

Key Point:
• The ADA Title III act requires that all public accommodations be accessible to everyone.

_____

☐ **LEARNING OBJECTIVE 6:** Describe the basic guidelines for waiting room environments.

_____

Infection Control Issues _____

_____

Key Point:
• Handwashing is the most important practice for preventing the transmission of diseases.

_____

☐ **LEARNING OBJECTIVE 7:** Describe the proper method for maintaining infection control standards in the waiting room.

_____

The End of the Patient Visit _____

_____

Key Point:
• As patients leave the office, they should feel they have been well cared for by a competent and courteous staff.

_____

Telephone _____

_____

_____

**Importance of the Telephone in the Medical Office** _____

_____

Key Point:
• You must be able to use the tone and quality of your voice and speech to project a competent and caring attitude over the telephone.

**Basic Guidelines for Telephone Use** _____

_____

_____

**Diction** _____

_____

Key Term: diction

**Pronunciation** _____

_____

_____

**Expression** _____

_____

_____

**Listening** _____

_____

_____

**Courtesy** _____

_____

Key Point:
• Remember, all information about and conversations with patients are confidential.

☐ **LEARNING OBJECTIVE 8:** Discuss the five basic guidelines for telephone use.

**Routine Incoming Calls** _____

_____

_____

Appointments _____

_____

_____

Billing Inquiries _____

_____

_____

Diagnostic Test Results _____

_____

_____

Routine and Satisfactory Progress Reports _____

_____

_____

Test Results _____

_____

_____

Unsatisfactory Progress Reports and Test Results _____

_____

Key Point:
• Never discuss unsatisfactory test results with a patient unless the doctor directs you to do so.

Prescription Refills _____

_____

Key Point:
• If there is any doubt, tell the pharmacy or the patient that you will check with the doctor and call back.

Other Calls _____

_____

☐ **LEARNING OBJECTIVE 9:** Describe the types of incoming telephone calls received by the medical office.

Challenging Incoming Calls _____

_____

Unidentified Callers _____

_____

Irate Patients _____

_____

Medical Emergencies _____

_____

Key Points:
- As a medical assistant, you must be able to differentiate between routine calls and emergencies.
- Determine the patient's name, location, and telephone number as quickly as possible in case you are disconnected or the patient is unable to continue the conversation.

☐ **LEARNING OBJECTIVE 10:** Discuss how to identify and handle callers with medical emergencies.

Triaging Incoming Calls _____

_____

Key Term: triage

☐ **LEARNING OBJECTIVE 11:** Describe how to triage incoming calls.

Taking Messages _____

_____

Key Point:
- The minimum information needed for a telephone message includes the name of the caller, date, and time of the call; telephone number where the caller can be reached; a short description of the caller's concern; and the person to whom the message is routed.

Outgoing Calls _____

_____

General Guidelines for Outgoing Calls _____

_____

Key Point:
- You should prepare for your calls carefully, have all information gathered, and know what you want to say before you dial the number.

Calling Emergency Medical Services _____

Key Term: emergency medical service (EMS)
Key Point:
- Reassure other patients in the waiting room. If the patient has any family members present, offer them assistance and reassurance.

☐ **LEARNING OBJECTIVE 12:** List the information that should be given to an emergency medical service dispatcher.

Services and Special Features _____

Telecommunication Relay Systems _____

Key Term: teletypewriter (TTY)

☐ **LEARNING OBJECTIVE 13:** Describe the types of telephone services and special features.

Content Review

FOUNDATIONAL KNOWLEDGE

1. A Lasting Impression

It's important for medical assistants to portray a professional image to patients and coworkers. Review the unprofessional actions below and explain what the medical assistant can do to correct each one and make a lasting professional impression.

a. Jacinda wears flowery perfume every day.

_____

b. Jorge's uniform has a hole at the seam and is wrinkled.

_____

c. Kate has beautiful long nails that are polished with bright red nail polish.

_____

Job Duties

2. Circle the six duties of a medical receptionist in the list below.

Prepare the office	Clean the examination rooms	Retrieve messages
Welcome patients and visitors	Update patient information in charts	Write prescriptions

| Prepare the charts | Register and orient patients | Manage waiting time |
| Create marketing materials | File paperwork for payroll | Call patients with test results |

3. Each morning a receptionist needs to collect messages. There are four different sources the receptionist needs to check to retrieve messages. Read the description of each message and then decide where the receptionist is most likely to find each message.

Message Retrieval System

a. Answering service

b. Voice mail system

c. E-mail

d. Fax machine

Descriptions

1. Dr. Orr's office sent a referral for patient Billy Waters.

2. Mr. Patel has a question about a blood test.

3. TGI health insurance has a question about a patient's billing charges.

4. The blood lab sent the results for five patients.

5. Lighthouse Nursing Home wants to tell the physician about a patient who fell out of bed early in the morning.

6. Mrs. Wright needs an appointment for her son who is complaining of an earache.

7. A pharmaceutical representative would like to discuss the release date of a new drug.

8. Mrs. Paul needs a prescription refill for her prenatal vitamins.

A Safe and Comfortable Place to Work

4. List four things a receptionist at a physician's office might do to avoid getting injured on the job.

a. _____

b. _____

c. _____

d. _____

5. The waiting room should be a comfortable and safe place for patients to wait. Review the list of guidelines below and determine which contribute to a comfortable and safe waiting room environment. Place a check in the "Yes" column for those guidelines that contribute to a comfortable and safe waiting room and place a check in the "No" column for those that do not.

Task	Yes	No
a. Sofas are preferable because they fit more people.		
b. Provide only chairs without arms.		
c. Bright, primary colors are more suitable and cheery.		
d. The room should be well ventilated and kept at a comfortable temperature.		
e. Soothing background music is acceptable.		
f. Reading material, like current magazines, should be provided.		
g. Patients should be allowed to control the television.		
h. In an office for adults, anything can be watched on the television.		
i. Closed captioning should be offered to patients with hearing impairments who want to watch television.		

6. Infection control is important to prevent the spread of disease among patients. List three things a medical assistant can do to help with infection control.

a. _____

b. _____

c. _____

7. A patient comes into the office with a severe bloody nose. He leaves bloody tissues in the waiting room and got blood on a magazine and a chair. Your supervisor says to you, "Come on! Get some gloves. We've got to clean this right away." Why do you need gloves? Why is it important that the waiting room be cleaned immediately?

_____

_____

8. Tatiana works as a receptionist in a busy medical office. During her review, her supervisor discusses her telephone skills and points out what telephone skills she has mastered and areas that need some improvement. Fill in the Comments section on the review sheet below. State one thing she is doing right for each "Satisfactory" mark and one thing she could do to improve each "Needs Improvement" mark.

Skill	Satisfactory	Needs Improvement	Comments
a. Courtesy	X		
b. Diction	X		
c. Expression		X	
d. Listening	X		
e. Pronunciation		X	

9. List four things you can do to maintain patient confidentiality within the reception area and waiting room.

a. _____

b. _____

c. _____

d. _____

Best Phone Practices

10. As a receptionist, you'll be answering incoming calls. Review the statements below and place a check in the "True" column for those that are true and place a check in the "False" column for those that are false.

Incoming Calls	True	False
a. Always ask new patients for their phone number in case you need to call them back.		
b. Always give patients an exact quote for services if asked.		
c. Patient information cannot be given to anyone without the patient's consent.		
d. All laboratory results phoned into the office must be immediately brought to the physician's attention.		
e. When a nursing home calls with a satisfactory report about a patient you should take the information down, record it in the patient's chart, and place it on the physician's desk for review.		
f. Never discuss unsatisfactory test results with a patient unless the doctor directs you to do so.		
g. Medical assistants are not allowed to take care of prescription refill requests.		

11. A woman calls the office frantic because she thinks she is having a heart attack. What information should you try to get first from the caller?

_____

_____

12. You are training a new receptionist. She doesn't understand why triaging calls is important. How would you explain this to her?

_____

_____

13. Triage the following calls:

   a. Line 1: A school nurse calls with a question about a medical form.

   b. Line 2: A mother calls about her child who is having an asthma attack.

   c. Line 3: A father calls with a question about his daughter's medication.

   d. Line 4: A patient calls complaining about a sore throat.

_____

_____

14. A patient in your office is having trouble breathing. You have been asked to call EMS. What five pieces of information will you need before you make the call?

   a. _____

   b. _____

   c. _____

   d. _____

   e. _____

15. Below are the steps that a receptionist should take to prepare the office for patient and other employee arrivals. However, they are not listed in the correct order. Review the steps and then place them in the correct order in which they should be performed.

   a. Turn on computers, printers, copiers, and other electronic devices.

   b. Disengage the alarm system.

   c. Restock your desk with necessary forms and office supplies.

   d. If the office uses a drop box to leave specimens for evening pickups, check the box to ensure that the specimens were taken.

   e. Turn on appropriate lights.

   f. Unlock doors as appropriate.

16. Dr. Porter is in a meeting, but he has instructed you to communicate with him via cell phone when you get the test results back for a certain patient. However, he does not like to have his cell phone ring while he is in meetings. How will you communicate with him?

_____

_____

17. It is an exceptionally hot day in spring. Because the air conditioner is not on yet, you take a chair from the waiting room and prop the door open with it. You also move the boxes that were delivered earlier away from the window so the air comes in. How is this a violation of the Americans with Disabilities Act?

_____

_____

18. Explain how a teletypewriter can help a hearing-impaired person communicate with a physician's office.

_____

_____

19. Match the following key terms to their definitions.

Key Terms

a. attitude _____

b. closed captioning _____

c. diction _____

d. diplomacy _____

e. emergency medical service (EMS) _____

f. ergonomic _____

g. receptionist _____

h. teletypewriter (TTY) _____

i. triage _____

Definitions

1. a person who performs administrative tasks and greets patients as they arrive at an office

2. the art of handling people with tact and genuine concern

3. a group of health care workers who care for sick and injured patients on the way to a hospital

4. printed words displayed on a television screen to help people with hearing disabilities or impairments

5. describing a workstation designed to prevent work-related injuries

6. the style of speaking and enunciating words

7. the sorting of patients into categories based on their level of sickness or injury

8. a state of mind or feeling regarding some matter

9. a special machine that allows communication on a telephone with a hearing-impaired person

20. True or False? Determine whether the following statements are true or false. If false, explain why.

a. An ergonomic workstation is nice, but not essential, for a medical office receptionist.

_____

_____

b. Jewelry such as dangling earrings and large rings are not appropriate for employees in a medical office.

_____

_____

c. Information about patients should never be transmitted using a fax machine.

_____

_____

d. It is not appropriate to have a television in a medical office waiting area.

_____

_____

APPLICATION

Critical Thinking Practice

1. You work as the office receptionist in a pediatrician's office. The physician has requested the purchase of new videos that can be used as teaching tools for parents. What kind of videos should you consider purchasing?

_____

_____

2. You receive a call from a patient who complains of being short of breath. What questions will you ask to determine whether this is an emergency?

_____

Patient Education

1. Mrs. Gonzalez calls to schedule her annual check-up. She is put on hold, and when the receptionist comes back to her call, she is upset that she was placed on hold. When she comes in for her appointment, she says that the receptionist should deal with every call individually and that no one should be placed on hold. How would you explain the phone call triage system to her?

_____

_____

Documentation

1. Ms. Wheeler calls the office in the morning complaining of dizziness and nausea. She comes in for a 10:30 AM appointment. While she's in the waiting room, she faints and falls on the floor. She wakes up and says that she is still dizzy. The physician asks you to call for an ambulance to take Ms. Wheeler to the local hospital. Write a narrative note describing the situation to be included in the patient's chart.

_____

_____

Active Learning

1. You have accepted a job as the receptionist for a physician opening a new office. She asks you to develop a plan for the waiting room and to make a list of all the necessary furniture and equipment she will need to purchase. Type up a plan including a brief description of the room, and then research the costs of the furniture and equipment on your list to provide the physician with a budget.

2. Working with two classmates, role-play a medical emergency in the physician's office waiting room. Have one person play the role of the patient, the second person play the role of the receptionist, and the third person play the role of the EMS call operator. The patient should describe his or her condition, and the receptionist is responsible for conveying these details to EMS. Switch roles so that everyone gets a chance to play each role.

3. Many individuals with disabilities rely on service animals to assist them with daily activities. A number of patients in your office have service animals and routinely bring them in to the office. The new receptionist says that it is against the law to have animals in a place of business. Visit the website for the U.S. Department of Justice/Americans with Disabilities Act at www.usdoj.gov/crt/ada. Research any rules that apply to service animals in businesses and organizations. Then create a pamphlet for your office educating staff about this topic.

Professional Journal

Reflect

(Prompts and Ideas: Think about your past experiences as a patient. What do you like about the waiting rooms at medical offices you have visited in the past? What do you dislike? Have you ever had a negative experience with medical office staff either over the phone or in the reception area? How did it make you feel? What do you wish you could change about the experience?)

_____

_____

_____

_____

_____

_____

PONDER AND SOLVE

1. Mr. Johnson is a difficult patient and frequently makes angry phone calls to the office. Today, he called yelling that his prescription refill had not been called in by the office. He demanded to speak to the person responsible, who is Nurse Karen. Nurse Karen had to leave early. What should you do?

_____

_____

_____

_____

2. Your office shows videos about healthy living, exercise, and nutrition throughout the day. It seems that most of the adults watch and enjoy the programming. One crowded afternoon, a patient comes up to the desk to complain that the programming is distracting and he would prefer having the television turned off. However, there are people in the room watching the television. What would you say to the upset patient?

_____

_____

_____

_____

_____

EXPERIENCE

Skills related to this chapter include:

1. Handling Incoming Calls (Procedure 5-1).
2. Calling Emergency Medical Services (Procedure 5-2).
3. Explaining General Office Policies (Procedure 5-3).

Record any common mistakes, lessons learned, and/or tips you discovered during your experience of practicing and demonstrating these skills:

_____

_____

_____

_____

_____

Skill Practice

PERFORMANCE OBJECTIVES:

1. Handle incoming calls (Procedure 5-1).
2. Call Emergency Medical Services (Procedure 5-2).
3. Explain general office policies (Procedure 5-3).

Name _____ Date _____ Time _____

HANDLING INCOMING CALLS

EQUIPMENT/SUPPLIES: Telephone, telephone message pad, writing utensil (pen or pencil), headset (if applicable)

STANDARDS: Given the needed equipment and a place to work, the student will perform this skill with _____% accuracy in a total of _____ minutes. (*Your instructor will tell you what the percentage and time limits will be before you begin.*)

KEY: 4 = Satisfactory   0 = Unsatisfactory   NA = This step is not counted

PROCEDURE STEPS	SELF	PARTNER	INSTRUCTOR
1. Gather the needed equipment.	☐	☐	☐
2. Answer the phone within two rings.	☐	☐	☐
3. Greet caller with proper identification (your name and the name of the office).	☐	☐	☐
4. Identify the nature or reason for the call in a timely manner.	☐	☐	☐
5. Triage the call appropriately.	☐	☐	☐
6. Communicate in a professional manner and with unhurried speech.	☐	☐	☐
7. Clarify information as needed.	☐	☐	☐
8. Record the message on a message pad. Include the name of caller, date, time, telephone number where the caller can be reached, description of the caller's concerns, and person to whom the message is routed.	☐	☐	☐
9. Give the caller an approximate time for a return call.	☐	☐	☐
10. Ask the caller whether he or she has any additional questions or needs any other help.	☐	☐	☐
11. Allow the caller to disconnect first.	☐	☐	☐
12. Put the message in an assigned place.	☐	☐	☐
13. Complete the task within 10 minutes.	☐	☐	☐

CALCULATION

Total Possible Points: _____
Total Points Earned: _____ Multiplied by 100 = _____ Divided by Total Possible Points = _____%

Pass   **Fail**
☐   ☐   Comments:

Student's signature _____ Date _____
Partner's signature _____ Date _____
Instructor's signature _____ Date _____

Name _____   Date _____   Time _____

| Procedure 5-2: | **CALLING EMERGENCY MEDICAL SERVICES** |

EQUIPMENT/SUPPLIES: Telephone, patient information, writing utensil (pen, pencil)

STANDARDS: Given the needed equipment and a place to work, the student will perform this skill with _____% accuracy in a total of _____ minutes. (*Your instructor will tell you what the percentage and time limits will be before you begin.*)

KEY: 4 = Satisfactory   0 = Unsatisfactory   NA = This step is not counted

PROCEDURE STEPS	SELF	PARTNER	INSTRUCTOR
1. Obtain the following the information before dialing: patient's name, age, sex, nature of medical condition, type of service the physician is requesting, any special instructions or requests the physician may have, your location, and any special information for access.	☐	☐	☐
2. Dial 911 or other EMS number.	☐	☐	☐
3. Calmly provide the dispatcher with the above information.	☐	☐	☐
4. Answer the dispatcher's questions calmly and professionally.	☐	☐	☐
5. Follow the dispatcher's instructions, if applicable.	☐	☐	☐
6. End the call as per dispatcher instructions.	☐	☐	☐
7. Complete the task within 10 minutes.	☐	☐	☐

CALCULATION

Total Possible Points: _____
Total Points Earned: _____ Multiplied by 100 = _____ Divided by Total Possible Points = _____%

Pass   **Fail**
☐   ☐   Comments:

Student's signature _____ Date _____
Partner's signature _____ Date _____
Instructor's signature _____ Date _____

Name_____ Date _____ Time _____

| Procedure 5-3: | **EXPLAIN GENERAL OFFICE POLICIES** |

EQUIPMENT/SUPPLIES: Patient's chart, office brochure

STANDARDS: Given the needed equipment and a place to work, the student will perform this skill with _____% accuracy in a total of _____ minutes. (*Your instructor will tell you what the percentage and time limits will be before you begin.*)

KEY: 4 = Satisfactory   0 = Unsatisfactory   NA = This step is not counted

PROCEDURE STEPS	SELF	PARTNER	INSTRUCTOR
1. Assess the patient's level of understanding.	☐	☐	☐
2. Review important areas and highlight these in the office brochure.	☐	☐	☐
3. Ask the patient if he or she understands or has any questions.	☐	☐	☐
4. Give the patient the brochure to take home.	☐	☐	☐
5. Put in place a procedure for updating information and letting patients know of changes.	☐	☐	☐

CALCULATION

Total Possible Points: _____
Total Points Earned: _____ Multiplied by 100 = _____ Divided by Total Possible Points = _____%

Pass   **Fail**
☐   ☐ | Comments:

Student's signature _____ Date _____
Partner's signature _____ Date _____
Instructor's signature _____ Date _____

Chapter Self-Assessment Quiz

1. Which of the following creates a professional image?

   a. Arguing with a patient

   b. Clean, pressed clothing

   c. Brightly colored fingernails

   d. Referring to physicians by first name

   e. Expensive flowery perfume

2. How can you exercise diplomacy?

   a. Treat patients as they treat you.

   b. Treat patients as you would like to be treated.

   c. Ignore patients who complain about their illnesses.

   d. Answer patients' questions about other patients they see in the waiting room.

   e. Disclose confidential information if a patient or relative asks for it tactfully.

3. When preparing the charts for the day, the charts should be put in order by:

   a. age.

   b. last name.

   c. chart number.

   d. reason for visit.

   e. appointment time.

4. The receptionist should check phone messages:

   a. at night before leaving.

   b. in the morning when coming in.

   c. when on the phone and knows a call has gone to voice mail.

   d. only after breaks, because each call coming in should be answered.

   e. when the office opens, after breaks, and periodically throughout the day.

5. Triaging calls is important because:

   a. it reduces the amount of time that callers wait.

   b. it places the calls in order of most urgent to least urgent.

   c. it lets the receptionist take care of the calls as quickly as possible.

   d. it puts the calls in time order so the receptionist knows who called first.

   e. it makes it easier for the receptionist to see which calls will be the easiest to handle.

6. There is a sign in the pediatrician's office that says "Do not throw dirty diapers in the garbage." Which of the following choices best explains the reason for the sign?

   a. Dirty diapers cannot be recycled.

   b. Dirty diapers are biohazard waste.

   c. Dirty diapers could leave an offensive odor.

   d. Dirty diapers could make the garbage too heavy.

   e. Dirty diapers take up too much room in the garbage.

7. Chewing gum or eating while on the phone could interfere with a person's:

   a. diction.

   b. attitude.

   c. ergonomics.

   d. expression.

   e. pronunciation.

8. Which of the following activities should a receptionist do in the morning to prepare the office for patients?

   a. Vacuum the office.

   b. Stock office supplies.

   c. Disinfect examination rooms.

   d. Turn on printers and copiers.

   e. Clean the patient restrooms.

9. Which of the following statements about telephone courtesy is correct?

   a. If two lines are ringing at once, answer one call and let the other go to voice mail.

   b. If you are on the other line, it is acceptable to let the phone ring until you can answer it.

   c. If a caller is upset, leaving him or her on hold will help improve the caller's attitude.

   d. If you need to answer another line, ask if the caller would mind holding and wait for a response.

   e. If someone is on hold for more than 90 seconds, they must leave a message and someone will call them back.

10. An ergonomic workstation is beneficial because it:

   a. prevents injuries to employees.

   b. educates patients about disease.

   c. maintains patients' confidentiality.

   d. creates a soothing, relaxed atmosphere.

   e. prevents the spread of contagious diseases.

11. Which feature fosters a positive waiting room environment?

    a. Abstract artwork on the walls

    b. Only sofas for patients to sit in

    c. Soap operas on the waiting room television

    d. Prominent display of the office fax machine

    e. Patient education materials in the reception area

12. How does a physician's pager system work?

    a. The pager sends a typed message that can be read by the physician.

    b. The pager has a "listen only" mode so the physician can hear messages.

    c. The pager will beep every two minutes until the physician answers it.

    d. The pager calls the physician over an intercom, so he/she can pick up a phone and call.

    e. The pager informs the physician of calls, but it cannot communicate messages.

13. A five-year-old girl has just come into the office with her mother. She has the flu and is vomiting into a plastic bag. Which of the following should the receptionist do?

    a. Get the patient into an examination room.

    b. Call the hospital and request an ambulance.

    c. Tell her to sit near the bathroom so she can vomit in the toilet.

    d. Place a new plastic bag in your garbage can and ask the girl to use it.

    e. Ask the patient to wait outside and you will get her when it is her turn.

14. An angry patient calls the office demanding to speak to the physician. The physician is not in the office. What should the receptionist do?

    a. Page the physician immediately.

    b. Try to calm the patient and take a message.

    c. Give the caller the physician's cell phone number.

    d. Tell the patient to calm down and call back in an hour.

    e. Place the patient on hold until he or she has calmed down.

15. Which of the following statements about e-mail is true?

    a. Patient e-mails should be deleted from the computer.

    b. The receptionist does not generally have access to e-mail.

    c. Actions taken in regard to e-mail do not need to be documented.

    d. Patients should not e-mail the office under any circumstances.

    e. E-mails should not be printed because the wrong person could view them.

16. The best technique for preventing the spread of disease is:

    a. washing your hands after any contact with patients.

    b. placing very sick patients immediately in an exam room.

    c. removing all reading materials or toys from the waiting room.

    d. keeping the window to the reception area closed at all times.

    e. preventing patients from changing channels on the TV in the waiting room.

17. One way to ensure patient privacy in the reception area is to:

    a. take all the patient's information at the front desk.

    b. ask the patient's permission before placing her name on the sign-in sheet.

    c. use computers in examination rooms only.

    d. make telephone calls regarding referrals at the front desk.

    e. close the privacy window when you are not speaking with a patient.

18. When receiving a call from a lab regarding a patient's test results, you should post the information:

    a. as an e-mail to the physician.

    b. in the receptionist's notebook.

    c. in the front of the patient's chart.

    d. as an e-mail to the patient's insurance company.

    e. in the front of the physician's appointment book.

19. In case of an emergency in the physician's office, who is usually responsible for calling emergency medical service (EMS)?

    a. Physician

    b. Dispatcher

    c. Receptionist

    d. Clinical staff

    e. Patient's relatives

20. What is a benefit of the teletypewriter (TTY)?

    a. Physicians can have verbal orders recorded in print.

    b. EMS crews can send messages from remote locations.

    c. Patients with hearing or speech impairments can type messages.

    d. A receptionist can write messages to patients on a television screen.

    e. Clinical staff can communicate with hearing-impaired patients within the medical office.

6 Managing Appointments

☐ Read textbook chapter and take notes within the Chapter Notes outline. Answer the Learning Objectives as you reach them in the content, and then check them off.

☐ Work the Content Review questions—both Foundational Knowledge and Application.

☐ Perform the Active Learning exercise(s).

☐ Complete Professional Journal entries.

☐ Complete Skill Practice Activity(s) using Competency Evaluation Forms and Work Products, when appropriate.

☐ Take the Chapter Self-Assessment Quiz.

☐ Insert all appropriate pages into your Portfolio.

1. Spell and define the key terms.
2. Describe the various systems for scheduling patient office visits, including manual and computerized scheduling.
3. Identify the factors that affect appointment scheduling.
4. Explain guidelines for scheduling appointments for new patients, return visits, inpatient admissions, and outpatient procedures.

5. List three ways to remind patients about appointments.
6. Describe how to triage patient emergencies, acutely ill patients, and walk-in patients.
7. Describe how to handle late patients.
8. Explain what to do if the physician is delayed.
9. Describe how to handle patients who miss their appointments.
10. Describe how to handle appointment cancellations made by the office or by the patient.

Note: Bold-faced headings are the major headings in the text chapter; headings in regular font are lower-level headings (i.e., the content is subordinate to, or falls "under," the major headings). Make sure you understand the key terms used in the chapter, as well as the concepts presented as Key Points.

TEXT SUBHEADINGS	NOTES

Introduction _____

_____

Key Term: providers
Key Point:
• Your responsibility is to manage all of this while maintaining a calm, efficient, and polite attitude.

☐ **LEARNING OBJECTIVE 1:** Spell and define the key terms.

Appointment Scheduling Systems _____

_____

Manual Appointment Scheduling _____

_____

The Appointment Book _____

_____

Establishing a Matrix _____

_____

Key Term: matrix
Key Point:
• Along with the notations in a patient's chart, the pages of the appointment book provide documentation of a patient's visits and any changes, such as cancellations and rescheduled appointments.

Computerized Appointment Scheduling _____

_____

Key Point:
• Once the daily schedule is printed, this important document is referred to as the daily activity sheet or the day sheet and is the guide for everyone involved in the flow of patient care. Figure 6-2 shows a computer-generated daily activity sheet.

☐ **LEARNING OBJECTIVE 2:** Describe the various systems for scheduling patient office visits, including manual and computerized scheduling.

Types of Scheduling _____

_____

_____

Structured Appointments _____

_____

Key Term: buffer

Clustering _____

_____

Key Term: clustering

Wave and Modified Wave _____

_____

Key Term: wave scheduling system

Fixed Scheduling _____

_____

_____

Streaming _____

_____

Key Term: streaming

Double Booking _____

_____

Key Term: double booking

Flexible Hours _____

_____

_____

Open Hours _____

_____

_____

Factors That Affect Scheduling _____

_____

_____

Patients' Needs _____

_____

Key Terms: acute, chronic
Key Point:
• With a patient in an emotional state, even the slightest real or imagined miscommunication can lead to a negative response from the patient.

Providers' Preferences and Needs _____

_____

_____

Physical Facilities _____

_____

Key Point:
• You must thoroughly understand the requirements for procedures to be performed in the office to schedule appointments accurately.

☐ **LEARNING OBJECTIVE 3:** Identify the factors that affect appointment scheduling.

Scheduling Guidelines _____

_____

_____

New Patients _____

_____

Key Point:
• The information you exchange at this encounter is crucial, and entering the patient's data accurately is imperative.

Established Patients _____

_____

☐ **LEARNING OBJECTIVE 4:** Explain guidelines for scheduling appointments for new patients, return visits, inpatient admissions, and outpatient procedures.

Preparing a Daily or Weekly Schedule _____

_____

_____

Patient Reminders _____

_____

_____

Appointment Cards _____

_____

_____

Telephone Reminders _____

_____

Key Point:
• All new patients and patients with appointments scheduled in advance should receive a telephone reminder the day before their appointment.

Mailed Reminder Cards _____

_____

Key Term: tickler file

☐ **LEARNING OBJECTIVE 5:** List three ways to remind patients about appointments.

Adapting the Schedule _____

_____

_____

Emergencies _____

_____

Key Terms: STAT; constellation of symptoms
Key Point:
• When a patient calls with an emergency (Fig. 6-5), your first responsibility is to determine whether the problem can be treated in the office.

Patients Who Are Acutely Ill _____

_____

Key Point:
• Obtain as much information about the patient's medical problem as you can so your message to the physician will allow him or her to decide how soon the patient should be seen.

Walk-in Patients _____

_____

☐ **LEARNING OBJECTIVE 6:** Describe how to triage patient emergencies, acutely ill patients, and walk-in patients.

Late Patients _____

_____

_____

☐ **LEARNING OBJECTIVE 7:** Describe how to handle late patients.

Physician Delays _____

_____

Key Point:
• If patients are waiting in the office, inform them immediately if the physician will be delayed.

☐ **LEARNING OBJECTIVE 8:** Explain what to do if the physician is delayed.

Missed Appointments _____

_____

Key Point:
• Continued failure to keep appointments should be brought to the attention of the physician, who may want to call the patient personally (particularly if the patient is seriously ill) or send a letter expressing concern for the patient's welfare.

☐ **LEARNING OBJECTIVE 9:** Describe how to handle patients who miss their appointments.

Cancellations _____

_____

_____

Cancellations by the Office _____

_____

Key Point:
• These cancellations should be noted in the patient's medical record.

Cancellations by the Patient _____

_____

_____

☐ **LEARNING OBJECTIVE 10:** Describe how to handle appointment cancellations made by the office or by the patient.

Making Appointments for Patients in Other Facilities _____

_____

_____

Referrals and Consultations _____

_____

Key Terms: consultation; referral; precertification
Key Point:
• Be sure the physician you are calling is on the preferred provider list for the patient's insurance company.

Diagnostic Testing _____

_____

_____

Surgery _____

_____

_____

When the Appointment Schedule Does Not Work _____

_____

Key Point:
• Since the work flow of the office affects every staff member, involve all employees in your study.

Content Review

FOUNDATIONAL KNOWLEDGE

Know Your Schedule

1. Medical offices may either use a manual or computerized appointment scheduling system. There are characteristics specific to each type of system. In the table below, read each characteristic, and then decide which type of system it describes. Place a check in the appropriate column.

Characteristic	Manual	Computerized
a. An appointment book		
b. Feature that allows you to search the appointment database for the next available timeslot		
c. Easy access to billing information		
d. Matrix created by crossing out unavailable times		

2. Identify each type of scheduling system in the chart below.

Description	Type of Scheduling System
a. several patients are scheduled for the first 30 minutes of each hour	
b. appointments are given based on the needs of individual patients	
c. each hour is divided into increments of 15, 30, 45, or 60 minutes for appointments depending on the reason for the visit	
d. patients are grouped according to needs or problems	
e. two patients are scheduled for the same period with the same physician	

3. List four advantages to clustering patients.

a. _____

b. _____

c. _____

d. _____

Schedule S.O.S.

4. Mr. Gonzalez requests an appointment for 1 PM on Wednesday. You already have a patient scheduled on that day and time slot. What should you do?

_____

_____

5. Name the three factors that can affect scheduling.

a. _____

b. _____

c. _____

6. The allotted time for each service will vary among different medical offices. However, you can estimate how long each service should take when creating a schedule. Match each service below with the estimated amount of time needed for each one.

Service

a. blood pressure check

b. complete physical exam

c. dressing change

d. recheck

e. school physical

Estimated Time

1. 5 minutes

2. 10 minutes

3. 15 minutes

4. 30 minutes

5. 1 hour

7. Below are the steps for making a return appointment. Some of the steps are false or incomplete. Review each step and then decide if it is correct or incorrect. If incorrect, rewrite the statement to make it true and complete.

a. Carefully check your appointment book or screen before offering an appointment time. If a specific examination, test, or x-ray is to be performed on the return visit, avoid scheduling two patients for the same examination at the same time.

_____

_____

b. Ask the patient when he or she would like to return.

_____

_____

c. Write the patient's name and telephone number in the appointment book or enter the information in computer.

_____

_____

d. Transfer the information to an appointment card that you will mail out to the patient at a later date.

_____

_____

e. Double-check your book or screen to be sure there are no errors.

_____

_____

f. End your conversation with a pleasant word and a smile.

_____

_____

8. Don't Forget. . .

List the three ways to remind patients about appointments.

a. _____

b. _____

c. _____

9. When a patient calls with an emergency, your first responsibility is to:

a. determine if the patient has an appointment.

b. decide whether the problem can be treated in the office.

c. verify that the physician can see the patient.

d. identify the patient's constellation of symptoms.

10. What should you do if the physician decides not to see a walk-in patient?

a. Ask the patient to schedule an appointment to return later.

b. Explain that the physician is too busy.

c. Tell the patient to try a different medical office.

d. Tell the patient to go to the hospital.

11. Tardy Party

Like the rabbit in "Alice in Wonderland," some patients always seem to be running just behind schedule. Patients who are routinely late might benefit by having their appointments _____ for a time at the _____ of the day.

a. rescheduled; end

b. suspended; beginning

c. revoked; afternoon

d. renewed; middle

12. Time on the Mind

Sometimes, the physician will be the person who is running late. Explain what you would do in each situation.
The physician calls in to the office to say he is delayed. What would you do if:

a. Office hours have not yet begun.

_____

_____

b. Patients are waiting in the office.

_____

_____

13. **No-Show**

Sometimes, a patient may neglect to keep an appointment. When this happens, you should call the patient. What should you do if you are unable to reach the patient by phone?

_____

_____

14. When might you write a letter to a patient who has an appointment that you must cancel?

   a. when you can't reach the patient by phone

   b. when the physician leaves the office abruptly

   c. when you have advance notice from the physician

   d. when you want to use written communication

15. Maria has just called into the office to cancel her appointment for today. Explain what you should do.

_____

_____

16. When calling another physician's office for an appointment for your patient, you'll need to provide certain information. Review the list below and circle the information that you should provide to another physician's office.

Physician's name	Patient's name	Physician's telephone number	Insurance company's telephone number
Reason for the referral	Patient's allergies	Patient's Social Security number	Patient's address and telephone number
Patient's next of kin	Degree of urgency	Patient's insurance information	If patient needs a consultation or referral

17. If diagnostic testing requires preparation from the patient, what should you do?

_____

_____

18. Preadmission testing for surgery may include:

   a. _____

   b. _____

   c. _____

19. Match the following key terms to their definitions.

Key Terms

   a. acute _____

   b. buffer _____

   c. chronic _____

   d. clustering _____

   e. constellation of symptoms _____

   f. consultation _____

   g. double booking _____

   h. matrix _____

   i. precertification _____

Definitions

   1. a group of clinical signs indicating a particular disease process

   2. the practice of booking two patients for the same period with the same physician

   3. term used in the medical field to indicate that something should be done immediately

   4. a system for blocking off unavailable patient appointment times

   5. a flexible scheduling method that allows time for procedures of varying lengths and the addition of unscheduled patients, as needed

   6. referring to a longstanding medical problem

   7. grouping patients with similar problems or needs

j. providers _____

k. referral _____

l. STAT _____

m. streaming _____

n. tickler file _____

o. wave scheduling system _____

8. a method of allotting time for appointments based on the needs of the individual patient that helps minimize gaps in time and backups

9. extra time booked on the schedule to accommodate emergencies, walk-ins, and other demands on the provider's daily time schedule that are not considered direct patient care

10. health care workers who deliver medical care

11. referring to a medical problem with abrupt onset

12. request for assistance from one physician to another

13. approved documentation prior to referrals to specialists and other facilities

14. instructions to transfer a patient's care to a specialist

15. a file that provides a reminder to do a given task at a particular date and time

20. True or False? Determine whether the following statements are true or false. If false, explain why.

a. Fixed scheduling is the most commonly used method.

_____

_____

b. A medical office that operates with open hours for patient visits is open 24 hours a day, 7 days a week.

_____

_____

c. Most appointments for new patients are made in person.

_____

_____

d. Patients with medical emergencies need to be seen immediately.

_____

_____

APPLICATION

Critical Thinking Practice

1. An elderly patient walks into the medical office. His constellation of symptoms includes chest discomfort, shortness of breath, and nausea. He doesn't have an appointment. Explain what you would do.

_____

_____

2. The appointment book below is divided into half-hour increments. The spaces below each time slot are empty. Fill in the appointment book with the following information: Dr. Brown has hospital rounds from 8:00 AM to 9:00 AM He has the following appointments: Cindy Wallis at 9:30 AM; Bill Waters at 10:00 AM; Rodney Kingston at 10:30 AM

8:00	8:30	9:00	9:30	10:00	10:30

Janet Pele calls the office and requests an emergency morning appointment because of a high fever. Can you accommodate her? Explain.

_____

_____

Patient Education

1. Juan is consistently late for appointments. You've spoken with him several times. What should you do next? Explain what you will you say to him and the information you will provide him with.

_____

_____

Documentation

1. Write a narrative charting note describing your interactions with Juan from the question above.

_____

_____

Active Learning

1. Record all of the activities you take part in on a typical day. Then, practice scheduling by placing these activities in a matrix.

2. Pretend that you're a new patient. Make a list of questions you might have about the medical office. Now as a medical assistant, answer your questions. If you don't know the answer to a question, find out. Then tape this "Q and A" list somewhere around your desk, and use it when new patients come into the office.

3. If you work in a medical office, place a "suggestions box" in the waiting room. Patients can place their suggestions concerning waiting times, scheduling, etc., into the box anonymously and at their leisure. After two weeks, open the box and discuss the suggestions with your coworkers. Decide which suggestions are possible and discuss ways of implementing these changes. Create a report for the medical office discussing the suggestions and how they may be addressed.

Professional Journal

REFLECT

(Prompts and Ideas: Are you concerned about controlling the appointment schedule effectively? How will you keep track of appointments, missed patients, physician delays, etc? Think about the medical office that you visit as a patient. In what ways does the medical assistant keep the schedule running smoothly? What changes would you like to see?)

_____

_____

_____

_____

_____

_____

PONDER AND SOLVE

1. Patients may come and go without your direct involvement in their care. Even so, why is it important for you to understand the reason for a patient's appointment?

_____

_____

_____

_____

_____

_____

_____

2. Would you rather use a manual or computerized appointment scheduling system? Explain your reasons and give advantages and disadvantages for each.

_____

_____

_____

_____

_____

_____

_____

_____

EXPERIENCE

Skills related to this chapter include:

1. Making an Appointment for a New Patient (Procedure 6-1).
2. Making an Appointment for an Established Patient (Procedure 6-2).
3. Making an Appointment for a Referral to an Outpatient Facility (Procedure 6-3).
4. Arranging for Admission to an Inpatient Facility (Procedure 6-4).

Record any common mistakes, lessons learned, and/or tips you discovered during your experience of practicing and demonstrating these skills:

_____

_____

_____

_____

_____

_____

_____

**Skill
Practice**

PERFORMANCE OBJECTIVES:

1. Schedule an appointment for a new patient (Procedure 6-1).
2. Schedule an appointment for a return visit (Procedure 6-2).
3. Schedule an appointment for a referral to an outpatient facility (Procedure 6-3).
4. Arrange for admission to an inpatient facility (Procedure 6-4).

Name _____   Date _____   Time _____

Procedure 6-1:	MAKING AN APPOINTMENT FOR A NEW PATIENT

EQUIPMENT/ITEMS NEEDED: Patient's demographic information, patient's chief complaint, appointment book or computer with appointment software

STANDARDS: Given the needed equipment and a place to work, the student will perform this skill with _____ % accuracy in a total of _____ minutes. (*Your instructor will tell you what the percentage and time limits will be before you begin.*)

KEY: 4 = Satisfactory   0 = Unsatisfactory   NA = This step is not counted

PROCEDURE STEPS	SELF	PARTNER	INSTRUCTOR
1. Obtain as much information as possible from the patient, such as: • Full name and correct spelling • Mailing address (not all offices require this) • Day and evening telephone numbers • Reason for the visit • Name of the referring person	☐	☐	☐
2. Determine the patient's chief complaint or the reason for seeing the physician.	☐	☐	☐
3. Explain the payment policy of the practice. Instruct patients to bring all pertinent insurance information.	☐	☐	☐
4. Give concise directions if needed.	☐	☐	☐
5. Ask the patient if it is permissible to call at home or at work.	☐	☐	☐
6. Confirm the time and date of the appointment.	☐	☐	☐
7. Check your appointment book to be sure that you have placed the appointment on the correct day in the right time slot.	☐	☐	☐
8. If the patient was referred by another physician, call that physician's office before the appointment for copies of laboratory work, radiology, pathology reports, and so on. Give this information to the physician prior to the patient's appointment.	☐	☐	☐

CALCULATION

Total Possible Points: _____
Total Points Earned: _____ Multiplied by 100 = _____ Divided by Total Possible Points = _____%

Pass   **Fail**
☐   ☐   Comments:

Student's signature _____ Date _____
Partner's signature _____ Date _____
Instructor's signature _____ Date _____

Name _____ Date _____ Time _____

MAKING AN APPOINTMENT FOR AN ESTABLISHED PATIENT

EQUIPMENT: Appointment book or computer with appointment software, appointment card

STANDARDS: Given the needed equipment and a place to work, the student will perform this skill with _____ % accuracy in a total of _____ minutes. (*Your instructor will tell you what the percentage and time limits will be before you begin.*)

KEY: 4 = Satisfactory   0 = Unsatisfactory   NA = This step is not counted

PROCEDURE STEPS	SELF	PARTNER	INSTRUCTOR
1. Determine what will be done at the return visit. Check your appointment book or computer system before offering an appointment.	☐	☐	☐
2. Offer the patient a specific time and date. Avoid asking the patient when he or she would like to return, as this can cause indecision.	☐	☐	☐
3. Write the patient's name and telephone number in the appointment book or enter it in the computer.	☐	☐	☐
4. Transfer the pertinent information to an appointment card and give it to the patient. Repeat aloud the appointment day, date, and time to the patient as you hand over the card.	☐	☐	☐
5. Double-check your book or computer to be sure you have not made an error.	☐	☐	☐
6. End your conversation with a pleasant word and a smile.	☐	☐	☐

CALCULATION

Total Possible Points: _____
Total Points Earned: _____ Multiplied by 100 = _____ Divided by Total Possible Points = _____%

Pass   **Fail**
☐   ☐   Comments:

Student's signature _____ Date _____
Partner's signature _____ Date _____
Instructor's signature _____ Date _____

Name _____ Date _____ Time _____

Procedure 6-3:	**MAKING AN APPOINTMENT FOR A REFERRAL TO AN OUTPATIENT FACILITY**

EQUIPMENT: Patient's chart with demographic information; physician's order for services needed by the patient and reason for the services; patient's insurance card with referral information, referral form, and directions to office

STANDARDS: Given the needed equipment and a place to work, the student will perform this skill with _____ % accuracy in a total of _____ minutes. (*Your instructor will tell you what the percentage and time limits will be before you begin.*)

KEY: 4 = Satisfactory   0 = Unsatisfactory   NA = This step is not counted

PROCEDURE STEPS	**SELF**	**PARTNER**	**INSTRUCTOR**
1. Make certain that the requirements of any third-party payers are met.	☐	☐	☐
2. Refer to the preferred provider list for the patient's insurance company. Allow the patient to choose a provider from the list.	☐	☐	☐
3. Have the following information available when you make the call: • Physician's name and telephone number • Patient's name, address, and telephone number • Reason for the call • Degree of urgency • Whether the patient is being sent for consultation or referral	☐	☐	☐
4. Record in the patient's chart the time and date of the call and the name of the person who received your call.	☐	☐	☐
5. Tell the person you are calling that you wish to be notified if your patient does not keep the appointment. If this occurs, be sure to tell your physician and enter this information in the patient's record.	☐	☐	☐
6. Write down the name, address, and telephone number of the doctor you are referring your patient to and include the date and time of the appointment. Give or mail this information to your patient. Be certain that the information is complete, accurate, and easy to read.	☐	☐	☐
7. If the patient is to call the referring physician to make the appointment, ask the patient to call you with the appointment date, then document this in the chart.	☐	☐	☐

CALCULATION

Total Possible Points: _____
Total Points Earned: _____ Multiplied by 100 = _____ Divided by Total Possible Points = _____%

Pass   **Fail**
☐   ☐

Comments:

Student's signature _____ Date _____
Partner's signature _____ Date _____
Instructor's signature _____ Date _____

Name _____ Date _____ Time _____

ARRANGING FOR ADMISSION TO AN INPATIENT FACILITY

EQUIPMENT: Physician's order with diagnosis, patient's chart with demographic information, contact information for inpatient facility

STANDARDS: Given the needed equipment and a place to work, the student will perform this skill with _____ % accuracy in a total of _____ minutes. (*Your instructor will tell you what the percentage and time limits will be before you begin.*)

KEY: 4 = Satisfactory   0 = Unsatisfactory   NA = This step is not counted

PROCEDURE STEPS	SELF	PARTNER	INSTRUCTOR
1. Determine the place patient and/or physician wants the admission arranged.	☐	☐	☐
2. Gather information for the other facility, including demographic and insurance information.	☐	☐	☐
3. Determine any precertification requirements. If needed, locate contact information on the back of the insurance card and call the insurance carrier to obtain a precertification number.	☐	☐	☐
4. Obtain from the physician the diagnosis and exact needs of the patient for an admission.	☐	☐	☐
5. Call the admissions department of the inpatient facility and give information from step 2.	☐	☐	☐
6. Obtain instructions for the patient and call or give the patient instructions and information.	☐	☐	☐
7. Provide the patient with the physician's orders for their hospital stay, including diet, medications, bed rest, etc.	☐	☐	☐
8. Document time, place, etc. in patient's chart, including any precertification requirements completed.	☐	☐	☐

CALCULATION

Total Possible Points: _____
Total Points Earned: _____ Multiplied by 100 = _____ Divided by Total Possible Points = _____ %

Pass   **Fail**
☐   ☐   Comments:

Student's signature _____ Date _____
Partner's signature _____ Date _____
Instructor's signature _____ Date _____

1. If your medical office uses a manual system of scheduled appointments for patient office visits, you will need a(n):

    a. toolbar.

    b. appointment book.

    c. computer.

    d. buffer time.

    e. fixed schedule.

2. How much time should be blocked off each morning and afternoon to accommodate emergencies, late arrivals, and other delays?

    a. 5 to 10 minutes

    b. 10 to 20 minutes

    c. 15 to 30 minutes

    d. 45 minutes to one hour

    e. one to two hours

3. When scheduling an appointment, why should you ask the patient the reason she needs to see the doctor?

    a. To know the level of empathy to give the patient

    b. To anticipate the time needed for the appointment

    c. To confront the patient about his personal choices

    d. To manipulate the patient's needs

    e. To determine who should see the patient

4. Which of the following is an advantage to clustering?

    a. Efficient use of employee's time

    b. Increased patient time for the physician

    c. Reduced staff costs for the office

    d. Shorter patient appointments

    e. Greater need for specialists in the office

5. In fixed scheduling, the length of time reserved for each appointment is determined by the:

    a. physician's personal schedule.

    b. number of hours open on a given day.

    c. reason for the patient's visit.

    d. type of insurance provider.

    e. patient's age.

6. Double booking works well when patients are being sent for diagnostic testing because:

    a. it gives each patient enough time to prepare for testing.

    b. it leaves time to see both patients without keeping either one waiting unnecessarily.

    c. the physician enjoys seeing two patients at one time.

    d. it challenges the medical practice's resources.

    e. it gives the physician more "downtime."

7. Which of the following is a disadvantage to open hours?

    a. Patients with emergencies cannot be seen quickly.

    b. Scheduling patients is a challenge.

    c. Effective time management is almost impossible.

    d. Walk-ins are encouraged.

    e. Patient charts aren't properly updated.

8. You should leave some time slots open during the schedule each day to:

    a. allow patients to make their own appointments online.

    b. make the schedule more well rounded.

    c. leave some time for personal responsibilities.

    d. provide the staff some flex time.

    e. make room for emergencies and delays.

9. Most return appointments are made:

    a. before the patient leaves the office.

    b. before the patient's appointment.

    c. after the patient leaves the office.

    d. during the patient's next visit.

    e. when the patient receives a mailed reminder.

10. Reminder cards be mailed:

    a. the first day of every month.

    b. a week before the date of the appointment.

    c. the beginning of the year.

    d. with all billing statements.

    e. only when the patient requests one.

11. A condition that is abrupt in onset is described as:

    a. chronic.

    b. commonplace.

    c. lethal.

    d. acute.

    e. uncurable.

12. Who is authorized to make the decision whether to see a walk-in patient or not?

    a. Medical assistant

    b. Emergency medical technician

    c. Physician

    d. Reception

    e. Nurse

13. If you reschedule an appointment, you should note the reason for the cancellation or rescheduling in:

    a. the patient's chart.

    b. the patient's immunization record

    c. the patient's insurance card

    d. the patient's billing form.

    e. the office's appointment book.

14. If you have to cancel on the day of an appointment because of a physician's illness:

    a. send the patient an apology letter.

    b. give the patient a detailed excuse.

    c. e-mail the patient a reminder.

    d. call the patient and explain.

    e. offer the patient a discount at his next appointment.

15. If you find that your schedule is chaotic nearly every day, then you should:

    a. evaluate the schedule over time.

    b. keep that information private.

    c. tell your supervisor that you would like a new job.

    d. stop the old schedule and make a new one.

    e. let the patients know that the schedule isn't working.

16. An instruction to transfer a patient's care to a specialist is a(n):

    a. precertification.

    b. consultation.

    c. transfer.

    d. referral.

    e. payback.

17. Established patients are:

    a. patients who are new to the practice.

    b. patients who have been to the practice before.

    c. patients who are over the age of 65.

    d. patients who are chronically ill.

    e. patients with insurance.

18. A flexible scheduling method that schedules patients for the first 30 minutes of an hour and leaves the second half of each hour open is called:

    a. clustering.

    b. wave scheduling system.

    c. streaming.

    d. fixed schedule system.

    e. doublebooking.

19. A chronic problem is one that is:

    a. not very serious.

    b. occurring for a short period of time.

    c. longstanding.

    d. easily cured.

    e. difficult to diagnose.

20. Which of the following is true of a constellation of symptoms?

    a. It can only be assessed by a physician.

    b. It is only an emergency if a patient is having a heart attack.

    c. It means a patient is suffering from appendicitis.

    d. It is a group of clinical signs indicating a particular disease.

    e. It probably requires a call to emergency medical services.

Written Communications

Chapter Checklist

- [ ] Read textbook chapter and take notes within the Chapter Notes outline. Answer the Learning Objectives as you reach them in the content, and then check them off.
- [ ] Work the Content Review questions—both Foundational Knowledge and Application.
- [ ] Perform the Active Learning exercise(s).
- [ ] Complete Professional Journal entries.
- [ ] Complete Skill Practice Activity(s) using Competency Evaluation Forms and Work Products, when appropriate.
- [ ] Take the Chapter Self-Assessment Quiz.
- [ ] Insert all appropriate pages into your Portfolio.

Learning Objectives

1. Spell and define key terms.
2. Discuss the basic guidelines for grammar, punctuation, and spelling in medical writing.
3. Discuss the 11 key components of a business letter.
4. Describe the process of writing a memorandum.
5. List the items that must be included in an agenda.
6. Identify the items that must be included when typing minutes.
7. Cite the various services available for sending written information.
8. Discuss the various mailing options.
9. Identify the types of incoming written communication seen in a physician's office.
10. Explain the guidelines for opening and sorting mail.

Chapter Notes

Note: Bold-faced headings are the major headings in the text chapter; headings in regular font are lower-level headings (i.e., the content is subordinate to, or falls "under," the major headings). Make sure you understand the key terms used in the chapter, as well as the concepts presented as Key Points.

TEXT SUBHEADINGS   **NOTES**

Introduction _____

_____

_____

☐ **LEARNING OBJECTIVE 1:** Spell and define key terms.

Guidelines for Producing Professional and Medical Documents _____

_____

_____

Basic Grammar and Punctuation Guidelines _____

_____

_____

Basic Spelling Guidelines _____

_____

Key Point:
• Remember, spell check will not recognize words that are spelled correctly but misused.

Accuracy _____

_____

Key Point:
• Inaccurate information in some letters can lead to injury of a patient and lawsuits and can harm the physician's practice.

Capitalization _____

_____

Key Terms: BiCaps, intercaps
Key Point:
• Ask for clarification and mark the proof letter with a question mark for the physician to assist.

Abbreviations and Symbols _____

_____

Key Point:
• When in doubt, spell it out.

Plural and Possessive _____

_____

Numbers _____

☐ **LEARNING OBJECTIVE 2:** Discuss the basic guidelines for grammar, punctuation, and spelling in medical writing.

Professional Letter Development _____

> **Key Point:**
> • The goal of professional writing is to get information communicated in a concise, accurate, and comprehensible manner.

Components of a Letter _____

> **Key Terms:** template; salutation; enclosure

☐ **LEARNING OBJECTIVE 3:** Discuss the eleven key components of a business letter.

Letter Formats _____

> **Key Terms:** full block; semiblock; block

Composing a Business Letter _____

Composition _____

> **Key Point:**
> • The goal of composition is to ensure that your message is transmitted clearly, concisely, and accurately to your reader. As you did during preparation, focus on the message, not on the mechanics.

Editing _____

Proofreading _____

_____

Key term: proofread

_____

Corrections _____

_____

_____

Types of Business Letters _____

_____

_____

Memorandum Development _____

_____

Key term: memorandum

_____

Components of a Memorandum _____

_____

☐ **LEARNING OBJECTIVE 4:** Describe the process of writing a memorandum.

_____

Composing Agendas and Minutes _____

_____

_____

Agendas _____

_____

Key Term: agenda
Key Point:
• It allows the meeting participants to prepare any necessary reports before the meeting and to anticipate questions.

_____

☐ **LEARNING OBJECTIVE 5:** List the items that must be included in an agenda.

_____

Minutes _____

_____

Key Point:
• Record only motions, seconds, and the results of a vote.

_____

☐ **LEARNING OBJECTIVE 6:** Identify the items that must be included when typing minutes.

_____

Sending Written Communication _____

_____

Key Point:
• All attempts must be made to ensure patient confidentiality.

Facsimile Machines _____

_____

_____

Electronic Mail _____

_____

_____

United States Postal Service _____

_____

_____

☐ **LEARNING OBJECTIVE 7:** Cite the various services available for sending written information.

Addressing Envelopes _____

_____

Key Term: font

Affixing Postage _____

_____

_____

USPS Mailing Options _____

_____

_____

USPS Special Services _____

_____

Key Point:
• It does not provide proof that the letter was received by the addressee.

Other Delivery Options _____

_____

_____

☐ **LEARNING OBJECTIVE 8:** Discuss the various mailing options.

Receiving and Handling Incoming Mail _____

_____

_____

Types of Incoming Mail _____

_____

☐ **LEARNING OBJECTIVE 9:** Identify the types of incoming written communication seen in a physician's office.

_____

Opening and Sorting Mail _____

_____

Key Point:
• Mail that pertains to patient care issues should be opened and handled appropriately.

☐ **LEARNING OBJECTIVE 10:** Explain the guidelines for opening and sorting mail.

_____

Annotation _____

_____

Key Term: annotation

Content Review

FOUNDATIONAL KNOWLEDGE

1. **Check Your Spelling**

   Read the following sentences. If the sentence is free of errors, write "correct" on the line. If the sentence contains errors, circle the problem and explain how you would fix the sentence.

   a. The patient has a cold and is bothered by the postnasal drip.

   _____

   _____

   b. The patient complained of constipation and has not had a bowl movement in three days.

   _____

   _____

   c. The patient, Mrs. Philips, sought weight-loss advise from the physician.

   _____

   _____

   d. The nurse applied antiseptic to the wounded elbow.

   _____

   _____

2. Capitalize

Review the list of terms below and place a check mark to indicate whether each term must always be capitalized.

Name	Always	Not always
a. Streptococcus		
b. Tylenol		
c. Benadryl		
d. Diagnosis		
e. Analgesic		
f. Merck		
g. Antihistamine		
h. Tampax		

3. Details, Details

Which charting note is written correctly?

a. Patient is a forty-four-year-old Hispanic man with two sprained fingers.

b. Patient is a 44-year-old hispanic man with 2 sprained fingers.

c. Patient is a 44-year-old Hispanic man with 2 sprained fingers.

d. Patient is a 44-year-old hispanic man with two sprained fingers.

4. Which of these statements is both clear and concise?

a. Mr. Jensen entered the office in the early evening complaining of stomach pain unlike any he had felt before.

b. Mr. Jensen complained of severe stomach pain.

c. Mr. Jensen came to the office complaining about pain.

d. Mr. Jensen complained about stomach pain before leaving the office.

5. Parts of a Letter

Identify the 11 key components of a business letter shown on the next page.

1.	**7.**
2.	**8.**
3.	**9.**
4.	**10.**
5.	**11.**
6.	

Benjamin Matthews, M.D.
999 Oak Road, Suite 313
Middletown, Connecticut 06457
860-344-6000

February 2, 2008 ②

Dr. Adam Meza ③
Medical Director
Family Practice Associates
134 N. Tater Drive
West Hartford, Connecticut 06157

Re: Ms. Beatrice Suess ④

Dear Doctor Meza: ⑤

Thank you for asking me to evaluate Ms. Suess. I agree with your diagnosis of rheumatoid arthritis. Her prodromal symptoms include vague articular pain and stiffness, weight loss, and general malaise. Ms. Suess states that the joint discomfort is most prominent in the mornings, gradually improving throughout the day.

My physical examination shows a 40-year-old female patient in good health. Heart sounds normal, no murmurs or gallops noted. Lung sounds clear. Enlarged lymph nodes were noted. Abdomen soft, bowel sounds present, and the spleen was not enlarged. Extremities showed subcutaneous nodules and flexion contractures on both hands.

⑥

Laboratory findings were indicative of rheumatoid arthritis. See attached laboratory data. I do not feel x-rays are warranted at this time.

My recommendations are to continue Ms. Suess on salicylate therapy, rest, and physical therapy. I suggest that you have Ms. Suess attend physical therapy at the American Rehabilitation Center on Main Street.

Thank you for this interesting consultation.

Yours truly, ⑦

Benjamin Matthews, MD
Benjamin Matthews, MD ⑧

BM/es ⑨

Enc. (2) ⑩

cc: Dr. Samuel Adams ⑪

6. The words "Dear Mr. Larson" compose a:

    a. salutation.

    b. closing.

    c. valediction.

    d. letter.

7. The office manager has asked you to compose a letter explaining why the waiting room should be renovated. He hopes your letter will convince the physician to invest in the new waiting room. Of the three organizational formats described in the chapter, which is most appropriate? Why?

_____

_____

8. Of the following, which is an appropriate salutation for a professional letter? Answer *Yes* or *No* in the chart below.

Salutation	Yes	No
a. Dear Denise		
b. To whom it may concern		
c. Dear Mr. Hernandez		
d. Dear Sam Landers		
e. Hi Dr. Kingston		
f. Greetings		
g. Dear Ms. Carter, Mr. Hollings, and Mr. Tan		

9. What will the identification line look like on a letter dictated by Dr. Harriet Unger to her assistant, Byron Coleman?

    a. UNGER/coleman

    b. HU/bc

    c. COLEMAN/unger

    d. HU/BC

10. Dr. Chen asks you to prepare a memorandum for distribution to the entire office. She hands you a note to use as the body. It reads as follows:

> On May 9, Jerry Henderson, a representative of Conrad Insurance, will be visiting the office during the morning. Please extend him the utmost courtesy and introduce yourself if you have not yet met him. Jerry is a wonderful man who has been very helpful to our practice. I will be unavailable during the morning as a result of his visit. Please direct questions to Shelly or Dr. Garcia. Of course, I may be contacted in case of an emergency.

What would be the BEST subject line for the memorandum?

    a. Jerry Henderson is a helpful man

    b. Dr. Chen unavailable in morning on May 9

    c. Introduce yourself to Jerry Henderson

    d. Conrad Insurance person in office May 9

11. What must you do after composing a piece of written communication? Why?

_____

_____

12. A Look at Written Communication

You have been asked to send a summary of a patient's recent visit to a specialist. Review the list of forms of written communication below and place a check mark to indicate whether it is an appropriate means of written communication.

Form	Appropriate	Not Appropriate
a. A formal letter labeled confidential		
b. An e-mail marked urgent		
c. A memorandum		
d. A fax with a confidentiality statement		
e. A memorandum labeled urgent		

13. Every Minute Counts

You always take the minutes at the staff meeting, but you'll be on vacation during the next meeting. Explain to your coworker what information belongs in the minutes.

_____

_____

14. On the Agenda

Why is an agenda useful for meetings?

_____

_____

15. The physician has asked you to prepare an agenda for the November 9, 2008, meeting of the Doctors and Nurses Fraternal Association in Wheaton, Pennsylvania. He asks you to include the following:

- a panel discussion entitled *Improving Health Care Access for Low-Income Families.*
- an introduction to the panel by Dr. Marion Pope.
- announcements.
- adjournment.

Fill in the blanks in the agenda below with the information above.

_____

_____

_____

_____

Meeting Agenda

_____

_____

Call to Order
President
Reading of the Minutes of October Mtg.
Secretary
Introduction of Panel

_____

_____

Panel:

_____

_____

Officers' Reports
Officers

_____

_____

_____

_____

16. The Pony Express

Dr. Epstein is at a week-long conference in another state. She needs a patient's complete history to present to the conference one day from now, but has forgotten it at the office. Name three suitable delivery options.

a. _____

b. _____

c. _____

17. Sorting Mail

Which of the following is/are good practice(s) in regard to handling mail? Place a check mark in the correct box below to answer "Yes" or "No."

	Yes	No
a. handling promotional materials last		
b. opening mail addressed to a physician marked "confidential"		
c. asking a physician or office manager about a piece of mail you are unsure about		
d. leaving patient correspondence in an external mailbox		
e. disposing of a physician's personal mail if he or she is away		
f. informing a covering physician about mail requiring urgent attention		
g. prioritizing patient care related mail over pharmaceutical samples		

18. What three things must be included on every piece of mail before sending it?

a. _____

b. _____

c. _____

19. Match the following key terms to their definitions.

Key Terms

a. agenda _____
b. annotation _____
c. BiCaps/intercaps _____
d. block _____

Definitions

1. an informal intra-office communication, generally used to make brief announcements
2. a typographic style
3. a type of letter format in which the first sentence is indented
4. additional information intended to highlight key points in a document, typically written in margins

e. enclosure _____

f. font _____

g. full block _____

h. margin _____

i. memorandum _____

j. proofread _____

k. salutation _____

l. semiblock _____

m. template _____

n. transcription _____

5. the process of reading a text to check grammatical and factual accuracy

6. a model used to ensure consistent format in writing

7. abbreviations, words, or phrases with unusual capitalization

8. a type of letter format in which all letter components are justified left

9. something that is included with a letter

10. the process of typing a dictated message

11. a brief outline of the topics discussed at a meeting

12. a type of letter format in which the date, subject line, closing, and signatures are justified right, and all other lines are justified left

13. the greeting of a letter

14. the blank space around the edges of a piece of paper that has been written on

20. True or False? Determine whether the following statements are true or false. If false, explain why.

a. You must always use full block formatting when generating business letters.

_____

_____

b. When you are unsure of the gender of the recipient of a letter, your salutation should read "Dear Sir or Madam."

_____

_____

c. Slang and idioms should be avoided when writing business letters.

_____

_____

d. Minutes should include extensive documentation of the discussion surrounding a vote.

_____

_____

APPLICATION

Critical Thinking Practice

1. You are taking minutes at a meeting of several doctors and nurses. They are discussing whether to hold an office holiday party. Doctor Metsoulos expresses the opinion that it is important for office morale, but Doctors Jones and Ramirez think it is an unnecessary expense. Irene, one of the nurses, is concerned that the party will not reflect the religious diversity of the office. Eventually, a vote is held, resulting in a decision not to hold the party. What kind of information should you record in the minutes? Explain your answer.

_____

_____

2. The physician is out of town and has requested that she not be contacted except in the case of emergency. You are inundated with mail. There is a variety of material including several letters addressed to the physician marked "Urgent," "Confidential," and "Personal." Some of the other mail is from patients, but it is not marked in any unusual fashion. Other letters are from insurance companies with which your office is associated. There are also several advertisements and promotional mailings from medical supply companies, pharmaceutical companies, and insurance companies. In addition, there are pieces of mail that do not include a return address. Explain the procedure you would follow in dealing with this mail.

_____

_____

Patient Education

1. The office's policy is to mail a welcome letter to new patients. Make a list of information that should be included in this letter so the patient is prepared for her first visit.

_____

_____

Documentation

1. The physician asks you to send a letter to a patient regarding the results from her Pap smear. The test results came back normal. What should you write in the patient's chart?

_____

_____

Active Learning

1. When writing, it is important to know your audience. The way you write for a physician is different from the way you write for a patient. In the case of a physician, you can assume he or she understands medical terminology, but this is not so of a patient. Do some Internet research to better understand the possible side effects of a common medication like simvastatin (Zocor) or esomeprazole (Nexium). Then, write two letters discussing the side effects, one to a physician and one to a patient. Think about what you must do differently when writing to a patient.

2. On certain occasions, you may need to write on behalf of a physician to a person occupying an important civic function, such as a judge or elected official. Using the Internet or another reference source, determine how such a person is properly addressed and write a brief letter on a relevant subject. For example, the physician may hold an opinion on a bill affecting state funding of health care and wish to express it to a state legislator.

3. Taking dictation can be a difficult task, especially if the speaker is unclear or talks very fast. Practice will help you record dictation rapidly and accurately. Have a friend dictate a letter to you and record the letter as he or she does so. Developing a shorthand system of notes might help you keep up, although it may be less accurate. You must transcribe your notes carefully. Remember, you can always ask the speaker to slow down.

Professional Journal

REFLECT

(Prompts and Ideas: Have you ever received a communication that you felt was not sufficiently professional? How did it make you feel to receive an informal communication when you were expecting a formal one? What does this tell you about the importance of professionalism in communication?)

_____

_____

_____

_____

PONDER AND SOLVE

1. The physician has informed you that he is canceling an appointment with a patient because of a sensitive personal issue (for example, a medical problem, court date, business appointment) and will reschedule as soon as possible. How would you structure a letter to the patient? What information should you tell the patient? What should you withhold? What is an appropriate tone for the letter?

_____

_____

_____

_____

_____

_____

2. One of your coworkers has been tasked with writing an important letter. As he prepares to seal it in an envelope and send it off, you ask whether it has been proofread. He says it has not. What should you do in this situation?

_____

_____

_____

_____

_____

_____

EXPERIENCE

Skills related to this chapter include:
1. Composing a Business Letter (Procedure 7-1).
2. Opening and Sorting Mail (Procedure 7-2).

Record any common mistakes, lessons learned, and/or tips you discovered during your experience of practicing and demonstrating these skills:

_____

_____

_____

_____

_____

_____

Skill Practice

PERFORMANCE OBJECTIVES:

1. Compose a business letter (Procedure 7-1).
2. Open and sort mail (Procedure 7-2).

Name _____ Date _____ Time _____

Procedure 7-1: COMPOSING A BUSINESS LETTER

EQUIPMENT/SUPPLIES: Computer with word processing software, 8½ × 11 white paper, #10 sized envelope

STANDARDS: Given the needed equipment and a place to work, the student will perform this skill with _____ % accuracy in a total of _____ minutes. (*Your instructor will tell you what the percentage and time limits will be before you begin.*)

KEY: 4 = Satisfactory   0 = Unsatisfactory   NA = This step is not counted

PROCEDURE STEPS	SELF	PARTNER	INSTRUCTOR
1. Move cursor down 2 lines below the letterhead and enter today's date, flush right.	☐	☐	☐
2. Flush left, move cursor down 2 lines and enter the inside address using the name and address of the person to whom you are writing.	☐	☐	☐
3. Double space and type the salutation followed by a colon.	☐	☐	☐
4. Enter a reference line.	☐	☐	☐
5. Double space between paragraphs.	☐	☐	☐
6. Double space and flush right, enter the complimentary close.	☐	☐	☐
7. Move cursor down 4 spaces and enter the sender's name.	☐	☐	☐
8. Double space and enter initials of the sender in all caps.	☐	☐	☐
9. Enter a slash and your initials in lower case letters.	☐	☐	☐
10. Enter c: and names of those who get copies of the letter.	☐	☐	☐
11. Enter Enc: and the number and description of each enclosed sheet.	☐	☐	☐
12. Print on letterhead.	☐	☐	☐
13. Proofread the letter.	☐	☐	☐
14. Attach the letter to the patient's chart.	☐	☐	☐
15. Submit to the sender of the letter for review and signature.	☐	☐	☐
16. Make a copy of the letter for the patient's chart.	☐	☐	☐
17. Address envelopes using all caps and no punctuation.	☐	☐	☐

CALCULATION

Total Possible Points: _____
Total Points Earned: _____ Multiplied by 100 = _____ Divided by Total Possible Points = _____%

Pass **Fail**
☐   ☐   Comments:

Student's signature _____ Date _____
Partner's signature _____ Date _____
Instructor's signature _____ Date _____

Name _____ Date _____ Time _____

OPENING AND SORTING INCOMING MAIL

EQUIPMENT/SUPPLIES: Letter opener, paper clips, directional tabs, date stamp

STANDARDS: Given the needed equipment and a place to work, the student will perform this skill with _____ % accuracy in a total of _____ minutes. (*Your instructor will tell you what the percentage and time limits will be before you begin.*)

KEY: 4 = Satisfactory 0 = Unsatisfactory NA = This step is not counted

PROCEDURE STEPS	SELF	PARTNER	INSTRUCTOR
1. Gather the necessary equipment.	☐	☐	☐
2. Open all letters and check for enclosures.	☐	☐	☐
3. Paper clip enclosures to the letter.	☐	☐	☐
4. Date-stamp each item.	☐	☐	☐
5. Sort the mail into categories and deal with it appropriately. Generally, you should handle the following types of mail as noted: *Correspondence regarding a patient:* **a.** Use a paper clip to attach letters, test results, etc. to the patient's chart. **b.** Place the chart in a pile for the physician to review. *Payments and other checks:* **a.** Record promptly all insurance payments and checks and deposit them according to office policy. **b.** Account for all drug samples and appropriately log them into the sample book.	☐	☐	☐
6. Dispose of miscellaneous advertisements unless otherwise directed.	☐	☐	☐
7. Distribute the mail to the appropriate staff members. For example, mail might be for the physician, nurse manager, office manager, billing clerk, or other personnel.	☐	☐	☐

CALCULATION

Total Possible Points: _____
Total Points Earned: _____ Multiplied by 100 = _____ Divided by Total Possible Points = _____ %

Pass   **Fail**
☐   ☐   Comments:

Student's signature _____ Date _____
Partner's signature _____ Date _____
Instructor's signature _____ Date _____

Work Products

Respond to and initiate written communications.

Compose a letter from Dr. Essen Mahlzeit, 321 Gasthaus Lane, Germantown, PA 87641, to Mr. Ligero Delgado, 888 La Sala Boulevard, Germantown, PA 87642.

The letter should inform Mr. Delgado of the following:
- The results of the biopsy taken during his sigmoidoscopy were negative.
- While these initial results are encouraging, his medical complaints need to be investigated further. Dr. Mahlzeit would like to refer Mr. Delgado to a specialist, Dr. Douloureux.
- Dr. Douloureux's practice is in Suite 100 of the Atroce Medical Center, 132 West Broadway, Germantown, PA 87642.
- With Mr. Delgado's consent, his records can be forwarded to Dr. Douloureux and an appointment will be arranged.

Prepare the letter on a sheet of letterhead if available. If this is not available to you, print the letter on a standard 8½ × 11 white paper and attach to this sheet.

Chapter Self-Assessment Quiz

1. In a letter, the word "Enc." indicates the presence of a(n):
  a. summary.
  b. abstract.
  c. enclosure.
  d. review.
  e. invitation.

2. If you are instructed to write using the semiblock format, then you should:
  a. indent the first line of each paragraph.
  b. use left justification for everything.
  c. use right justification for the date only.
  d. write the recipient's full name in the salutation.
  e. indent the first line of the first paragraph.

3. Which of the following items can be abbreviated in an inside address?
  a. City
  b. Town
  c. Recipient's name
  d. Business title
  e. State

4. Which sentence is written correctly?
  a. "We will have to do tests" said Doctor Mathis, "Then we will know what is wrong."
  b. "We will have to do tests" said Doctor Mathis. "Then we will know what is wrong."
  c. "We will have to do tests," said Doctor Mathis "Then we will know what is wrong."
  d. "We will have to do tests", said Doctor Mathis "Then we will know what is wrong."
  e. "We will have to do tests," said Doctor Mathis. "Then we will know what is wrong."

5. Which term should be capitalized?
  a. morphine
  b. fluoxetine
  c. zithromax
  d. antibiotic
  e. catheter

6. If the fax machine is busy when sending a fax, you should:
  a. mail the document instead.
  b. call the recipient and ask him to contact you when the machine is available.
  c. ask a coworker to send the document.
  d. make a note in the patient's chart.
  e. wait with the document until you receive confirmation that it was sent.

7. Which sentence is written correctly?

   a. The patient is 14 years old and is urinating 3 times more than normal.

   b. The patient is 14 years old and is urinating three times more than normal.

   c. The patient is fourteen years old and is urinating 3 times more than normal.

   d. The patient is fourteen years old and is urinating three times more than normal.

   e. The patient is fourteen years old and is urinating three times more than normally.

8. Which of the following always belongs on a fax cover sheet?

   a. The number of pages, not including the cover sheet

   b. The number of pages, including the cover sheet

   c. A summary of the content of the message

   d. A summary of the content of the message, less confidential portions

   e. The name of the patient discussed in the message

9. The USPS permit imprint program:

   a. guarantees overnight delivery.

   b. provides receipt of delivery.

   c. offers physicians cheaper postage.

   d. deducts the postage charges from a prepaid account.

   e. addresses envelopes for no additional charge.

10. Which USPS service will allow you to send a parcel overnight?

   a. Registered mail

   b. First-class mail

   c. Presorted mail

   d. Priority mail

   e. Express mail

11. Which is the best way to highlight a list of key points in a business letter?

   a. Use boldface text.

   b. Use a larger font.

   c. Use bulleted text.

   d. Use a highlighter.

   e. Use italicized test.

Scenario: You are tasked with writing a letter to a patient on the basis of a chart from his last visit. Most important is a diagnosis listed as "HBV infection."

12. Which is an appropriate course of action?

   a. Including the words "HBV infection" in the letter

   b. Consulting the physician on the meaning of the term

   c. Omitting the diagnosis from the otherwise complete letter

   d. Guessing the meaning of the term and writing about that

   e. Asking the office manager what to do about the letter

13. Having learned that HBV means hepatitis B virus, you should:

   a. research HBV infection.

   b. give the patient your condolences.

   c. write a letter based on the physician's instructions.

   d. immediately schedule an appointment for the patient.

   e. ask the patient to visit the office to learn his or her condition.

End Scenario

14. Who might receive a memorandum you have written?

   a. A nurse in your office

   b. A drug sales representative

   c. An insurance agent

   d. An outside specialist

   e. A recently admitted patient

15. Which closing is written correctly?

   a. Best Regards

   b. Sincerely Yours,

   c. Best regards,

   d. Sincerely yours

   e. Best Regards,

16. The purpose of an agenda is to:

   a. summarize the opinions expressed at a meeting.

   b. provide a brief outline for topics to be discussed at a meeting.

   c. inform participants of any changes since the last meeting.

   d. remind group members about an upcoming meeting.

   e. communicate key issues that should be addressed at future meetings.

17. Correspondence that contains information about a patient should be marked:

   a. personal.

   b. confidential.

   c. urgent.

   d. classified.

   e. top secret.

18. Which of these should be included in minutes?

   a. Individuals' statements

   b. Your opinion of the vote

   c. Names of those voting against

   d. Names of those voting in favor

   e. Date and time of the next meeting

19. Which type of mail provides the greatest protection for valuables?

   a. Certified mail

   b. International mail

   c. Registered mail

   d. Standard mail

   e. First class mail

20. Among these, which type of mail should be handled first?

   a. Medication samples

   b. Professional journals

   c. Insurance information

   d. Patient correspondence

   e. Waiting room magazines

Health Information Management: Electronic and Manual

- ☐ Read textbook chapter and take notes within the Chapter Notes outline. Answer the Learning Objectives as you reach them in the content, and then check them off.
- ☐ Work the Content Review questions—both Foundational Knowledge and Application.
- ☐ Perform the Active Learning exercise(s).
- ☐ Complete Professional Journal entries.
- ☐ Complete Skill Practice Activity(s) using Competency Evaluation Forms and Work Products, when appropriate.
- ☐ Take the Chapter Self-Assessment Quiz.
- ☐ Insert all appropriate pages into your Portfolio.

1. Spell and define the key terms.
2. Explain the requirements of the Health Insurance Portability and Accountability Act relating to the sharing and saving of personal and protected health information.
3. Describe standard and electronic health record systems.
4. Explain the process for releasing medical records to third-party payers and individual patients.
5. List and explain the EHR guidelines established to protect computerized records.
6. List the standard information included in medical records.
7. Identify and describe the types of formats used for documenting patient information in outpatient settings.
8. Explain how to make an entry in a patient's medical record, using abbreviations when appropriate.
9. Explain how to make a correction in a standard and electronic health record.
10. Compare and contrast the differences between alphabetic and numeric filing systems and give an example of each.
11. Identify the various ways medical records can be classified for storage.
12. Explain the guidelines of sound policies for record retention.

Note: Bold-faced headings are the major headings in the text chapter; headings in regular font are lower-level headings (i.e., the content is subordinate to, or falls "under," the major headings). Make sure you understand the key terms used in the chapter, as well as the concepts presented as Key Points.

TEXT SUBHEADINGS	NOTES

Introduction _____

_____

Key Points:
- A thorough and accurate medical record furnishes documented evidence of the patient's evaluation, treatment, change in condition, and communication with the physician and staff.
- In 1996, HIPAA was enacted to provide consumers with greater access to health care insurance, to protect the privacy of health care data, and to promote more standardization and efficiency in the health care industry.

☐ **LEARNING OBJECTIVE 1:** Spell and define the key terms.

The Health Insurance Portability and Accountability Act of 1996 _____

_____

Key Point:
- In addition to these issues addressed by HIPAA, the rapid advancement of technology in medical information maintenance caused the need for strict regulations to keep electronically-transmitted and stored protected health information (PHI) safe from unauthorized release.

Covered Entities _____

_____

Key Terms: covered entity; clearinghouses; electronic health record (EHR)
Key Point:
- Covered entities are subject to individual state laws, but if a state and federal law are different, you must follow the strictest laws.

Administrative Simplification _____

_____

The HIPAA Officer _____

_____

Key Points:
- In most cases, as long as reasonable care is taken to comply with the intent of the ruling and that effort is documented, providers are considered compliant with HIPAA.
- HIPAA requires that at least one employee be designated as the HIPAA Officer and one as Privacy Officer.

☐ **LEARNING OBJECTIVE 2:** Explain the requirements of the Health Insurance Portability and Accountability Act relating to the sharing and saving of personal and protected health information.

Releasing Medical Records _____

Key Point:
• Any release of records must first be authorized by the patient or the patient's legal guardian.

HIPAA's Privacy Rule _____

Releasing Records to Patients _____

Proper Authorization _____

Key Point:
• Patients may release only information relating to a specific disorder, or they may specify a time limit. They may not, however, ask that the physician leave out information pertinent to the situation.

Legally Required Disclosures _____

Key Point:
• Certain information is crucial to the patient, needed for the protection of the public, or involves criminal activity, and is released without the patient's permission.

☐ **LEARNING OBJECTIVE 3:** Describe standard and electronic health record systems.

Adopting Electronic Health Records Technology _____

Making the Transition _____

Features and Capabilities of Electronic Health Records _____

_____

Key Term: demographic data

Billing and Coding Using Electronic Health Records _____

_____

The Medical Assistant's Role _____

_____

Electronic Health Record Security _____

_____

Key Point:
- The physician should take care in keeping a personal data system, just as he or she protects the prescription pad.

☐ **LEARNING OBJECTIVE 4:** Explain the process for releasing medical records to third-party payers and individual patients.

Standard Medical Records _____

_____

Contents of the Medical Record _____

_____

☐ **LEARNING OBJECTIVE 5:** List and explain the EHR guidelines established to protect computerized records.

Medical Record Organization _____

_____

Key Term: reverse chronological order

Provider Encounters _____

_____

Narrative Format _____

_____

Key Term: narrative

SOAP Format _____

_____

Key Point:
• SOAP (subjective-objective-assessment-plan)

POMR Format _____

_____

Key Term: problem-oriented medical record (POMR)

☐ **LEARNING OBJECTIVE 6:** List the standard information included in medical records.

Electronic Health Records _____

_____

☐ **LEARNING OBJECTIVE 7:** Identify and describe the types of formats used for documenting patient information in outpatient settings.

Documentation Forms _____

_____

Medical History Forms _____

_____

Key Term: medical history forms
Key Point:
• Whether the patient brings the completed form or fills out the history form in the office, you will review the information with the patient to clarify any questions and add additional information gathered in the interview.

Flow Sheets _____

_____

Key Term: flow sheet

Progress Notes _____

_____

Key Point:
• This immediate availability makes patient care more efficient and convenient for the physician and the patient.

Medical Record Entries _____

_____

Key Point:
• If the documentation is accurate, timely, and legible, it can help win a lawsuit or prevent one altogether.

☐ **LEARNING OBJECTIVE 8:** Explain how to make an entry in a patient's medical record, using abbreviations when appropriate.

Charting Communications with Patients _____

_____

Key Term: chronological order
Key Point:
• Dates that are out of order and gaps between entries may confuse the reader and give the appearance of poor service. For this reason, entries should be made immediately after communications with the patient.

Additions to Medical Records _____

_____

Key Point:
• All additions to the medical record (e.g., laboratory results, radiographic reports, consultation reports) should be read and initialed by the physician before you put them in the chart.

☐ **LEARNING OBJECTIVE 9:** Explain how to make a correction in a standard and electronic health record.

Workers' Compensation Records _____

_____

Key Term: workers' compensation

Storing Medical Records _____

_____

Medical Record Preparation _____

_____

Filing Procedures _____

_____

Filing Systems _____

_____

Alphabetic Filing _____

_____

> **Key Term:** alphabetic filing

Numeric Filing _____

_____

> **Key Terms:** numeric filing; cross-reference

Other Filing Systems _____

_____

> **Key Term:** subject filing
> **Key Point:**
> • A well-kept, complete, and accurate medical record and the ability to quickly retrieve information are reflections of the quality and efficiency of the medical facility in which they are generated.

☐ **LEARNING OBJECTIVE 10:** Compare and contrast the differences between alphabetic and numeric filing systems and give an example of each.

Storing Health Information _____

_____

_____

Electronic Data Storage _____

_____

> **Key Point:**
> • The speed of computer technology promises changes and new practices. In order to optimize efficiency, you must keep abreast of these new technologies.

Storage of Standard Medical Records _____

_____

_____

Classification of Records _____

_____

Key Terms: microfilm; microfiche
Key Point:
• You will still keep these records in the office, but they do not have to be as accessible as the active files.

☐ **LEARNING OBJECTIVE 11:** Identify the various ways medical records can be classified for storage.

Record Retention _____

_____

Key Points:
• You must observe the statute of limitations in your particular state to know how long medical and business records should be kept in storage.
• At the least, every reasonable attempt should be made to notify patients and disseminate the information maintained by the retiring or deceased physician.

☐ **LEARNING OBJECTIVE 12:** Explain the guidelines of sound policies for record retention.

Content Review

FOUNDATIONAL KNOWLEDGE

Upholding Patients' Rights

1. HIPAA is the law for the health care industry. Those who must abide by HIPAA are called "covered entities." List the three groups that are considered covered entities.

a. _____

b. _____

c. _____

2. HIPAA has privacy rules that protect your personal health information. Under HIPAA, covered entities must take certain safety measures to protect patients' information. Read the paragraph below. For each blank, there are two choices. Circle the correct word or phrase for each sentence.

Covered entities must designate a ___(a)___ to keep track of who has access to health information (HIPAA officer, privacy officer). They must also adopt written ___(b)___ procedures (privacy, health care). Under HIPAA, patients have the right to decide if they provide ___(c)___ before their health information can be used or shared for certain purposes (permission, marketing). They also have the right to get a ___(d)___ on when and why their health care information was shared for certain purposes (narrative, report).

It's Electric

3. Describe the difference between standard and electronic health record systems.

_____

_____

4. Making the transition from a paper-based office environment to one using advanced technology has advantages and disadvantages. Complete the chart below with two more advantages and disadvantages of the electronic health care system. The first box has been completed for you.

ELECTRONIC HEALTH CARE SYSTEM	
Advantages	**Disadvantages**
a. **Point-of-care charting**	a. **Cost**
b.	b.
c.	c.

Record Release Party!

5. Sharing information can be fun; but, not so fast: do you know who you can share it with? And who will see it? Releasing medical records to patients and others shouldn't be like a gossip chain. The rules for releasing medical records and authorization are meant to protect patients' privacy rights. Read the questions below regarding the release of medical records and circle "Yes" or "No" for each question.

a. May an 18-year-old patient get copies of his own medical records?	**Yes**	**No**
b. May all minors seek treatment for STDs and birth control without parental knowledge or consent?	**Yes**	**No**
c. When a patient requests copies of her own records, does the doctor make the decision about what to copy?	**Yes**	**No**
d. Must the authorization form give the patient the opportunity to limit the information released?	**Yes**	**No**
e. When a patient authorizes the release of information, may he request that the physician leave out information pertinent to the situation?	**Yes**	**No**

Securing the System

6. HIPAA requirements provide guidelines and suggestions for safe computer practices when storing or transferring patient information. The following is a list of guidelines that medical facilities are urged to follow. Complete each sentence with the appropriate word from the word bank below.

   a. Store _____ in a bank safe-deposit box.

   b. Change log-in _____ and passwords every 30 days.

   c. Turn _____ away from areas where information may be seen by patients.

   d. Use _____ with _____ other than letters.

   e. Prepare a back-up _____ for use when the computer system is down.

Word Bank

characters	plan	disks	information
codes	passwords	template	terminals

*Note: Not all words will be used.

Piles of Files

7. A standard medical record in an outpatient facility, known as a chart or file, contains clinical information as well as billing and insurance information. In the clinical section of the file, you will often find certain types of information. In the chart below, match the clinical type of information with its correct description.

Name of Clinical Information	Description
a. Chief complaint	**1.** Documentation of each patient encounter
b. Family and personal history	**2.** Provider's opinion of the patient's problem
c. Progress notes	**3.** Symptoms that led the patient to seek the physician's care
d. Diagnosis or medical impression	**4.** Letters or memos generated in the facility and sent out
e. Correspondence pertaining to patient	**5.** Review of major illnesses of family members

Documentation

8. Every medical office may use a different documentation format, depending on physician preference and type of patient (e.g., established, new). As a medical assistant, you should be familiar with the three most common formats. Read the chart below and match the format name with its description.

Format Name	Description
1. Narrative	**a.** A paragraph indicating the contact with the patient, what was done for the patient, and the outcome of any action
2. SOAP	**b.** Lists each problem of the patient, and references each problem with a number throughout the folder
3. POMR	**c.** Has a subjective and an objective component

9. POMR documents are divided into four components. List them below.

a. _____

b. _____

c. _____

d. _____

To Document, or Not to Document?

10. Documentation is a large part of your job as a medical assistant. Legible, correct, and thorough documentation is necessary. List three instances, other than patient visits, when documentation is required.

a. _____

b. _____

c. _____

11. When documenting in a medical record or file, why should you use caution when using abbreviations? Explain.

_____

_____

12. Fill in the chart below to explain how to make a correction in a standard and electronic health record.

Corrections in Standard Health Record	Corrections in Electronic Health Record

13. How does a numeric filing system help a medical office meet HIPAA's privacy requirements?

_____

_____

14. Your medical office uses an alphabetic filing system. Place the following names in the correct order to show how you would place each record in a filing system.

Brandon P. Snow	Kristen F. Darian-Lewes	Shante L. Dawes	Emil S. Faqir, Jr.
Shaunice L. DeBlase	Juan R. Ortiz	Kim Soo	Fernando P. Vasquez, D.O.

a. _____

b. _____

c. _____

d. _____

e. _____

f. _____

g. _____

h. _____

Filing Frenzy

15. List the four steps you should take to ensure that files are filed and retrieved quickly and efficiently.

a. _____

b. _____

c. _____

d. _____

16. For the Record. . .

For the purpose of storing records, they may be classified in three categories. In the chart below, match the type of record with its patient description.

Type of Record	Patient Description
a. Active	**1.** Mr. Arnold hasn't been seen by the physician in the last six years.
b. Inactive	**2.** Mrs. Lin was seen last month by the physician.
c. Closed	**3.** Mr. Angelos has passed away.

17. When a health care provider's practice ends, either from retirement or death, what happens to the records?

_____

_____

18. Organizational Hierarchy

Though there are some exceptions, most information in the paper medical record is placed in a standard order. Do you know the general order of information? Complete the graphic organizer below.

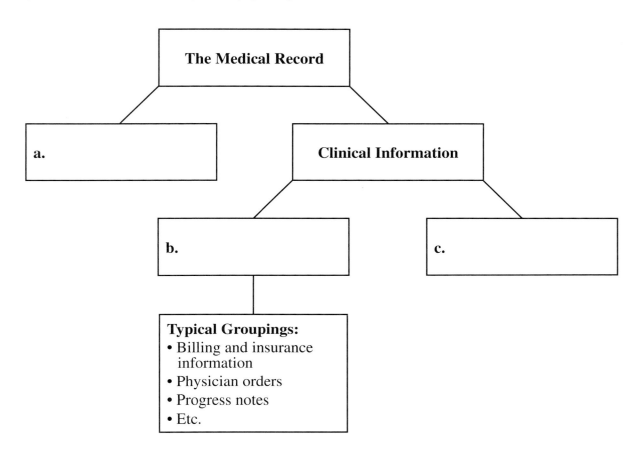

19. Match the following key terms to their definitions.

Key Terms

a. alphabetic filing _____

b. chief complaint _____

c. chronological order _____

d. clearinghouse _____

e. covered entity _____

f. cross-reference _____

g. demographic data _____

h. electronic health records (EHR) _____

i. flow sheet _____

j. medical history forms _____

k. microfiche _____

Definitions

1. information about patients that is recorded and stored on computer

2. photographs of records in a reduced size

3. a paragraph indicating the contact with the patient, what was done for the patient, and the outcome of any action

4. a specific account of the chief complaint, including time frames and characteristics

5. a common method of compiling information that lists each problem of the patient, usually at the beginning of the folder, and references each problem with a number throughout the folder

6. notation in a file indicating that a record is stored elsewhere and giving the reference; verification to another source; checking the tabular list against the alphabetic list in ICD-9 coding

7. entity that takes claims and other electronic data from providers and verifies the information and forwards the proper forms to the payors for physicians

l. microfilm _____

m. narrative _____

n. numeric filing _____

o. protected health information (PHI) _____

p. present illness _____

q. problem-oriented medical record (POMR) _____

r. reverse chronological order _____

s. SOAP _____

t. subject filing _____

u. workers' compensation _____

8. employer insurance for treatment of an employee's injury or illness related to the job

9. any information that can be linked to a specific person

10. items placed with oldest first

11. sheets of microfilm

12. arranging files according to their title, grouping similar subjects together

13. a style of charting that includes subjective, objective, assessment, and planning notes

14. arranging of names or titles according to the sequence of letters in the alphabet

15. health plan; health care clearinghouse; or health care provider who transmits any health information in electronic form in connection with a transaction covered under HIPAA

16. placing in order of time; usually the most recent is placed foremost

17. information relating to the statistical characteristics of populations

18. color-coded sheets that allow information to be recorded in graphic or tabular form for easy retrieval

19. arranging files by a numbered order

20. main reason for the visit to the medical office

21. record containing information about a patient's past and present health status

20. True or False? Determine whether the following statements are true or false. If false, explain why.

a. HIPAA allows patients to ask to see and get a copy of their health records.

_____

_____

b. To maintain secure files, you should change log-in codes and passwords every ten days.

_____

_____

c. Medical history forms are commonly used to gather information from the patient before the visit with the physician.

_____

_____

d. Before treating a patient for a possible workers' compensation case, you must first obtain verification from the employer unless the situation is life-threatening.

_____

_____

APPLICATION

Critical Thinking Practice

1. A mother is accused of physically abusing her 16-year-old daughter, a patient with your facility. A police officer who has been asked to investigate visits the medical office and asks for the patient's medical records. What should you do?

_____

_____

2. You're in the medical office and you suddenly realize that you've forgotten to document a telephone conversation you had with a patient 2 days ago. What should you do?

_____

_____

Patient Education

1. Dr. Minato is retiring and will be closing her practice. Write a letter to her patients explaining what they should do about their medical records.

_____

_____

Documentation

1. Maria Juaneza comes to the physician's office complaining of chest congestion and a deep cough. The physician examines the patient and notes that she is straining to breathe. The physician also notes that the patient's throat is red and irritated. The physician suspects that the patient has bronchitis, but he also wants Mrs. Juaneza to have a chest x-ray to rule out pneumonia. He prescribes an antibiotic and tells the patient to take an over-the-counter cough medicine. He also tells Mrs. Juaneza to call the office if her symptoms worsen and come back for a recheck if the symptoms are not cleared up by the end of the week. Use the SOAP method to document this interaction in the patient's chart.

_____

_____

Active Learning

1. If you were opening a new medical facility, consider whether you would want staff members using abbreviations in patient records. Then create a list of acceptable abbreviations that may be used in your new facility. Then create a "Do Not Use" list for abbreviations that may be confusing and should not be included in records. Visit the website for the JCAHO at www.jcaho.gov and include all of those abbreviations in addition to five other abbreviations of your own choice.

2. Choose a filing system that you learned about in this chapter (e.g., chronological, alphabetical, etc.) and practice it using household items. For example, you might organize your music collection or clothing drawers.

3. Make a KWL chart about Patients' Privacy Rights. Fill out the "What I Know" and "What I Would Like To Know" columns first. Then visit HIPAA's website at: http://www.hhs.gov/ocr/hipaa/. Click on "Fact Sheets" at the top, and then "Your Health Information Privacy Rights." Read the sheet and fill out the "What I Learned" column of your chart. Think about how you will apply this new information when you record, retrieve, and store patient health information.

Professional Journal

REFLECT

(Prompts and Ideas: Are you concerned about the prospect of transitioning from a paper-based medical facility to an electronic health record system? How will you make the transition smooth and efficient for yourself and your coworkers? Are there any advantages or disadvantages to using electronic health records that seem especially important to you? Explain.)

_____

_____

_____

_____

_____

_____

_____

PONDER AND SOLVE

1. The golden rule in documentation is, "If it is not documented, it was not done." Explain what this means in regard to a potential malpractice suit.

_____

_____

_____

_____

_____

_____

_____

2. Should a medical facility keep paper health records during the transition to electronic health records? Why or why not?

_____

_____

_____

_____

_____

_____

_____

EXPERIENCE

Skills related to this chapter include:

1. Establishing, Organizing, and Maintaining a Medical File (Procedure 8-1).

2. Filing a Medical Record (Procedure 8-2).

Record any common mistakes, lessons learned, and/or tips you discovered during your experience of practicing and demonstrating these skills:

_____

_____

_____

_____

_____

_____

_____

Skill Practice

PERFORMANCE OBJECTIVES:

1. Establish, organize, and maintain a patient's medical record (Procedure 8-1).
2. File a medical record (Procedure 8-2).

Name_____   Date_____   Time_____

Procedure 8-1:	ESTABLISHING, ORGANIZING, AND MAINTAINING A MEDICAL FILE

EQUIPMENT/SUPPLIES: File folder; metal fasteners; hole punch; five divider sheets with tabs, title, year, and alphabetic or numeric labels

STANDARDS: Given the needed equipment and a place to work the student will perform this skill with _____% accuracy in a total of _____ minutes. (*Your instructor will tell you what the percentage and time limits will be before you begin.*)

KEY: 4 = Satisfactory   0 = Unsatisfactory   NA = This step is not counted

PROCEDURE STEPS	SELF	PARTNER	INSTRUCTOR
1. Place the label along the tabbed edge of the folder so that the title extends out beyond the folder itself. (Tabs can be either the length of the folder or tabbed in various positions, such as left, center, and right.)	☐	☐	☐
2. Place a year label along the top edge of the tab before the label with the title. This will be changed each year the patient has been seen. *Note:* Do not automatically replace these labels at the start of a new year; remove the old year and replace with a new one only when the patient comes in for the first visit of the new year.	☐	☐	☐
3. Place the appropriate alphabetic or numeric labels below the title.	☐	☐	☐
4. Apply any additional labels that your office may decide to use.	☐	☐	☐
5. Punch holes and insert demographic and financial information on the left side of the chart using top fasteners across the top.	☐	☐	☐
6. Make tabs for: Ex. H&P, Progress Notes, Medication Log, Correspondence, and Test Results.	☐	☐	☐
7. Place pages behind appropriate tabs.	☐	☐	☐

CALCULATION

Total Possible Points: _____
Total Points Earned: _____ Multiplied by 100 = _____ Divided by Total Possible Points = _____%

Pass   **Fail**
☐   ☐   Comments:

Student's signature _____ Date _____
Partner's signature _____ Date _____
Instructor's signature _____ Date _____

Name _____ Date _____ Time _____

Procedure 8-2:	**FILING MEDICAL RECORDS**

EQUIPMENT/SUPPLIES: Simulated patient file folder, several single sheets to be filed in the chart, file cabinet with other files

STANDARDS: Given the needed equipment and a place to work the student will perform this skill with _____% accuracy in a total of _____ minutes. (*Your instructor will tell you what the percentage and time limits will be before you begin.*)

KEY: 4 = Satisfactory 0 = Unsatisfactory NA = This step is not counted

PROCEDURE STEPS	SELF	PARTNER	INSTRUCTOR
1. Double check spelling of names on the chart and any single sheets to be placed in the folder.	☐	☐	☐
2. Condition any single sheets, etc.	☐	☐	☐
3. Place sheets behind proper tab in the chart.	☐	☐	☐
4. Remove outguide.	☐	☐	☐
5. Place the folder between the two appropriate existing folders, taking care to place the folder between the two charts.	☐	☐	☐
6. Scan color coding to ensure none of the charts in that section are out of order.	☐	☐	☐

CALCULATION

Total Possible Points: _____
Total Points Earned: _____ Multiplied by 100 = _____ Divided by Total Possible Points = _____%

Pass   **Fail**
☐   ☐   Comments:

Student's signature _____ Date _____
Partner's signature _____ Date _____
Instructor's signature _____ Date _____

Chapter Self-Assessment Quiz

1. Who coordinates and oversees the various aspects of HIPAA compliance in a medical office?

   a. Medicaid and Medicare

   b. HIPAA officer

   c. Privacy officer

   d. Office manager

   e. Law enforcement

2. A release of records request must contain the patient's:

   a. next of kin.

   b. home phone number.

   c. original signature.

   d. medical history.

   e. date of birth.

3. Which is an example of protected health information?

   a. Published statistics by a credible source

   b. Insurance company's mailing address

   c. Physician's pager number

   d. First and last name associated with a diagnosis

   e. Poll published in a medical journal

4. If patients believe their rights have been denied or their health information isn't being protected, they can file a complaint with the:

   a. Journal of American Medical Assistants.

   b. American Medical Association.

   c. provider or insurer.

   d. medical assistant.

   e. state's attorney.

5. The only time an original record should be released is when the:

   a. patient asks for the record.

   b. patient is in critical condition.

   c. record is subpoenaed by the court of law.

   d. physician is being sued.

   e. patient terminates the relationship with the physician.

6. Do medical records have the same content if they are on paper or a computer disk?

   a. Yes

   b. No

   c. Sometimes

   d. Most of the time

   e. Never

7. Documentation of each patient encounter is called:

   a. consultation reports.

   b. medication administration.

   c. correspondence.

   d. narrative.

   e. progress notes.

8. Improved medication management is a feature of:

   a. SOAP.

   b. electronic health records.

   c. clearinghouses.

   d. protected health information.

   e. workers' compensation.

9. To maintain security, a facility should:

   a. design a written confidentiality policy for employees to sign.

   b. provide public access to medical records.

   c. keep a record of all passwords and give a copy to each employee.

   d. keep doors unlocked during the evening hours only.

   e. have employees hide patient information from other coworkers.

10. Under source-oriented records, the most recent documents are placed on top of previous sheets. This is called:

    a. chronological order.

    b. reverse chronological order.

    c. alphabetical order.

    d. subject order.

    e. numeric order.

11. The acronym "SOAP" stands for:

    a. subjective-objective-adjustment-plan.

    b. subjective-objective-accounting-plan.

    c. subjective-objective-assessment-plan.

    d. subjective-objective-accounting-problem.

    e. subjective-objective-assessment-problem.

12. The acronym "POMR" stands for:

    a. presentation-oriented medical record.

    b. protection-oriented medical record.

    c. performance-oriented medical record.

    d. professional-oriented medical record.

    e. problem-oriented medical record.

13. Which of the following is contained in a POMR database?

    a. Marketing tools

    b. Field of interest

    c. Job description

    d. Review of systems

    e. Accounting review

14. Which of the following will reflect each encounter with the patient chronologically, whether by phone, by e-mail, or in person?

    a. Microfilm

    b. Narrative

    c. Progress notes

    d. Subject filing

    e. Flow sheet

15. Shingling is:

    a. printing replies to a patient's e-mail.

    b. recording laboratory results in the patient's chart.

    c. telephone or electronic communications with patients.

    d. taping the paper across the top to a regular-size sheet.

    e. filing records in chronological order.

16. How long are workers' compensation cases kept open after the last date of treatment for any follow-up care that may be required?

    a. 6 months

    b. 1 year

    c. 2 years

    d. 5 years

    e. 10 years

17. A cross-reference in numeric filing is called a(n):

    a. open file.

    b. locked file.

    c. straight digit file.

    d. master patient index.

    e. duplication index.

18. Security experts advise storing backup disks:

    a. in the office.

    b. off-site.

    c. at the physician's home.

    d. on every computer.

    e. at the library.

19. Drawer files are a type of:

    a. filing cabinet.

    b. storage container.

    c. computer system.

    d. shelving unit.

    e. subject filing.

20. The statute of limitations is:

    a. the end of a provider's ability to legally practice.

    b. the record retention system.

    c. a miniature photographic system.

    d. the legal time limit set for filing suit against an alleged wrongdoer.

    e. the number of records a storage system is able to hold.

Computer Applications in the Medical Office

Chapter Checklist

- [ ] Read textbook chapter and take notes within the Chapter Notes outline. Answer the Learning Objectives as you reach them in the content, and then check them off.
- [ ] Work the Content Review questions—both Foundational Knowledge and Application.
- [ ] Perform the Active Learning exercise(s).

- [ ] Complete Professional Journal entries.
- [ ] Complete Skill Practice Activity(s) using Competency Evaluation Forms and Work Products, when appropriate.
- [ ] Take the Chapter Self-Assessment Quiz.
- [ ] Insert all appropriate pages into your Portfolio.

Learning Objectives

1. Spell and define the key words.
2. Identify the basic computer components.
3. Explain the basics of connecting to the Internet.
4. Discuss the safety concerns for online searching.
5. Describe how to use a search engine.
6. List sites that can be used by professionals and sites geared for patients.
7. Describe the benefits of an intranet and explain how it differs from the Internet.

8. Describe the various types of clinical software that might be used in a physician's office.
9. Describe the various types of administrative software that might be used in a physician's office.
10. Describe the benefits of a handheld computer.
11. Describe the considerations for purchasing a computer.
12. Describe various training options.
13. Discuss the ethics related to computer access.

Chapter Notes

Note: Bold-faced headings are the major headings in the text chapter; headings in regular font are lower-level headings (i.e., the content is subordinate to, or falls "under," the major headings). Make sure you understand the key terms used in the chapter, as well as the concepts presented as Key Points.

TEXT SUBHEADINGS	**NOTES**

Introduction _____

_____

Key Point:
• You will need excellent computer skills to work as a medical assistant.

☐ **LEARNING OBJECTIVE 1:** Spell and define the key words.

The Computer _____

_____

_____

Hardware _____

_____

Key Points:
• These cells read, analyze, and process data, and instruct the computer how to operate a given program.
• Keep in mind that you need to adhere to copyright laws.

Peripherals _____

_____

Key Term: Ethernet

☐ **LEARNING OBJECTIVE 2:** Identify the basic computer components.

Care and Maintenance of the System and Equipment ____

_____

Key Point:
• As with any piece of equipment in the medical office, it is necessary to maintain your computer on a regular basis.

Internet Basics _____

_____

Key Term: Internet

Getting Started and Connected _____

_____

_____

☐ **LEARNING OBJECTIVE 3:** Explain the basics of connecting to the Internet.

Security of Electronically-Shared Health Information

Key Point:
• The HIPAA legislation mandates that when a health care provider and health plan transmit and receive PHI (personal health information) electronically, the transmission must comply with certain standards.

Internet Security

Key Term: cookies
Key Point:
• By examining your cookies, a website can learn what sites you have visited, products for which you have been searching, and files that you have downloaded.

Viruses

Key Term: virus

☐ **LEARNING OBJECTIVE 4:** Discuss the safety concerns for online searching.

Downloading Information

Key Term: downloading

Working Offline

Key Point:
• Remember, Web pages are regularly updated, and a page that you have saved to view off-line may not be the latest version.

Electronic Mail

Key Term: encryption

Access _____

_____

Composing Messages _____

_____

Address Books _____

_____

Attachments _____

_____

Opening Electronic Mail _____

_____

Medical Applications of the Internet _____

Key Term: surfing
Key Point:
• Besides e-mail, the Internet offers the World Wide Web, which provides health care professionals with great resources and information.

Search Engines _____

Key Term: search engine

☐ **LEARNING OBJECTIVE 5:** Describe how to use a search engine.

Professional Medical Sites _____

Key Point:
• The Internet can help you communicate with patients who speak a foreign language.

☐ **LEARNING OBJECTIVE 6:** List sites that can be used by professionals and sites geared for patients.

Literary Searches _____

_____

Key Term: literary search
Key Point:
- Your local hospital librarian is often available to assist you with literary searches and may be able to get the article for free.

Health-Related Calculators _____

_____

_____

Insurance-Related Sites _____

_____

_____

Patient Teaching Issues Regarding the Internet _____

_____

Key Point:
- Keep in mind that patients often turn to the Internet when they feel confused or hopeless about their disease or anger about the medical profession.

Buying Medications Online _____

_____

Key Point:
- A good Internet pharmacy will provide information on what the medication is used for, possible side effects, dosage recommendation, and safety concerns.

Financial Assistance for Medications _____

_____

_____

Medical Records _____

_____

_____

Medical Records Forms _____

_____

Key Point:
- Advance directives and legal forms for medical power of attorney are also available online.

Injury Prevention _____

_____

_____

Intranet _____

_____

Key Term: intranet
Key Point:
- The only people with access to an intranet home page are people with an affiliation to the practice.

☐ **LEARNING OBJECTIVE 7:** Describe the benefits of an intranet and explain how it differs from the Internet.

Medical Software Applications _____

_____

_____

Clinical Applications _____

_____

Key Term: virtual
Key Points:
- Clinical software is designed to help the physician, nurse, medical assistant, or other health care professional provide the most efficient, safest, and most reliable health care available.
- A good program that focuses on pharmaceutical information will decrease medication errors, increase patient satisfaction, and provide better patient care; and it can be financially beneficial to the patient and to the practice.

☐ **LEARNING OBJECTIVE 8:** Describe the various types of clinical software that might be used in a physician's office.

Administrative Applications _____

_____

Key Point:
- Again, programs must aim to comply with HIPAA's Privacy Rule; these programs allow you to document your adherence to these rules and regulations.

Paging System Software _____

_____

PowerPoint _____

_____

_____

Meeting Maker _____

_____

☐ **LEARNING OBJECTIVE 9:** Describe the various types of administrative software that might be used in a physician's office.

Handheld Computers _____

_____

Key Point:
- A handheld device can do almost anything that your desktop computer can do.

☐ **LEARNING OBJECTIVE 10:** Describe the benefits of a handheld computer.

Purchasing A Computer _____

_____

Key Point:
- All key members of the staff should be consulted prior to such a purchase and should be actively involved in selecting the hardware and software.

☐ **LEARNING OBJECTIVE 11:** Describe the considerations for purchasing a computer.

Training Options _____

_____

☐ **LEARNING OBJECTIVE 12:** Describe various training options.

Computer Ethics _____

_____

Key Point:
- Its capabilities are endless. It can, however, lead to an invasion of patients' privacy and unethical behavior.

☐ **LEARNING OBJECTIVE 13:** Discuss the ethics related to computer access.

FOUNDATIONAL KNOWLEDGE

Computer Basics

1. A computer system is divided into two areas: hardware and peripherals. Take a look at the chart and decide which category each component fits into. Place a check mark in the appropriate box.

Name of component	Hardware	Peripheral
a. Keyboard		
b. Modem		
c. Central processing unit		
d. Printer		
e. Mouse		
f. Monitor		

2. Match these methods of connecting to the Internet with the statements below them.

Method of Connecting to Internet

a. ISP

b. cable television company

c. DSL

Description

1. This is the fastest connection, but it is the most expensive and it is not available in all areas.
2. This is a subscriber system that provides a faster connection than dial-up.
3. This system connects your computer's modem to the Internet through the phone line and is the slowest, but cheapest service.

3. Your office has started converting many of your paper files into digital online files to save time. Recently, you have realized that accessing these records through your ISP is taking a very long time. Check the box next to the solutions to this problem.

Solution

a. Upgrade your office's ISP to cable.	
b. Switch your Web browser.	
c. Switch your search engine.	
d. Upgrade your printer.	
e. Eliminate viruses with a virus scan.	
f. Upgrade your monitor.	
g. Upgrade your office's ISP to DSL.	

Professional Journal

REFLECT

(Prompts and Ideas: Are you comfortable with computer technology, or do you find it intimidating? Do you currently use any specialized software? Was it difficult to learn how to use that software? Have you found that computer technology has made your life simpler or more complicated?)

_____

_____

_____

_____

_____

_____

_____

PONDER AND SOLVE

1. One of your coworkers has a habit of getting up from her computer and leaving confidential patient information visible on the screen. She says that she sits too far away from patients for them to read anything on the screen, but you have seen several patients near the computer while your coworker is away from her desk. What do you say to her?

_____

_____

_____

_____

_____

_____

_____

2. A patient tells you that she has found a miracle medical cure for her child's cancer on the Internet. She is extremely excited about the treatment and tells you the website address. When you take a look, you notice that the information looks suspicious and is not endorsed by any medical professional. Explain what actions you would take and what you would say to the patient.

_____

_____

_____

_____

_____

_____

_____

EXPERIENCE

Skills related to this chapter include:

1. Care For and Maintain Computer Hardware (Procedure 9-1).

2. Searching on the Internet (Procedure 9-2).

Record any common mistakes, lessons learned, and/or tips you discovered during your experience of practicing and demonstrating these skills:

_____

_____

_____

_____

_____

_____

_____

Skill
Practice

PERFORMANCE OBJECTIVES:

1. Care for and maintain computer hardware (Procedure 9-1).
2. Search a given topic on the Internet (Procedure 9-2).

Name _____ Date _____ Time _____

Procedure 9-1:	CARE FOR AND MAINTAIN COMPUTER HARDWARE

EQUIPMENT/SUPPLIES: Computer CPU, monitor, keyboard, mouse, printer, duster, simulated warranties

STANDARDS: Given the needed equipment and a place to work, the student will perform this skill with _____% accuracy in a total of _____ minutes. (*Your instructor will tell you what the percentage and time limits will be before you begin.*)

KEY: 4 = Satisfactory   0 = Unsatisfactory   NA = This step is not counted

PROCEDURE STEPS	SELF	PARTNER	INSTRUCTOR
1. Place the monitor, keyboard, and printer in a cool, dry area out of direct sunlight.	☐	☐	☐
2. Place the computer desk on an antistatic floor mat or carpet.	☐	☐	☐
3. Clean the monitor screen with antistatic wipes.	☐	☐	☐
4. Use dust covers for the keyboard and the monitor when they were not in use.	☐	☐	☐
5. Lock the hard drive when moving the computer.	☐	☐	☐
6. Keep keyboard and mouse free of debris and liquids; dust and/or vacuum the keyboard.	☐	☐	☐
7. Create a file for maintenance and warranty contracts for the computer system.	☐	☐	☐
8. Handle data storage disks with special care.	☐	☐	☐

CALCULATION

Total Possible Points: _____
Total Points Earned: _____ Multiplied by 100 = _____ Divided by Total Possible Points = _____%

Pass   **Fail**
☐   ☐ | Comments: |

Student's signature _____ Date _____
Partner's signature _____ Date _____
Instructor's signature _____ Date _____

Name _____ Date _____ Time _____

Procedure 9-2:	**SEARCHING ON THE INTERNET**

PURPOSE: To quickly and effectively search the Internet as necessary for good time management.

EQUIPMENT/SUPPLIES: Computer with Web browser software, modem, active Internet connection account

STANDARDS: Given the needed equipment and a place to work, the student will perform this skill with _____% accuracy in a total of _____ minutes. (*Your instructor will tell you what the percentage and time limits will be before you begin.*)

KEY: 4 = Satisfactory   0 = Unsatisfactory   NA = This step is not counted

PROCEDURE STEPS	SELF	PARTNER	INSTRUCTOR
1. Connect computer to the Internet.	☐	☐	☐
2. Locate a search engine.	☐	☐	☐
3. Select two or three key words and type them at the appropriate place on the Web page.	☐	☐	☐
4. View the number of search results. If no sites are found, check spelling and retype or choose new key words.	☐	☐	☐
5. If the search produces a long list, do an advanced search and refine key words.	☐	☐	☐
6. Select an appropriate site and open its home page.	☐	☐	☐
7. If satisfied with the site's information, either download the material or bookmark the page. If unsatisfied with its information, either visit a site listed on the results page or return to the search engine.	☐	☐	☐

CALCULATION

Total Possible Points: _____
Total Points Earned: _____ Multiplied by 100 = _____ Divided by Total Possible Points = _____%

Pass   **Fail**
☐   ☐   Comments:

Student's signature _____ Date _____
Partner's signature _____ Date _____
Instructor's signature _____ Date _____

Perform routine maintenance of administrative and clinical equipment.

Clean the monitor, keyboard, and mouse of a computer in your office, school, or home. If you are currently working in a medical office, use a maintenance log sheet from your office. If this is not available to you, use the sample maintenance log below. Document cleaning the specific computer parts on the maintenance log.

Computer Maintenance Log

Model No: _____

Date Purchased: _____

Manufacturer: _____

_____

Telephone: _____

Warranty: _____   **Expiration Date** _____

Technical Service Representative _____

Cleaning Log

Date	Initials	Action Taken	Comments

Chapter
Self-Assessment
Quiz

1. Another name for a central processing unit is a:
   a. silicon chip.
   b. USB port.
   c. modem.
   d. microprocessor.
   e. handheld computer.

2. The purpose of a zip drive in a computer is to:
   a. scan information.
   b. delete information.
   c. store information.
   d. research information.
   e. translate information.

3. The acronym *DSL* stands for:

    a. data storage location.

    b. digital subscriber line.

    c. digital storage link.

    d. data saved/lost.

    e. digital software link.

4. In a physician's practice, the HIPAA officer:

    a. checks for security threats or gaps in electronic information.

    b. purchases new technological equipment.

    c. maintains computer equipment and fixes problems.

    d. trains staff in how to use computer equipment.

    e. monitors staff who may be misusing computer equipment.

Scenario: A parent approaches you and asks how he can keep his 9-year-old daughter safe on the Internet.

5. Which of these actions would you recommend to the parent?

    a. Don't allow the daughter on the Internet after 7 PM

    b. Stand behind the daughter the entire time she is using the Internet.

    c. Don't permit the daughter to use the Internet until she is ten years old.

    d. Add a filter to the daughter's computer to only allow safe sites as decided by the parent.

    e. Ask other parents for advice.

6. Which of these websites might be helpful to the parent?

    a. www.skyscape.com

    b. www.pdacortec.com

    c. www.ezclaim.com

    d. www.cyberpatrol.com

    e. www.nextgen.com

End Scenario

7. To protect your computer from a virus, you should:

    a. make sure that your computer is correctly shut down every time you use it.

    b. avoid opening any attachments from unknown websites.

    c. only download material from government websites.

    d. consult a computer technician before you use new software.

    e. only open one website at a time.

8. What is the advantage of encrypting an e-mail?

    a. It makes the e-mail arrive at its intended destination faster.

    b. It marks the e-mail as urgent.

    c. It scrambles the e-mail so that it cannot be read until it reaches the recipient.

    d. It translates the e-mail into another language.

    e. It informs the sender when the e-mail has been read by the recipient.

9. Which of these is an example of an inappropriate e-mail?

    a. "There will be a staff meeting on Wednesday at 9 AM."

    b. "Please return Mrs. Jay's call: her number is 608-223-3444."

    c. "If anyone has seen a lost pair of sunglasses, please return them to reception."

    d. "Mr. Orkley thinks he is having a stroke. Please advise."

    e. "Mrs. Jones called to confirm her appointment."

10. Which of the following is a peripheral?

    a. Zip drive

    b. Monitor

    c. Keyboard

    d. Internet

    e. Modem

11. Which of these would you most likely find on an intranet?

    a. Advice about health insurance

    b. Minutes from staff meetings

    c. Information about Medicare

    d. Descriptions of alternative treatments

    e. National guidelines on medical ethics

12. What is the difference between clinical and administrative software packages?

    a. Clinical software helps provide good medical care, while administrative software keeps the office efficient.

    b. Administrative software is designed to be used by medical assistants, while clinical software is used by physicians.

    c. Clinical software is cheaper than administrative software because it offers fewer technical features.

    d. Administrative software lasts longer than clinical software because it is of higher quality.

    e. Clinical software does not allow users to access it without a password, while anyone can use administrative software.

13. Which of these should you remember to do when paging a physician?

    a. Follow up the page with a phone call to make sure the physician got the message.

    b. Keep track of what time the message is sent and re-page if there is no response.

    c. Document the fact that you sent a page to the physician.

    d. Contact the person who left the message to let them know you have paged the physician.

    e. E-mail the physician with a copy of the paged message.

14. You can use the Meeting Maker software program to:

    a. contact patients about appointment changes.

    b. coordinate internal meetings and calendars.

    c. print patient reminders for annual checkups.

    d. create slideshow presentations for meetings.

    e. page office staff when a meeting is about to start.

15. Which of these is an important consideration when purchasing a new computer for the office?

    a. Whether the computer's programs are HIPAA compliant

    b. Whether the computer will be delivered to the office

    c. The number of people who will be using the computer

    d. The amount of space the computer will take up in the office

    e. Which is the best-selling computer on the market

16. When assigning computer log-in passwords to staff, a physician should:

    a. make sure that everyone has the code for the hospital computers.

    b. give staff two log-in passwords: one for professional use and one for personal use.

    c. issue all new employees with their own password.

    d. make sure that everyone has access to his or her e-mails, in case he or she is out of the office.

    e. use a standard log-in password for all the office computers.

17. It is a good idea to lock the hard drive when you are moving a computer to:

    a. prevent the zip drive from falling out.

    b. make sure that no information is erased.

    c. stop viruses from attacking the computer.

    d. protect the CPU and disk drives.

    e. avoid damaging the keyboard.

18. A modem is a(n):

    a. communication device that connects a computer to other computers, including the Internet.

    b. piece of software that enables the user to perform advanced administrative functions.

    c. name for the Internet.

    d. method of storing data on the computer.

    e. type of networking technology for local area networks.

19. Which of the following is true of an abstract found during a literary search?

    a. Abstracts are only found on government websites.

    b. Only physicians can access an abstract during a literary search.

    c. An abstract is a summary of a journal article.

    d. Most medical offices cannot afford to download an abstract.

    e. Abstracts can only be printed at a hospital library.

20. If a computer is exposed to static electricity, there is the potential risk of:

    a. electrical fire.

    b. memory loss.

    c. dust accumulation.

    d. slow Internet connection.

    e. viruses.

Management of the Medical Office

☐ Read textbook chapter and take notes within the Chapter Notes outline. Answer the Learning Objectives as you reach them in the content, and then check them off.

☐ Work the Content Review questions—both Foundational Knowledge and Application.

☐ Perform the Active Learning exercise(s).

☐ Complete Professional Journal entries.

☐ Complete Skill Practice Activity(s) using Competency Evaluation Forms and Work Products, when appropriate.

☐ Take the Chapter Self-Assessment Quiz.

☐ Insert all appropriate pages into your Portfolio.

Learning Objectives

1. Spell and define the key terms.
2. Describe what is meant by organizational structure.
3. List seven responsibilities of the medical office manager.
4. Explain the five staffing issues that a medical office manager will be responsible for handling.
5. List the types of policies and procedures that should be included in a medical office's policy and procedures manual.
6. List five types of promotional materials that a medical office may distribute.
7. Discuss financial concerns that the medical office manager must be capable of addressing.
8. Describe the duties regarding office maintenance, inventory, and service contracts.
9. Discuss the need for continuing education.

10. Discuss the need for general liability and medical malpractice insurance. List three services provided by most medical malpractice companies.
11. List six guidelines for completing incident reports.
12. List four regulatory agencies that require medical offices to have quality improvement programs.
13. Describe the accreditation process of the Joint Commission on Accreditation of Healthcare Organizations.
14. Describe the steps to developing a quality improvement program.
15. Explain how quality improvement programs and risk management work together in a medical office to improve overall patient care and employee needs.

Chapter Notes

Note: Bold-faced headings are the major headings in the text chapter; headings in regular font are lower-level headings (i.e., the content is subordinate to, or falls "under," the major headings). Make sure you understand the key terms used in the chapter, as well as the concepts presented as Key Points.

TEXT SUBHEADINGS   **NOTES**

Introduction _____

_____

_____

☐ **LEARNING OBJECTIVE 1:** Spell and define the key terms.

Overview of Medical Office Management _____

_____

_____

Organizational Structure _____

_____

Key Term: organizational chart
Key Point:
- The medical office's organizational structure, or chain of command, is depicted in an **organizational chart**, a flow sheet that allows the manager and employees to identify their team members and to see where they fit into the team.

☐ **LEARNING OBJECTIVE 2:** Describe what is meant by organizational structure.

The Medical Office Manager _____

_____

Key Point:
- The medical office manager must be multiskilled, multitalented, and able to prioritize a variety of issues, juggle responsibilities, and communicate effectively with patients, staff, and physicians. In some settings, the medical office manager may be referred to as the business manager.

☐ **LEARNING OBJECTIVE 3:** List seven responsibilities of the medical office manager.

Responsibilities of the Medical Office Manager _____

_____

_____

Communication _____

_____

Key Point:
- You must be a good listener, have good interpersonal skills, and be aware of your own nonverbal language.

Communicating with Patients _____

Key Point:
• Your goal should be to correct the problem in a timely and professional manner and to alleviate any negative feelings the patient may have.

Communicating with Staff _____

Key Term: job description
Key Point:
• To be an effective manager, you should communicate not only bad news but also positive messages to your employees.

Staffing Issues _____

Writing Job Descriptions _____

Key Point:
• Each employee should receive a copy of his or her job description at the time of hiring and after any revisions to the description are made.

Hiring and Interviewing Employees _____

Key Point:
• Any employee application form should be reviewed by legal counsel prior to its use.

Evaluating Employees _____

Key Point:
• Employee evaluations must be fair, accurate, and objective.

Taking Disciplinary Action _____

_____

Key Point:
- Determine whether the employee's credentialing agency should be notified of serious infractions.

Terminating Employees _____

_____

_____

Scheduling _____

_____

☐ **LEARNING OBJECTIVE 4:** Explain the five staffing issues that a medical office manager will be responsible for handling.

Policy and Procedures Manuals _____

_____

Key Terms: policy; procedure; mission statement; quality improvement; compliance officer
Key Points:
- Every business needs written rules and regulations to ensure that its practices are within legal and ethical boundaries.
- A **mission statement** describes the goals of the practice and whom it serves.

☐ **LEARNING OBJECTIVE 5:** List the types of policies and procedures that should be included in a medical office's policy and procedures manual.

Developing Promotional Materials _____

_____

Key Point:
- The medical office manager is often responsible for developing and distributing promotional literature for the practice.

☐ **LEARNING OBJECTIVE 6:** List five types of promotional materials that a medical office may distribute.

Financial Concerns _____

_____

_____

Budgets _____

_____

Key Term: budget

Payroll _____

_____

☐ **LEARNING OBJECTIVE 7:** Discuss financial concerns that the medical office manager must be capable of addressing.

Office Maintenance _____

_____

Management of Inventory and Supplies _____

_____

Service Contracts _____

_____

☐ **LEARNING OBJECTIVE 8:** Describe the duties regarding office maintenance, inventory, and service contracts.

Education _____

_____

Staff Education _____

_____

Patient Education _____

_____

Manager Education _____

_____

☐ **LEARNING OBJECTIVE 9:** Discuss the need for continuing education.

Risk Management _____

_____

> **Key Point:**
> • Risk management is an internal process geared to identifying potential problems before they cause injury to patients or employees.

Liability Insurance _____

_____

☐ **LEARNING OBJECTIVE 10:** Discuss the need for general liability and medical malpractice insurance. List three services provided by most medical malpractice companies.

Incident Reports _____

_____

> **Key Term:** incident reports
> **Key Point:**
> • **Incident reports,** sometimes referred to as occurrence reports, are written accounts of untoward (negative) patient, visitor, or staff events.

When to Complete an Incident Report _____

_____

> **Key Point:**
> • The rule of thumb is, when in doubt, always complete an incident report.

Information Included on an Incident Report _____

_____

Guidelines for Completing an Incident Report _____

_____

> **Key Point:**
> • State only the facts. Do not draw conclusions or summarize the event.

☐ **LEARNING OBJECTIVE 11:** List six guidelines for completing incident reports.

Trending Incident Reports _____

_____

Quality Improvement Programs _____

_____

_____

Regulatory Agencies _____

_____

_____

Occupational Safety and Health Administration _____

_____

> **Key Point:**
> • OSHA's mission is to save lives, prevent injuries, and protect the health of America's workers.

Joint Commission on Accreditation of Healthcare Organizations (JCAHO) _____

_____

> **Key Term:** sentinel event
> **Key Points:**
> • JCAHO is a private agency that sets health care standards and evaluates an organization's implementation of these standards for health care settings.
> • Participation in JCAHO is voluntary for health care organizations; without accreditation, however, the health care organization may not be eligible to participate in particular federal and state funding programs, such as Medicare and Medicaid.
> • A sentinel event is an unexpected death or serious physical or psychological injury to a patient.

☐ **LEARNING OBJECTIVE 12:** List four regulatory agencies that require medical offices to have quality improvement programs.

Centers for Medicare & Medicaid Services _____

_____

_____

State Health Departments _____

_____

☐ **LEARNING OBJECTIVE 13:** Describe the accreditation process of the Joint Commission on Accreditation of Healthcare Organizations.

Developing a Quality Improvement Program _____

_____

_____

Seven Steps for a Successful Program _____

_____

Key Terms: task force; expected threshold
Key Points:
- Problems given top priority are those that are high risk (most likely to occur) and those that are most likely to cause injury to patients, family members, or employees.
- A **task force** is a group of employees with different roles within the organization brought together to solve a given problem.
- Thresholds must be realistic and achievable.
- After implementation, the solution must be evaluated to determine whether it worked and if so, how well.

☐ **LEARNING OBJECTIVE 14:** Describe the steps to developing a quality improvement program.

Putting It All Together: A Case Review _____

_____

☐ **LEARNING OBJECTIVE 15:** Explain how quality improvement programs and risk management work together in a medical office to improve overall patient care and employee needs.

Content Review

FOUNDATIONAL KNOWLEDGE

1. Organizational Structure

Circle every item that would be an appropriate part of a medical organizational chart.

Salaries	Job titles	Who supervises whom
Employees' names	Physicians' names	Social security numbers

2. A Day in the Life of a Medical Office Manager

Circle all the following tasks that are the responsibility of the medical office manager.

a. scheduling staff

b. ordering supplies

c. writing the budget

d. keeping up to date on legal issues

e. assisting with medical procedures

f. cleaning the office and waiting room

g. revising policy and procedures manuals

h. presenting continuing education seminars

i. developing HIPAA and OSHA regulations

j. developing promotional pamphlets or newsletters

Writing Job Descriptions

3. List six of the elements that should be included in any job description.

a. _____

b. _____

c. _____

d. _____

e. _____

f. _____

4. In addition to writing job descriptions and managing employee evaluations, what are three other staffing issues that are the responsibility of the medical office manager?

a. _____

b. _____

c. _____

5. Employee Evaluations

Answer "Yes," "No," or "Yes But" to the following questions about evaluating employees. If you answer "No" or "Yes But," be able to explain why.

	Yes	No	Yes But. . .
a. Are employee evaluations your responsibility as a medical office manager?			
b. Should new employees be evaluated annually?			
c. Should you coach new employees about how to do their jobs well?			
d. Can annual performance appraisals be done orally?			
e. Should you communicate with employees about performance problems when one of the physicians asks you to?			
f. Should you inform a good employee yearly that she or he is doing a good job?			

Office Policies

6. Indicate by a check mark in the "Yes" or "No" column whether an item should be included in a medical office's policy and procedures manual.

	Yes	No
a. a chain of command chart		
b. a list of employee benefits		
c. infection control guidelines		
d. the office operating budget		
e. annual employee evaluations		
f. procedures for bill collections		
g. copies of completed incident reports		
h. a description of the goals of the practice		
i. responsibilities and procedures for ordering supplies		
j. a list of responsibilities for the last employee to leave the office each day		

7. List five types of promotional materials that a medical office might use.

a. _____

b. _____

c. _____

d. _____

e. _____

8. Why might a medical office manager outsource payroll?

_____

_____

9. Service Contracts

   a. List three types of service contractors a medical office is likely to use.

_____

_____

_____

_____

   b. List three responsibilities of the office manager regarding service contractors.

_____

_____

_____

_____

_____

10. On Budget

Medical offices usually have an operating budget and a capital budget. Separate the following items into the two categories by checking the column for operating budget or capital budget.

Budget Item	Operating Budget	Capital Budget
a. payroll		
b. medical equipment		
c. office supplies		
d. Internet service		
e. medical supplies		
f. building maintenance		
g. telephone service		
h. electricity		
i. expensive furniture		
j. patient materials		
k. continuing education		

11. Controlling Inventory

Inventory control is the responsibility of the office manager. On the checklist below, put an **M** beside the inventory tasks the manager should do and an **A** beside the things an assistant or other office staff member can do.

_____ Receive supplies

_____ Initial the packing slip

_____ Develop a system to keep track of supplies

_____ Determine the procedures for ordering supplies

_____ Transfer supplies from packing boxes to supply shelves

_____ Check the packing slip against the actual supply contents

_____ Keep receipts or packing slips in a bills-pending file for payment

_____ Develop a process to check that deliveries of supplies are complete and accurate

12. Continuing Education

Give a practical reason, a psychological reason, and a professional reason for off-site seminars and other continuing education activities for medical office staff.

a. PRACTICAL:

_____

_____

b. PSYCHOLOGICAL:

_____

_____

c. PROFESSIONAL:

_____

_____

Avoiding Malpractice Suits

13. List three services provided by most medical malpractice companies.

a. _____

b. _____

c. _____

14. General liability and medical malpractice insurance is needed:

a. only by employees in offices that use new medical procedures.

b. by physicians sued for malpractice, but not by nurses or office personnel.

c. to protect medical professionals from financial loss due to lawsuits or settlements.

d. because visitors who are hurt in the waiting room can sue unless an incident report is completed.

15. Each of the following statements about incident reports is <u>false or incomplete</u>. Rewrite each statement to make it true and complete.

a. You should write up an incident report as the event was reported to you.

_____

_____

b. The witness should summarize and explain the event.

_____

_____

c. You should remain anonymous when you fill out a report.

_____

_____

d. The form should be completed within 48 hours of the event.

_____

_____

e. If a particular section of the report does not apply, it should be left blank.

_____

_____

f. Keep a copy of the incident report for your own personal record.

_____

_____

g. If the incident happened to a patient, put a copy of the report in the patient's chart.

_____

_____

h. The report should be reviewed by a supervisor to make sure the office is not liable.

_____

_____

i. Incident reports are written when negative events happen to patients or visitors.

_____

_____

16. Which Agency?

Below is a list of four regulatory agencies that require medical offices to have quality improvement programs.
Match the regulatory agency with its description.

Agencies

a. CMS

b. OSHA

c. JCAHO

d. state health department

Descriptions

1. federal agency that regulates and runs Medicare and Medicaid

2. nonfederal agency to license and monitor health care organizations and enforce regulations

3. federal agency that enforces regulations to protect the health and welfare of patients and employees

4. agency that sets voluntary health care standards and evaluates a health care organization's implementation of those standards

Quality Improvement

17. Below is a list of the steps for creating a quality improvement plan. Put the steps in logical order. Then explain the reason for each step.

Steps

Assign an expected threshold.

Document the entire process.

Establish a monitoring plan.

Explore the problem and propose solutions.

Form a task force.

Identify the problem.

Implement the solution.

Obtain feedback.

Step	Reason
1.	
2.	
3.	
4.	
5.	
6.	
7.	
8.	

18. Explain how QI programs and risk management work together in a medical office.

_____

_____

19. Match the following key terms to their definitions.

Key Terms

a. budget _____

b. compliance officer _____

c. expected threshold _____

d. incident report _____

e. job description _____

f. mission statement _____

g. organizational chart _____

h. policy _____

i. procedure _____

j. sentinel event _____

k. quality improvement _____

l. task force _____

Definitions

1. numerical goal for a given problem

2. statement of work-related responsibilities

3. series of steps required to perform a given task

4. written account of untoward patient, visitor, or staff event

5. description of the goals of the practice and whom it serves

6. statement regarding the organization's rules on a given topic

7. unexpected death or serious physical or psychological injury to a patient

8. financial planning tool used to estimate anticipated expenditures and revenues

9. staff member who ensures compliance with the rules and regulations of the office

10. implementation of practices that will help ensure high-quality patient care and service

11. flow sheet that allows staff to identify team members and see where they fit into the team

12. group of employees with different roles brought together to solve a problem

20. True or False? Determine whether the following statements are true or false. If false, explain why.

a. Health care organizations are required to follow the regulations of the Joint Commission on Accreditation of Healthcare Organizations (JCAHO).

_____

_____

b. Accreditation by JCAHO is valid for 5 years.

_____

_____

c. If JCAHO's initial site review identifies unsatisfactory areas, the health care organization may later prove that corrections have been made by passing a focus survey.

_____

_____

d. The health care organization should prepare for the JCAHO survey by assessing its compliance with OSHA standards.

_____

_____

APPLICATION

Critical Thinking Practice

1. As you enter the office on the first day of your new job as the medical office manager, you notice a thick layer of dust on the plastic plants in the waiting room and see that the magazines are old and tattered. The staff greets you with enthusiasm, saying you are just what they need to deal with the patients' complaints about spending too much time waiting to be seen. Someone has left the incident report file on your desk. You look through it right away and learn that a needlestick has been reported almost every Wednesday evening for a month. What should you do first, and why?

_____

_____

2. Your assistant is moving across the country and you need to find a replacement. The office policy and procedures manual contains a job interview questionnaire that has questions relating to gender, race, age, marital status, education, and experience. You think it's important to find out more about a potential employee's personality and how the job is likely to affect his or her other responsibilities, and vice versa. Which of these questions should you not ask, and why?

_____

_____

Patient Education

1. Influenza incidence is predicted to be high this year, and flu season is coming. You find an outdated flu prevention poster in storage but no other patient education materials about flu. Make a plan for this year's flu education effort. Describe the educational materials you want and how you want to use them. Explain any research you should and or any input you will need.

_____

_____

Documentation

1. The office is still running out of medium-sized examination gloves, even though you increased their number last time you ordered them from the supplier. How will better documentation help you solve this problem?

_____

_____

Active Learning

1. When you complete your program of study, you would like to find a job as a medical office manager. Write the job description for your ideal job. Be sure to include all the essential elements, including a position summary, hours, location, and duties.

2. Get a head start on outsourcing services for your office. Search the Internet for service contractors (such as payroll, biohazard collection, office machine maintenance), and compare and contrast the services you find. Prepare a list of questions you would want answered by any service contractor before you decided whether to do business with them.

3. Working together with a partner, search the local classified ads for an open job as a medical office manager. Then prepare to role-play the interview process with your partner, taking turns acting as the interviewer and the interviewee. Make a list of questions that you would ask as both the interviewer and the interviewee. Switch places so you both get to experience the job interview process from each perspective.

Professional Journal

REFLECT

(Prompts and Ideas: Have you ever gone on a job interview before? How did you prepare? Were you nervous beforehand, and, if so, what did you do to calm yourself down? Have you ever started a new job? What kind of information did you get the first week on the job [e.g., policy manual, handbook]? Could your supervisor have done anything else to make you feel more prepared and comfortable in your new position?)

_____

_____

_____

_____

_____

_____

_____

PONDER AND SOLVE

1. Mrs. Hadley, who is blind and walks with a cane, slipped on the wet floor near a leaky water cooler and fell, cutting her forearm. One of the nurses examined and treated her wound and apologized. Mrs. Hadley said it was no problem and left the office. The nurse told you she wasn't going to file an incident report because the wound was minor and Mrs. Hadley had accepted her apology. As the medical office manager, what should you do?

_____

_____

_____

_____

_____

_____

_____

2. One member of the office staff consistently uses all her sick days but she always does a great job when she does come to work. Most of the staff members come in even when they are sick; they brag about it and apparently disapprove of taking sick days. Is this a problem? As the medical office manager, what should your goal be and which staff members should you talk with to meet your goal?

_____

_____

_____

_____

_____

_____

_____

EXPERIENCE

Skills related to this chapter include:

1. Creating a Procedures Manual (Procedure 10-1).

2. Creating a Quality Improvement Plan (Procedure 10-2).

Record any common mistakes, lessons learned, and/or tips you discovered during your experience of practicing and demonstrating these skills.

_____

_____

_____

_____

_____

_____

_____

_____

Skill Practice

PERFORMANCE OBJECTIVES:

1. Create a policy and procedures manual (Procedure 10-1).
2. Create a quality improvement plan (Procedure 10-2).

Name_____   Date_____   Time_____

EQUIPMENT/SUPPLIES:

STANDARDS: Given the needed equipment and a place to work, the student will perform this skill with _____% accuracy in a total of _____ minutes. (*Your instructor will tell you what the percentage and time limits will be before you begin.*)

KEY: 4 = Satisfactory   0 = Unsatisfactory   NA = This step is not counted

PROCEDURE STEPS	SELF	PARTNER	INSTRUCTOR
1. Check the latest information from key governmental agencies, local and state health departments, and health care organizations, such as OSHA, CDC, JCAHO, etc. to make sure that the policies and procedures being written comply with federal and state legislation and regulations.	☐	☐	☐
2. Gather product information; consult government agencies, if needed. Secure educational pamphlets.	☐	☐	☐
3. Title the procedure properly.	☐	☐	☐
4. Number the procedure appropriately.	☐	☐	☐
5. Define the overall purpose of the procedure in a sentence or two explaining the intent of the procedure.	☐	☐	☐
6. List all necessary equipment and forms. Include everything needed to complete the task.	☐	☐	☐
7. List each step with its rationale.	☐	☐	☐
8. Provide spaces for signatures.	☐	☐	☐
9. Record the date the procedure was written.	☐	☐	☐

CALCULATION

Total Possible Points: _____
Total Points Earned: _____ Multiplied by 100 = _____ Divided by Total Possible Points = _____%

Pass   **Fail**
☐   ☐   Comments:

Student's signature _____ Date _____
Partner's signature _____ Date _____
Instructor's signature _____ Date _____

Name _____ Date _____ Time _____

Procedure 10-2:	CREATE A QUALITY IMPROVEMENT PLAN

EQUIPMENT/SUPPLIES:

STANDARDS: Given the needed equipment and a place to work, the student will perform this skill with _____% accuracy in a total of _____ minutes. (*Your instructor will tell you what the percentage and time limits will be before you begin.*)

KEY: 4 = Satisfactory   0 = Unsatisfactory   NA = This step is not counted

PROCEDURE STEPS	SELF	PARTNER	INSTRUCTOR
1. Identify the problem or potential problem.	☐	☐	☐
2. Form a task force from group of students.	☐	☐	☐
3. Explore the problem and proposed solutions.	☐	☐	☐
4. Assign an expected threshold using measurable, realistic goals.	☐	☐	☐
5. Implement the solution and write a memorandum to the employees with instructions for the implementation.	☐	☐	☐
6. Establish a QI monitoring plan by listing the source, frequency, and person responsible for collecting data.	☐	☐	☐
7. Obtained feedback. Review data collected in the monitoring process.	☐	☐	☐
8. Document the entire process.	☐	☐	☐

CALCULATION

Total Possible Points: _____
Total Points Earned: _____ Multiplied by 100 = _____ Divided by Total Possible Points = _____%

Pass   **Fail**
☐   ☐   Comments:

Student's signature _____ Date _____
Partner's signature _____ Date _____
Instructor's signature _____ Date _____

Work Product 1

Use methods of quality control.

Louise Baggins, a 55-year-old patient, was visiting the physician for a physical exam. While waiting for her appointment, she asked you to direct her to the restroom. On her way into the restroom, she slipped and fell on a magazine that had fallen on the floor in the reception area. You did not see her fall, but she yelled out in pain after she fell. She was able to get up on her own, but injured her wrist. Her wrist was immediately red, swollen, and painful to touch. Dr. Mikuski looked at her wrist and suggested she go to the hospital emergency room to have x-rays. You called an ambulance to transfer Mrs. Baggins to the hospital.

Fill in the incident report below to document this event.

Workplace Requirements Program for Safety and Health

SUPERVISOR'S ACCIDENT REPORT FORM

This form is to be completed by the supervisor and forwarded to the Payroll Coordinator along with a copy of the North Carolina Industrial Commission Form 19 (Workers Compensation Form) within five days of the accident. All accidents involving serious bodily injury or death must be reported to the safety and health officer immediately.

ACCIDENT DATA

1. NAME OF EMPLOYEE:
or Patient

2. ADDRESS AND PHONE NO:

3. WORK DEPT. OR DIVISION: 4. SEX: 5. DATE AND TIME OF INJURY:
☐ MALE ☐ FEMALE

6. NATURE OF INJURY: 7. PART OF BODY INJURED:

8. CAUSE OF INJURY: 9. LOCATION OF ACCIDENT:

10. OCCUPATION AND ACTIVITY OF PERSON AT TIME OF ACCIDENT: 11. STATUS OF JOB OR ACTIVITY: (CHOOSE ONE)
Halted

12. NAME AND PHONE NO. OF ACCIDENT WITNESS:

13. LIST UNSAFE ACT, IF ANY:

14. LIST UNSAFE PHYSICAL OR MECHANICAL CONDITION, IF ANY:

15. UNSAFE PERSONAL FACTOR:

16. LIST HAZARD CONTROLS IN EFFECT AT TIME OF INJURY DESIGNED TO PREVENT INJURY:

17. PERSONAL PROTECTIVE EQUIPMENT BEING USED AT TIME OF ACCIDENT:
GLOVES, SAFETY GLASSES, GOGGLES, FACE SHIELD, OTHER

18. BRIEF DESCRIPTION OF ACCIDENT:

19. CORRECTIVE ACTION TAKEN OR RECOMMENDED TO DEPARTMENT SAFETY COMMITTEE:

TREATMENT DATA

20. WAS INJURED TAKEN TO (CHOOSE ONE): Hospital

21. DIAGNOSIS AND TREATMENT, IF KNOWN:

22. ESTIMATED LOST WORKDAYS: 23. DATE OF REPORT:
(EXCLUDING DAY OF ACCIDENT)   Month   Day   Year

24. REPORT PREPARED BY:

25. SIGNATURE OF SUPERVISOR:

26. SIGNATURE OF AGENCY SAFETY AND HEALTH OFFICER:

Work Product 2

Use methods of quality control.

After Mrs. Baggins fell in the reception area (see Work Product 1), your supervisor asks you to review any other injuries in the reception area in the past 6 months. There are seven incident reports involving patient falls, and all of those occurred in some part of the reception area. Three patients slipped by the doorway on rainy days. Two more tripped on the corner of the doormat. The last two patients fell in the main lobby—one tripped over a children's toy and the other slipped on a magazine, just like Mrs. Baggins did.

You are named to represent the medical assistants on a task force addressing these complaints. Assign an expected threshold using measurable, realistic goals. Explore the problem and propose solutions. Establish a QI monitoring plan explaining how data will be collected. Document the entire process and print the information to attach to this sheet. Using the blank memorandum below, write a memo to the staff with instructions to implement the solutions.

Memo

To:

From:

Date:

Re:

....

Scenario: It's your first day on the job as the medical office manager, so there's a lot you don't know yet about this office.

1. You want to know who's responsible for what in the office. Where is the best place to find that information?

   a. Payroll records

   b. The work schedule

   c. The chain of command chart

   d. The recent employee evaluations

   e. The bulletin board

2. You know the office is running low on paper and syringes. You're most likely to find out how to order supplies in:

   a. the QI plan.

   b. the service contracts folder.

   c. the operating budget.

   d. the policy and procedures manual.

   e. the communication notebook.

3. What is the first thing you should do about employee evaluations once you have located the file?

   a. Commit them to memory.

   b. Schedule counseling sessions with the employees.

   c. Check that employee evaluations are all on schedule.

   d. See whether there are any incident reports in the files.

   e. Reorganize the evaluations so they are at the front of the file.

4. The office keeps running out of tongue depressors. Which action should you take first?

   a. Establish a recycling program.

   b. Determine whether someone is stealing supplies.

   c. Review the system for keeping track of supplies.

   d. Tell the physicians not to use so many tongue depressors.

   e. Borrow some tongue depressors from the nearest medical office.

End Scenario

5. Which item should be in any job description?

   a. Age requirements

   b. Salary or hourly pay

   c. Physical requirements

   d. The preferred gender of the applicant

   e. Medical and dental benefits

6. Which task should you be expected to perform as medical office manager?

   a. Clean the waiting room

   b. Assign someone to make coffee

   c. Develop promotional pamphlets

   d. Assist with simple medical procedures

   e. Sign prescription refills

7. Which of the following is a medical office manager's responsibility?

   a. Completing all incident reports

   b. Teaching CPR

   c. Evaluating the physicians

   d. Hiring and firing employees

   e. Teach employees about malpractice insurance

8. Which statement is true of an incident report about a patient?

   a. It should go in the patient's file.

   b. It should be written by a physician.

   c. It should be written within 24 hours of the incident.

   d. It should be written from the patient's point of view.

   e. It should be kept in the medical office.

9. Which action should be taken if an employee is stuck by a patient's needle?

   a. The patient should be informed.

   b. The physician should take disciplinary action against the employee.

   c. The employee should write an incident report.

   d. The employee should be kept away from patients.

   e. The employee should sign a form admitting liability.

10. Which of the following categories is part of a capital budget?

   a. Payroll

   b. Medical supplies

   c. Building maintenance

   d. Heating and air conditioning

   e. Electricity

11. Which item should be part of any medical office budget?

    a. Merit bonuses

    b. Billing service

    c. Continuing education

    d. Magazine subscriptions

    e. Children's play facility

12. Which agency licenses and monitors health care organizations and enforces regulations?

    a. CMS

    b. State health department

    c. JCAHO

    d. OSHA

    e. HCFA

13. General liability and medical malpractice insurance is for:

    a. all medical professionals.

    b. all physicians.

    c. physicians who perform risky procedures.

    d. medical professionals with high risk profiles.

    e. physicians and nurses.

14. The first step in creating a quality improvement plan is to:

    a. form a task force.

    b. identify the problem.

    c. establish a monitoring plan.

    d. assign an expected threshold.

    e. explore the problem.

15. A QI program is most likely to be begun because of:

    a. two needlesticks.

    b. five missed cases of nail fungus.

    c. two mislabeled biopsy specimens.

    d. four complaints about waiting time.

    e. a patient falling over in the waiting area.

16. If you fill out an incident report, you should:

    a. keep a copy of the report.

    b. have a supervisor review it.

    c. give your title but not your name.

    d. fill out only the sections that apply.

    e. summarize what happened in the report.

17. A sentinel event is a(n):

    a. untoward staff event.

    b. step required to perform a given task.

    c. unexpected death or serious injury to a patient.

    d. action taken to ensure high-quality patient care and service.

    e. annual performance review.

18. Which of the following is used to estimate expenditures and revenues?

    a. Budget

    b. Tracking file

    c. Expected threshold

    d. Financial statement

    e. Previous expenditures

19. Risk management is a(n):

    a. process begun only after a sentinel event.

    b. process intended to identify potential problems.

    c. external process that deals with OSHA violations.

    d. internal process that deals with recurring problems.

    e. process undertaken by managers to reduce annual expenditure.

20. Which of the following is true of an expected threshold for a quality improvement program?

    a. It is the expected percentage reduction in risk.

    b. It is a way to measure the success of the program.

    c. It should be set higher for more dangerous problems.

    d. It should be set lower than you think you can achieve.

    e. It should only be used for particularly severe problems.

Managing the Finances in the Practice

11

Credit and Collections

Chapter Checklist

- [ ] Read textbook chapter and take notes within the Chapter Notes outline. Answer the Learning Objectives as you reach them in the content, and then check them off.
- [ ] Work the Content Review questions—both Foundational Knowledge and Application.
- [ ] Perform the Active Learning exercise(s).

- [ ] Complete Professional Journal entries.
- [ ] Complete Skill Practice Activity(s) using Competency Evaluation Forms and Work Products, when appropriate.
- [ ] Take the Chapter Self-Assessment Quiz.
- [ ] Insert all appropriate pages into your Portfolio.

Learning Objectives

1. Spell and define the key terms.
2. Explain the physician fee schedule.
3. Discuss forms of payment.
4. Explain the legal considerations in extending credit.

5. Discuss the legal implications of credit collection.
6. Describe three methods of debt collection.

Chapter Notes

Note: Bold-faced headings are the major headings in the text chapter; headings in regular font are lower-level headings (i.e., the content is subordinate to, or falls "under," the major headings). Make sure you understand the key terms used in the chapter, as well as the concepts presented as Key Points.

TEXT SUBHEADINGS   **NOTES**

Introduction _____

☐ **LEARNING OBJECTIVE 1:** Spell and define the key terms.

Fees _____

_____

_____

_____

_____

Fee Schedules _____

_____

_____

Key Term: participating providers

☐ **LEARNING OBJECTIVE 2:** Explain the physician fee schedule.

Discussing Fees in Advance _____

_____

_____

Key Term: patient co-payment
Key Points:
• It is always a good policy to discuss fees with patients in advance.
• Ideally you should collect the entire amount due from a new patient on the first visit.

Forms of Payment _____

_____

_____

☐ **LEARNING OBJECTIVE 3:** Discuss forms of payment.

Payment by Insurance Companies _____

_____

_____

Key Point:
• Remember, always make a copy of both sides of the patient's insurance card and place it in the appropriate section of the chart for billing reference.

Adjusting Fees _____

_____

_____

Key Terms: adjustments; professional courtesy; write-off

Credit _____

_____

_____

Extending Credit _____

_____

Key Term: credit

Legal Considerations _____

_____

☐ **LEARNING OBJECTIVE 4:** Explain the legal considerations in extending credit.

Collections _____

_____

Legal Considerations _____

_____

☐ **LEARNING OBJECTIVE 5:** Discuss the legal implications of credit collection.

Collecting a Debt _____

_____

Monthly Billing _____

_____

Key Term: installment
Key Point:
• If your facility changes a billing cycle, you are legally required to notify patients of the change 3 months before the change takes effect.

Aging Accounts _____

_____

Key Term: aging schedule

Collecting Overdue Accounts _____

_____

☐ **LEARNING OBJECTIVE 6:** Describe three methods of debt collection.

Collection Alternatives _____

_____

Key Term: collections

_____

Content Review

FOUNDATIONAL KNOWLEDGE

1. Office visit fees are usually based on the UCR system. Match the letters in "UCR" with their explanations.

Fees

U (usual) _____

C (customary) _____

R (reasonable) _____

Explanations

a. The fee is a good balance between cost and the clients' expectations.

b. The fee is based on the actual value of the service being provided.

c. The fee is competitive with fees charged by other local practices.

2. Fee setting also considers RBRVS, by which fees are adjusted for geographical differences. What does RBRVS stand for?

_____

_____

3. There should be a sign posted in the office, where patients can see it, giving information about procedure fees. What should be on the sign?

_____

_____

4. Which third-party payers affect fee schedules if the physicians in your office are participating providers, and how many fee schedules might there be?

_____

_____

5. Fill in the missing parts with the things you should do to improve the success of fee collection.

What	When	Why
a. _____	Before any procedure is done	To ensure that patients are aware of the charges
Collect the entire co-pay or other amount due from a new patient.	**b.** _____	To lower your accounts receivable and improve cash flow
Get a picture identification and complete contact information from a new patient, including the names, numbers, and relationships of contacts who can give you information about the patient's location.	On the first visit	**c.** _____

6. Patients are usually allowed to pay for services with cash, a personal check, debit card, or credit card.

a. If a new patient is paying by check, what should you do?

_____

_____

b. The office pays a credit card company a percentage. Why is it still sometimes cost effective to accept payment by credit card?

_____

_____

7. How often should you ask the patient for his insurance card, and what should you do with it when you get it?

_____

_____

8. Compare and contrast fee adjustments and fee write-offs in the diagram below.

Professional Courtesy Fees	Both	Fee Write-offs
• _____	• result in reduced income	• _____
	• _____	

Cash or Credit?

9. Fill out the following 5W chart about extending credit.

Extending Credit

Who	For patients
What	
Where	
Why	
Watch out	

Collection Time

10. Your office employs a billing cycle based on patients' last names. Here is when patients are billed:
- A-H on the 1st of the month
- I-P on the 15th of the month
- Q-Z on the 22nd of the month

Organize the patients below in the chart to determine when you should send their bills in October.

October 1	October 15	October 22

Sanquetta Jones	Taylor Harris	Kim Dewar	Taneesha Rockfield
Imani Wilson	Haywood Barry	Valerie Angeles	Isabelle Smith
Tisha Matthews	Mekhi Currant	So Yin	Seth Noh

11. All the statements below are false or inaccurate. Rewrite each statement so that it accurately reflects the consumer protection laws regarding credit collection.

a. You cannot contact a patient directly about an unpaid bill.

_____

_____

b. You should not try to contact a debtor before 9:00 a.m. or after 5:00 p.m.

_____

_____

c. You have every right to call debtors at work.

_____

_____

d. You should keep calling a patient about a debt after turning the case over to a collection agency, in order to increase your chances of recovering the money.

_____

_____

e. It's okay to use abusive language to intimidate a debtor, as long as you don't give false or misleading information.

_____

_____

f. If a patient dies and the estate can't meet all her debts, the probate court will pay the medical bills first.

_____

_____

12. The three most common ways of collecting overdue accounts are:

a. _____

b. _____

c. _____

13. List three situations in which calling a patient to collect an overdue payment may be least helpful.

a. _____

b. _____

c. _____

14. What should be in a mailing that asks a patient to settle an overdue account?

_____

_____

15. What is a good way to use a patient's visit as an opportunity to try to collect payment on an overdue bill?

_____

_____

16. What should you say and not say if you call a patient to collect on a bill and you are asked to leave a message?

_____

_____

17. For each line in the box below, put an **X** in the "Office" column and/or the "Collection Agency" column to indicate who can take the action.

Action	Office	Collection Agency
Send overdue notices.		
Call patients who have overdue bills.		
Remind patients of bills during office visits.		
Sue in small claims court.		
List debtors with credit bureaus.		

18. How many times should you contact patients asking them to pay overdue bills? Why?

_____

_____

19. Match the following key terms to their definitions.

Key Terms	Definitions
a. adjustment _____	**1.** a change in a posted account
b. aging schedule _____	**2.** a total bill being paid off over time
c. collections _____	**3.** process of seeking payment for overdue bills
d. credit _____	**4.** arrangement for a patient to pay on an installment plan
e. installment _____	**5.** charging other health care professionals a reduced rate
f. participating provider _____	**6.** cancellation of an unpaid debt, usually claimed on the practice's federal taxes
g. patient co-payment _____	**7.** a certain share of the bill that a managed care company usually requires the patient to pay
h. professional courtesy _____	**8.** physician who agrees to participate with managed care companies and other third-party payers
i. write-off _____	**9.** record of a patient's name, balance, payments made, time of outstanding debt, and relevant comments

20. True of False? Determine whether the following statements are true or false. If false, explain why.

a. A physician's fee schedule takes into consideration the costs of operating the office, such as rent, utilities, malpractice insurance, and salaries.

_____

_____

b. If a patient has insurance, you must charge him the insurance carrier's allowed fee for a procedure.

_____

_____

c. To maintain good relations with patients, you should be vague and polite when you ask them to pay their bills.

_____

_____

d. You should monitor the activity on a patient's credit account in order to keep the collection ratio low.

APPLICATION

Critical Thinking Practice

1. What are some of the negative aspects of extending credit to patients? Consider costs, patient attitudes, and legal requirements in your answer.

2. You have several patients who have long-outstanding debts. They don't come into the office anymore, and they don't respond to your telephone calls or letters. The physicians in the practice are absolutely against using a collection agency. What avenues are open to you to help you collect the debts?

Patient Education

1. Mrs. Sanchez is seeing Dr. Roland for the first time and has asked you to explain the physician's fees. Explain to Mrs. Sanchez how Dr. Roland establishes the fees he charges his patients.

Documentation

1. If your office has a computerized billing system, it will automatically document any overdue notices you send to patients to collect fees. However, you have the options of calling patients and speaking to them while they're in the office. Those events won't be automatically input into the computer records, but it's very important that you keep track of them. How could you do that?

Active Learning

1. Use the Internet to research the three major credit bureaus and find out how to check a new patient's credit history. Specifically, find out what's available to help you decide how to handle payment from people without traditional credit histories. This group includes college students, young adults, recent immigrants, traditional housewives, and people who choose not to use credit cards.
2. Many people feel uncomfortable asking other people for money. However, you need to feel comfortable discussing finance and account information with patients. Working with a partner, role-play a scenario in which a patient has an overdue account that the medical assistant must address. Take turns playing the parts of the medical assistant and the patient to understand both perspectives.

3. In recent years, the government has called into question the practice of professional courtesy extended to other health care professionals. Perform research online or talk to health care professionals to find out more about the issues surrounding professional courtesy. Then write a viewpoint paper arguing for or against the practice of professional courtesy.

Professional Journal

REFLECT

(Prompts and Ideas: Have you or a loved one ever been unable to pay a bill right away or been in deep debt? How were you treated, or how do you wish you had been treated? How do you think you may be able to handle debt collections with the right amount of sensitivity toward your patients?)

_____

_____

_____

_____

_____

_____

PONDER AND SOLVE

1. Mr. Green has been a patient with your practice for more than 20 years and has always paid his co-payment or bill before he left the office. Recently, however, he has not been paying anything at all, and his outstanding bill is 60 days past due. You have called his home and left several phone messages, but you still haven't heard from him. What should you do?

_____

_____

_____

_____

_____

2. You outsourced your overdue billing to a collections agency in order to give yourself time to devise a better inventory system, but a few of your long-time patients have told you that they have been very upset by the "nastiness" of the collections people who contacted them. You spoke with a collections agency representative who assured you his employees were doing nothing illegal or inappropriate. However, a week later, another patient apologized for being late on a bill and confided to you that the unnerving call from the collector had gravely upset her. What should you do?

_____

_____

_____

_____

_____

_____

EXPERIENCE

Skills related to this chapter include:

1. Evaluating and Managing a Patient Account (Procedure 11-1).

2. Composing a Collection Letter (Procedure 11-2).

Record any common mistakes, lessons learned, and/or tips you discovered during your experience of practicing and demonstrating these skills.

_____

_____

_____

_____

_____

_____

_____

_____

Skill Practice

PERFORMANCE OBJECTIVES:

1. Evaluate and manage a patient account (Procedure 11-1).
2. Write a collection letter (Procedure 11-2).

Name _____   Date _____   Time _____

EQUIPMENT: Simulation including scenario; sample patient ledger card with transactions; yellow, blue, and red stickers (yellow for accounts 30 days past due; blue for accounts 60 days past due; red for accounts 90 days past due)

STANDARDS: Given the needed equipment and a place to work the student will perform this skill with _____% accuracy in a total of _____ minutes. (*Your instructor will tell you what the percentage and time limits will be before you begin.*)

KEY: 4 = Satisfactory   0 = Unsatisfactory   NA = This step is not counted

PROCEDURE STEPS	SELF	PARTNER	INSTRUCTOR
1. Review the patient's account history to determine the "age" of the account. If payment has not been made between 30 and 59 days from today's date, the account is 40 days past due, and so on.	☐	☐	☐
2. Flag the account for appropriate action. Place a yellow flag (sticker) on accounts that are 30 days old. Place a blue flag on accounts that are 60 days old. Place a red flag on accounts that are 90 days old.	☐	☐	☐
3. Set aside accounts that have had no payment in 91 days or longer.	☐	☐	☐
4. Make copies of the ledger cards.	☐	☐	☐
5. Sort the copies by category: 30, 60, 90 days.	☐	☐	☐
6. Write or stamp the copies with the appropriate message.	☐	☐	☐
7. Mail the statements to the patients.	☐	☐	☐
8. Follow through with the collection process by continually reviewing past due accounts.	☐	☐	☐

CALCULATION

Total Possible Points: _____
Total Points Earned: _____ Multiplied by 100 = _____ Divided by Total Possible Points = _____%

Pass   **Fail**
☐   ☐   Comments:

Student's signature _____ Date _____
Partner's signature _____ Date _____
Instructor's signature _____ Date _____

Name _____ Date _____ Time _____

<table>
<tr><td>Procedure 11-2:</td><td>**COMPOSING A COLLECTION LETTER**</td></tr>
</table>

EQUIPMENT: Ledger cards generated in Procedure 11-1, word processor, stationery with letterhead

STANDARDS: Given the needed equipment and a place to work the student will perform this skill with _____% accuracy in a total of _____ minutes. (*Your instructor will tell you what the percentage and time limits will be before you begin.*)

KEY: 4 = Satisfactory 0 = Unsatisfactory NA = This step is not counted

PROCEDURE STEPS	SELF	PARTNER	INSTRUCTOR
1. Review the patients' accounts and sort the accounts by age.	☐	☐	☐
2. Design a rough draft of a form letter that can be used for collections.	☐	☐	☐
3. In the first paragraph, tell the patient why you are writing.	☐	☐	☐
4. Inform the patient of the action you expect. For example: "To avoid further action, please pay $50.00 on this account by Friday, May 1, 20__."	☐	☐	☐
5. Proofread the rough draft for errors, clarity, accuracy, and retype.	☐	☐	☐
6. Take the collection letter to a supervisor or physician for approval.	☐	☐	☐
7. Fill in the appropriate amounts and dates on each letter. Ask for at least half of the account balance within a two-week period.	☐	☐	☐
8. Print, sign, and mail the letter.	☐	☐	☐

CALCULATION

Total Possible Points: _____
Total Points Earned: _____ Multiplied by 100 = _____ Divided by Total Possible Points = _____%

Pass   **Fail**
☐   ☐   Comments:

Student's signature _____ Date _____
Partner's signature _____ Date _____
Instructor's signature _____ Date _____

Work Product 1

Perform Accounts Receivable Procedures.

Your office's billing cycle posts bills on the first of every month. Review the list of outstanding payments and organize in the Aging of Accounts Receivable Report below.

- Oliver Santino visited the office on April 27 for a physical and blood work. The bill was $250.
- Warren Gates visited the office on May 8. His bill was $55.
- Tamara Jones visited the office on June 18 for a physical. The cost for the physical was $125, with an additional $55 for lab work.
- Amir Shell visited the office on June 25 for a physical exam and chest x-rays. The bill was $315.
- Nora Stevenson visited the office on July 9 to have a wound sutured. The bill was $100.

Below is an aging schedule as of August 30, 2008. Please fill in the information for these patients. Please enter an account number of 000-00-0000 for all patients.

Aging of Accounts Receivable Report: August 30, 2008

Patient Name	Account Number	Due Date	Amount

Accounts 30 Days Past Due:

Accounts 60 Days Past Due:

Accounts 90 Days Past Due:

Accounts 120 Days or More Past Due:

Total Overdue Accounts Receivable

Work Product 2

Perform Billing and Collection Procedures.

Caroline Cusick has an outstanding balance of $415 due to the medical office Pediatric Associates, 1415 San Juan Way, Santa Cruz, CA 95060. Write a collection letter to the patient to tell her about her overdue account. Her contact information is as follows: Caroline Cusick, 24 Beach Street, Santa Cruz, CA 95060. Print the letter and attach to this sheet.

Chapter Self-Assessment Quiz

1. The total of all the charges posted to patients' accounts for the month of May is $16,000. The revenues the practice received for May total $12,000. What is the collection percentage for May?

   a. 5 percent

   b. 25 percent

   c. 75 percent

   d. 80 percent

   e. 133 percent

2. Interest that may be charged to a patient account is determined by:

   a. the physician.

   b. the patient.

   c. the insurance company.

   d. the law.

   e. the state.

3. In the UCR concept, the letters stand for:

   a. user, customer, and regulation.

   b. usual, competitive, and regular.

   c. usage, consumption, and return.

   d. usual, customary, and reasonable.

   e. usage, complaint, and rationale.

4. When credit cards are accepted by a medical practice, the medical practice generally agrees to pay the credit card company:

   a. 5.2 percent.

   b. 1.8 percent.

   c. 15 percent.

   d. 3.1 percent.

   e. 25 percent.

5. Federal regulations require each medical office to describe its services and procedures and to give the procedure codes and prices by:

   a. giving a list to each patient at check in.

   b. offering the list to each patient at payment.

   c. posting a sign stating that a list is available.

   d. answering a patient's questions about billing.

   e. placing an ad in the newspaper describing the fees.

6. Physicians who chose to become participating providers with third-party payers usually do so in order to:

   a. charge higher fees.

   b. simplify fee schedules.

   c. build a solid patient base.

   d. reduce the time before payment.

   e. share a patient load with another physician.

7. It is a good and ethical business practice to:

   a. take payment in cash only.

   b. accept only patients who have insurance.

   c. refuse patients who have third-party payment plans.

   d. discuss fees with patients before they see a physician or nurse.

   e. charge the patient a small fee for paying with a credit card.

8. When dealing with a new patient, you should avoid:

   a. taking cash.

   b. taking a partial payment.

   c. taking a check with two picture IDs.

   d. taking co-payment with an insurance card.

   e. taking a payment by credit card.

9. Most fees for medical services:

    a. are paid by insurance companies.

    b. are paid by Medicare and Medicaid.

    c. are paid by patients who are private payers.

    d. are written off on the practice's federal taxes.

    e. are paid to the physician late.

10. When an insurance adjustment is made to a fee:

    a. the patient is charged less than the normal rate.

    b. the medical office receives more than its normal rate.

    c. the insurance carrier pays the adjustment rate.

    d. the insurance carrier's explanation of benefits shows how much the office may collect for the service.

    e. the difference between the physician's normal fee and the insurance carrier's allowed fee is written off.

11. Why would a medical office extend credit to a patient?

    a. To save money

    b. To accommodate the patient

    c. To postpone paying income tax

    d. To charge interest

    e. To make billing more cost effective

12. Why do many medical offices outsource their credit and billing functions?

    a. They don't want to ask their patients for money directly.

    b. They are not licensed to manage credit card transactions.

    c. Creating their own installment plans is too complicated legally.

    d. Managing patient accounts themselves costs about $5 per month per patient.

    e. Billing companies can manage the accounts more cost effectively.

13. It is illegal for a medical office to

    a. use a collection agency.

    b. disclose fee information to patients who have insurance.

    c. deny credit to patients because they receive public assistance.

    d. charge patients interest, finance charges, or late fees on unpaid balances.

    e. change their established billing cycle

14. If you are attempting to collect a debt from a patient, you must:

    a. use reasonable self-restraint.

    b. call the patient only at home.

    c. hire a licensed bill collection agency.

    d. first take the patient to small claims court.

    e. wait one year before you can ask for payment.

15. When first attempting to collect a debt by telephone, you should:

    a. ask the patient to come in for a checkup.

    b. contact the patient before 8:00 AM or after 9:00 PM

    c. contact the patient only at his place of employment.

    d. leave a message explaining the situation on the answering machine.

    e. speak only to the patient or leave only your first name and number.

16. When you are collecting a debt from an estate, it is best to:

    a. send a final bill to the estate's executor.

    b. take the matter directly to small claims court.

    c. try to collect within a week of the patient's death.

    d. allow the family a month to mourn before asking for payment.

    e. ask a collection agency to contact the family.

17. If a billing cycle is to be changed, you are legally required to notify patients:

    a. one month before their payment is due.

    b. before the next scheduled appointment.

    c. three months prior to the billing change.

    d. after you approve the change with the insurance company.

    e. only if they have outstanding payments.

18. When you age an account, you:

    a. write off debts that have been outstanding longer than 120 days.

    b. send bills first to the patients who had the most recent procedures.

    c. organize patient accounts by how long they have been seeing the physician.

    d. calculate the time between the last bill and the date of the last payment.

    e. determine the time between the procedure and the date of the last payment.

19. A cancellation of an unpaid debt is called a(n):

    a. professional courtesy.

    b. co-payment.

    c. write-off.

    d. adjustment.

    e. credit.

20. Which collections method takes the least staff time?

    a. Using a collection agency

    b. Going to small claims court

    c. Billing the patient monthly until paid

    d. Scheduling all payments on the first of the month

    e. Reporting patients to the credit bureaus

Accounting Responsibilities

CHAPTER
12

Chapter Checklist

☐ Read textbook chapter and take notes within the Chapter Notes outline. Answer the Learning Objectives as you reach them in the content, and then check them off.

☐ Work the Content Review questions—both Foundational Knowledge and Application.

☐ Perform the Active Learning exercise(s).

☐ Complete Professional Journal entries.

☐ Complete Skill Practice Activity(s) using Competency Evaluation Forms and Work Products, when appropriate.

☐ Take the Chapter Self-Assessment Quiz.

☐ Insert all appropriate pages into your Portfolio.

Learning Objectives

1. Spell and define the key terms.
2. Explain the concept of the pegboard book-keeping system.
3. Describe the components of the pegboard system.
4. Identify and discuss the special features of the pegboard day sheet.
5. Describe the functions of a computer account-ing system.
6. List the uses and components of computer accounting reports.
7. Explain banking services, including types of accounts and fees.
8. Describe the accounting cycle.
9. Describe the components of a record-keeping system.
10. Explain the process of ordering supplies and paying invoices.

Chapter Notes

Note: Bold-faced headings are the major headings in the text chapter; headings in regular font are lower-level headings (i.e., the content is subordinate to, or falls "under," the major headings). Make sure you understand the key terms used in the chapter, as well as the concepts presented as Key Points.

TEXT SUBHEADINGS **NOTES**

Introduction _____

_____

_____

☐ **LEARNING OBJECTIVE 1:** Spell and define the key terms.

Accounts Receivable and Daily Bookkeeping

Key Terms: bookkeeping; balance; debit; credit
Key Point:
- Because the two sides of the accounting equation must always **balance** (be equal), each transaction requires a **debit** (charge) on one side of the equation and a **credit** (payment) on the other side of the equation; the amount of the debit and credit must be equal.

Manual Accounting

Pegboard Bookkeeping System

Key Terms: day sheet; ledger card; charge slip
Key Point:
- At the end of the day, all of the transactions are added.

☐ **LEARNING OBJECTIVE 2:** Explain the concept of the pegboard bookkeeping system.

☐ **LEARNING OBJECTIVE 3:** Describe the components of the pegboard system.

Day Sheet

Key Terms: posting; adjustment
Key Points:
- The day sheet keeps track of daily patient transactions, such as charges for services to patients, payments received from patients and insurance carriers, and adjustments to patient accounts.
- You should perform a trial balance at the end of each month.

☐ **LEARNING OBJECTIVE 4:** Identify and discuss the special features of the pegboard day sheet.

Ledger Cards

Key Term: ledger card
Key Point:
- The ledger card is a legal document and should be kept for the same length of time as the patient's medical record.

Encounter Forms and Charge Slips _____

_____

Key Term: encounter form

Posting a Charge _____

_____

Key Point:
• The charge column of the day sheet is for original charges incurred for services received by the patient from the physician or staff on a specific date.

Posting a Payment _____

_____

_____

Processing a Credit Balance _____

_____

Key Point:
• Brackets indicate the opposite of the column's usual meaning.

Processing Refunds _____

_____

_____

Posting a Credit Adjustment _____

_____

_____

Posting a Debit Adjustment _____

_____

_____

Posting to Cash-Paid-Out Section of Day Sheet _____

_____

_____

Computerized Accounting _____

_____

_____

☐ **LEARNING OBJECTIVE 5:** Describe the functions of a computer accounting system.

Posting to Computer Accounts _____

_____

Key Point:
- If you understand the fundamentals of accounting and how to post entries manually, you will be able to use a computer system with ease.

Computer Accounting Reports _____

_____

☐ **LEARNING OBJECTIVE 6:** List the uses and components of computer accounting reports.

Banks and Their Services _____

_____

Types of Accounts _____

_____

Checking Accounts _____

_____

Key Point:
- A checking account allows you to write checks for funds that are deposited in the account.

Savings Accounts _____

_____

Money Market Accounts _____

_____

Bank Fees _____

_____

Monthly Service Fees _____

_____

Key Term: service charge

Overdraft Protection _____

_____

_____

Returned Check Fee _____

_____

Key Term: returned check fee

_____

☐ **LEARNING OBJECTIVE 7:** Explain banking services, including types of accounts and fees.

Types of Checks _____

_____

_____

Banking Responsibilities _____

_____

_____

Writing Checks for Accounts Payable _____

_____

Key Point:
- Banks require signature cards for each person authorized to sign checks.

Receiving Checks and Making Deposits _____

_____

Key Point:
- This way, if the payments are lost or stolen, no one else can cash them.

Reconciling Bank Statements _____

_____

Key Point:
- This bank statement must be reconciled, or compared for accuracy, with your records each month.

Petty Cash _____

_____

Key Point:
- The value of the petty cash account should always remain the same.

Overview of Accounting _____

_____

_____

Accounting Cycle _____

_____

Key Terms: accounting cycle; Internal Revenue Service (IRS); audit

☐ **LEARNING OBJECTIVE 8:** Describe the accounting cycle.

Record-Keeping Components _____

_____

Key Terms: payroll; liabilities; check register; summation reports; profit-and-loss statement
Key Points:
- The practice's financial records should include a running record of income, accounts receivable, and total expenditures, including **payroll** (employee salaries), cash on hand, and **liabilities** (amounts the practice owes).
- Software packages offer the most sophisticated way to maintain financial records, not just for the categorization of expenses but also for the rapid formation of financial reports.
- If financial data are entered diligently into the bookkeeping system, preparing monthly, quarterly, or yearly reports should not be a daunting task.

☐ **LEARNING OBJECTIVE 9:** Describe the components of a record-keeping system.

Accounts Payable _____

_____

Ordering Goods and Services _____

_____

Key Term: purchase order

Receiving Supplies _____

_____

Key Terms: packing slip; invoice

Paying Invoices _____

_____

Manual Payment _____

_____

Key Term: check stub
Key Point:
• Memos or notations on **check stubs** can be referenced later if a question arises concerning payment by a particular check.

Pegboard Payment _____

_____

Key Term: check register

Computer Payment _____

_____

☐ **LEARNING OBJECTIVE 10:** Explain the process of ordering supplies and paying invoices.

Preparation of Reports _____

_____

Assisting With Audits _____

_____

Key Term: audit

Content Review

FOUNDATIONAL KNOWLEDGE

Features of the Pegboard

1. What is the concept of the pegboard bookkeeping system?

_____

_____

2. A new assistant unfamiliar with the pegboard bookkeeping has asked you to explain the system to her. Briefly describe each component to her.

Component	Description
a. day sheet	
b. ledger card	
c. charge slip	
d. ledger tray	

3. Match the feature of the pegboard day sheet with the proper description.

Feature of Pegboard Day Sheet

a. deposit slip _____

b. distribution columns _____

c. payments _____

d. adjustments _____

e. posting proofs _____

Description

1. used to assign charges for various services

2. the section where you allow for reductions in fees, adding credit to an account, or reinstating charges when a check is returned

3. used to deposit all payments received from patients in the bank

4. the section where you enter the day's totals and balance the sheet

5. the section where you record all payments received

Computerized Accounting Functions

4. There are several advantages of a computerized system over a manual system. Read the selection below, and circle the functions that are computerized accounting functions only.

   a. Entries are recorded in a patient's file

   b. Quickly create invoices and receipts

   c. Calculation of each transaction is made, as well as a total at the end of the day

   d. Performs bookkeeping, making appointments, and generating office reports

   e. Daily activities are recorded

   f. Bill reminders are placed to keep track of expenses

5. The office you are working in has recently updated its bookkeeping system from pegboard to computer. Now, the physician wants to utilize all the capabilities the new system offers. One particular function that interests her is the computer accounting reports. List the different types of reports and briefly describe their uses.

   a. _____

   b. _____

   c. _____

Banking Ins and Outs

6. What are banking services?

_____

_____

7. A medical office is just starting up, and one of the first things the bookkeeper needs to do is find a bank. Fill in the chart below with descriptions of checking, savings, and money market accounts.

Checking Account	Savings Account	Money Market Account

8. What is a returned check fee?

_____

_____

9. The office you are working in has an accounting cycle that begins in June. Describe what the accounting cycle is, and what kind of year your office follows.

_____

_____

10. The office manager ordered a new endorsement stamp from the bank. In the meantime, you need to deposit a check for Rinku Banjere, MD, into account number 123-4567-890. Endorse the check below for deposit.

ENDORSE HERE

_____

_____

_____

DO NOT SIGN/WRITE/STAMP BELOW THIS LINE
FOR FINANCIAL INSTITUTION USE ONLY*

11. List four items that should be readily available in case your office is audited.

a. _____

b. _____

c. _____

d. _____

12. When is it unnecessary to use a charge slip?

_____

_____

13. Why is correction fluid not used in a medical office, and what is the proper procedure to correct a mistake?

_____

_____

14. Why might you run a trial daily report before you run a final daily report?

_____

_____

15. When a patient's check has been returned for insufficient funds, what do you do if the patient asks you to send it back through the bank?

_____

_____

Taking Stock of Supplies and Inventory

16. What are four steps you can take if an item you ordered was not delivered?

a. _____

b. _____

c. _____

d. _____

17. Explain the process of ordering supplies and paying invoices.

_____

_____

18. Where can you find the order number to confirm that an item has been shipped?

_____

_____

19. Match the following key terms to their definitions.

Key Terms	Definitions
a. accounting cycle _____	**1.** a preprinted three-part form that can be placed on a day sheet to record the patient's charges and payments along with other information in an encounter form
b. accounts payable _____	
c. adjustment _____	**2.** a charge or money owed to an account
d. audit _____	**3.** a record of all money owed to the business
e. balance _____	**4.** a document that accompanies a supply order and lists the enclosed items
f. bookkeeping _____	**5.** any report that provides a summary of activities, such as a payroll report or profit-and-loss statement
g. charge slip _____	
h. check register _____	**6.** a daily business record of charges and payments
i. check stub _____	**7.** a statement of income and expenditures; shows whether in a given period a business made or lost money and how much
j. credit _____	
k. day sheet _____	**8.** statement of debt owed; a bill
l. debit _____	**9.** a review of an account
m. encounter form _____	**10.** a consecutive 12-month period for financial record keeping following either a fiscal year or the calendar year
n. Internal Revenue Service (IRS) _____	
o. invoice _____	**11.** a balance in one's favor on an account; a promise to pay a bill at a later date; record of payment received

p. liabilities _____

q. ledger card _____

r. packing slip _____

s. posting _____

t. profit-and-loss statement _____

u. purchase order _____

v. returned check fee _____

w. service charge _____

x. summation report _____

12. listing financial transactions in a ledger

13. a continuous record of business transactions with debits and credits

14. change in a posted account

15. a federal agency that regulates and enforces various taxes

16. amount of money a bank or business charges for a check written on an account with insufficient funds

17. amounts of money the practice owes

18. organized and accurate record-keeping system of financial transactions

19. a document that lists required items to be purchased

20. preprinted patient statement that lists codes for basic office charges and has sections to record charges incurred in an office visit, the patient's current balance, and next appointment

21. that which is left over after the additions and subtractions have been made to an account

22. piece of paper that indicates to whom a check was issued, in what amount, and on what date

23. a document used to record the checks that have been written

24. a charge by a bank for various services

20. True or False? Determine whether the following statements are true or false. If false, explain why.

a. Once you have entered a patient transaction on the day sheet, you give the ledger to the patient as a receipt.

_____

_____

b. As long as your bookkeeping records are accurate and the figures balance, you do not need to save receipts.

_____

_____

c. You should always compare the prices and quality of office supplies when you are placing an order.

_____

_____

d. Audits are performed in the office yearly by the IRS.

_____

_____

APPLICATION

Critical Thinking Practice

1. During a staff meeting, the issue of ordering supplies comes up. The office has been buying small quantities of all supplies, causing some items to quickly run out, while others are stockpiled in disuse. The head physician wants to figure out a way to spend the budget more efficiently, and asks you to be in charge of the next order. What steps can you take to determine which items you will order in the office's next purchase? How can you further improve the office's expenditure?

_____

_____

2. Your office currently is using a checking account at a local bank. However, the physician you work for is thinking about changing over to a money market account, because he has heard the interest is much better in a money market account. He knows about an offer through another bank that will waive the minimum balance of $500 for 3 months. What important information should you look into before you give him your opinion? Discuss the differences between a checking account and a money market account, and include the advantages and disadvantages to switching accounts.

_____

_____

Patient Education

1. Your patient is a young woman who does not understand what happens to the difference between what a physician charges and what her insurance company will pay. In her case, the physician's charge is $100, but insurance only allows for $80. The insurance company will pay for 75% of the cost. How much will the patient pay? Explain to her how this works, and how the charge is determined.

_____

_____

Documentation

1. A patient comes in for an office visit, which costs $60. When he comes to pay his bill, he gives you his insurance information. The insurance company will pay for 60% of the procedure. How would you document this on his ledger and on the day sheet?

_____

_____

Active Learning

1. One of the most important aspects of maintaining an orderly office is making sure that the supplies are fully stocked and up to standards. You have been put in charge of ordering new supplies for the office, and you need to see what options are available to you. Go online and compare prices of two different medical suppliers. Make a note of how many units are sold per order, if there is a minimum purchase limit, how long shipping will take, and what shipping might cost. Select five items that you will order for your office, and fill out a purchasing order for those items.

2. Budgeting for new supplies and keeping track of the office budget is another important part of your job. However, this skill can be used in your own life to assess your spending habits. Whenever you go shopping for food or for other items, or whenever you pay the bills, you must take into account your own budget and need for that item. Over the next few weeks, keep track of your spending habits. List each item you buy, as well as the price of that item. Make a note if it was on sale, or if you paid full price for it. After you have made at least four separate entries, examine your results. Which items on the list were most important? Which items would you forgo if you were on a tighter budget? How would you change your spending habits?

3. Working with a fellow student, go through the process of using a pegboard system. Make sure you fill out the day sheet completely, and go through each step from start to finish. Take turns being the patient and the office assistant. Be sure to practice dealing with credit, debit, and returned check charges, and change methods of payment with each turn.

Professional Journal

REFLECT

(Prompts and Ideas: Do you have a natural talent and/or interest in working with numbers and accounting tasks? If so, what do you like about it? If not, what can you do to increase your comfort level?)

_____

_____

_____

_____

_____

_____

_____

_____

PONDER AND SOLVE

1. A patient whose checks have repeatedly bounced has come in for some minor surgery. The physician at your office does not want to perform the surgery without guarantee of payment. What do you say to both patient and physician in this instance? What steps can you take to prevent future situations similar to this?

_____

_____

_____

_____

_____

_____

_____

2. Another assistant in your office is responsible for maintaining the books and financial records in your office. One of her responsibilities is keeping track of the petty cash. You have noticed that recently she has been borrowing money from the petty cash to buy lunch. She always returns the money within the next few days, but you know that this is not standard office policy. How would you address this issue?

_____

_____

_____

_____

_____

_____

_____

EXPERIENCE

Skills related to this chapter include:

1. Posting Charges on a Daysheet (Procedure 12-1).
2. Posting Payments on a Daysheet (Procedure 12-2).
3. Processing a Credit Balance (Procedure 12-3).
4. Processing Refunds (Procedure 12-4).
5. Posting Adjustments (Procedure 12-5).
6. Posting Collection Agency Payments (Procedure 12-6).
7. Posting NSF Checks (Procedure 12-7).
8. Balancing a Daysheet (Procedure 12-8).
9. Completing a Bank Deposit Slip and Make a Deposit (Procedure 12-9).
10. Reconciling a Bank Statement (Procedure 12-10).
11. Maintaining a Petty Cash Account (Procedure 12-11).
12. Ordering Supplies (Procedure 12-12).
13. Writing a Check (Procedure 12-13).

Record any common mistakes, lessons learned, and/or tips you discovered during your experience of practicing and demonstrating these skills:

_____

_____

_____

_____

_____

_____

_____

_____

Skill Practice

PERFORMANCE OBJECTIVES:

1. Post charges on a daysheet (Procedure 12-1).
2. Post payments on a daysheet (Procedure 12-2).
3. Process a credit balance (Procedure 12-3).
4. Process refunds (Procedure 12-4).
5. Post adjustments (Procedure 12-5).
6. Post collection agency payments (Procedure 12-6).
7. Post NSF checks (Procedure 12-7).
8. Balance a daysheet (Procedure 12-8).
9. Complete a bank deposit slip and make a deposit (Procedure 12-9).
10. Reconcile a bank statement (Procedure 12-10).
11. Maintain a petty cash account (Procedure 12-11).
12. Order supplies (Procedure 12-12).
13. Write a check (Procedure 12-13).

Name _____ Date _____ Time _____

Procedure 12-1:	**POST CHARGES ON A DAYSHEET**

EQUIPMENT/SUPPLIES: Pen, pegboard, calculator, daysheet, encounter forms, ledger cards, previous day's balance, list of patients and charges, fee schedule

STANDARDS: Given the needed equipment and a place to work the student will perform this skill with _____% accuracy in a total of _____ minutes. (*Your instructor will tell you what the percentage and time limits will be before you begin.*)

KEY: 4 = Satisfactory 0 = Unsatisfactory NA = This step is not counted

PROCEDURE STEPS	SELF	PARTNER	INSTRUCTOR
1. Place a new daysheet on the pegboard and record the totals from the previous daysheet.	☐	☐	☐
2. Align the patient's ledger card with the first available line on the daysheet.	☐	☐	☐
3. Place the receipt to align with the appropriate line on the ledger card.	☐	☐	☐
4. Record the number of the receipt in the appropriate column.	☐	☐	☐
5. Write the patient's name on the receipt.	☐	☐	☐
6. Record any existing balance the patient owes in the previous balance column of the daysheet.	☐	☐	☐
7. Record a brief description of the charge in the description line.	☐	☐	☐
8. Record the total charges in the charge column. Press hard so that the marks go through to the ledger card and the daysheet.	☐	☐	☐
9. Add the total charges to the previous balance and record in the current balance column.	☐	☐	☐
10. Return the ledger card to appropriate storage.	☐	☐	☐

CALCULATION

Total Possible Points: _____
Total Points Earned: _____ Multiplied by 100 = _____ Divided by Total Possible Points = _____%

Pass **Fail**
☐ ☐

Comments:

Student's signature _____ Date _____
Partner's signature _____ Date _____
Instructor's signature _____ Date _____

Name _____ Date _____ Time _____

Procedure 12-2:	**POST PAYMENTS ON A DAYSHEET**

EQUIPMENT/SUPPLIES: Pen, pegboard, calculator, daysheet, encounter forms, ledger cards, previous day's balance, list of patients and charges, fee schedule

COMPUTER AND MEDICAL OFFICE SOFTWARE: Follow the software requirements for posting credits to patient accounts.

STANDARDS: Given the needed equipment and a place to work the student will perform this skill with _____% accuracy in a total of _____ minutes. (*Your instructor will tell you what the percentage and time limits will be before you begin.*)

KEY: 4 = Satisfactory   0 = Unsatisfactory   NA = This step is not counted

PROCEDURE STEPS	SELF	PARTNER	INSTRUCTOR
1. Place a new daysheet on the pegboard and record the totals from the previous daysheet.	☐	☐	☐
2. Align the patient's ledger card with the first available line on the daysheet.	☐	☐	☐
3. Place receipt to align with the appropriate line on the ledger card.	☐	☐	☐
4. Record the number of the receipt in the appropriate column.	☐	☐	☐
5. Write the patient's name on the receipt.	☐	☐	☐
6. Record any existing balance the patient owes in the previous balance column of the daysheet.	☐	☐	☐
7. Record the source and type of the payment in the description line.	☐	☐	☐
8. Record appropriate adjustments in adjustment column.	☐	☐	☐
9. Record the total payment in the payment column. Press hard so that marks go through to the ledger card and the daysheet.	☐	☐	☐
10. Subtract the payment and adjustments from the outstanding/previous balance, and record the current balance.	☐	☐	☐
11. Return the ledger card to appropriate storage.	☐	☐	☐

CALCULATION

Total Possible Points: _____
Total Points Earned: _____ Multiplied by 100 = _____ Divided by Total Possible Points = _____%

Pass   **Fail**
☐   ☐ | Comments: |

Student's signature _____ Date _____
Partner's signature _____ Date _____
Instructor's signature _____ Date _____

Name _____ Date _____ Time _____

Procedure 12-3:   PROCESS A CREDIT BALANCE

EQUIPMENT/SUPPLIES: Pen, pegboard, calculator, daysheet, ledger card

STANDARDS: Given the needed equipment and a place to work the student will perform this skill with _____% accuracy in a total of _____ minutes. (*Your instructor will tell you what the percentage and time limits will be before you begin.*)

KEY: 4 = Satisfactory   0 = Unsatisfactory   NA = This step is not counted

PROCEDURE STEPS	SELF	PARTNER	INSTRUCTOR
1. Determine the reason for the credit balance.	☐	☐	☐
2. Place brackets around the balance indicating that it is a negative number.	☐	☐	☐
3. Write a refund check and follow the steps in Procedure 12-7.	☐	☐	☐

CALCULATION

Total Possible Points: _____
Total Points Earned: _____ Multiplied by 100 = _____ Divided by Total Possible Points = _____%

Pass   **Fail**
☐   ☐   Comments:

Student's signature _____ Date _____
Partner's signature _____ Date _____
Instructor's signature _____ Date _____

Name _____ Date _____ Time _____

Procedure 12-4:	**PROCESS REFUNDS**

EQUIPMENT/SUPPLIES: Pen, pegboard, calculator, daysheet, ledger card, checkbook, check register, word processor letterhead, envelope, postage, copy machine, patient's chart, refund file

STANDARDS: Given the needed equipment and a place to work the student will perform this skill with _____% accuracy in a total of _____ minutes. (*Your instructor will tell you what the percentage and time limits will be before you begin.*)

KEY: 4 = Satisfactory   0 = Unsatisfactory   NA = This step is not counted

PROCEDURE STEPS	SELF	PARTNER	INSTRUCTOR
1. Determine who gets the refund, the patient or the insurance company.	☐	☐	☐
2. Pull patient's ledger card and place on current daysheet aligned with the first available line.	☐	☐	☐
3. Post the amount of the refund in the adjustment column in brackets indicating it is a debit, not a credit, adjustment.	☐	☐	☐
4. Write "Refund to Patient" or "Refund to _____" (name of insurance company) in the description column.	☐	☐	☐
5. Write a check for the credit amount made out to the appropriate party.	☐	☐	☐
6. Record the amount and name of payee in the check register.	☐	☐	☐
6. Mail check with letter of explanation to patient or insurance company.	☐	☐	☐
8. Place copy of check and copy of letter in the patient's record or in refund file.	☐	☐	☐
9. Return the patient's ledger card to its storage area.	☐	☐	☐

CALCULATION

Total Possible Points: _____
Total Points Earned: _____ Multiplied by 100 = _____ Divided by Total Possible Points = _____%

Pass   **Fail**
☐   ☐

Comments:

Student's signature _____ Date _____
Partner's signature _____ Date _____
Instructor's signature _____ Date _____

Name _____ Date _____ Time _____

Procedure 12-5:	**POST ADJUSTMENTS**

EQUIPMENT/SUPPLIES: Pen, pegboard, calculator, daysheet, encounter forms, ledger cards, previous day's balance, list of patients and charges, fee schedule

COMPUTER AND MEDICAL OFFICE SOFTWARE: Follow the software requirements for posting credits to patient accounts.

STANDARDS: Given the needed equipment and a place to work the student will perform this skill with _____% accuracy in a total of _____ minutes. (*Your instructor will tell you what the percentage and time limits will be before you begin.*)

KEY: 4 = Satisfactory   0 = Unsatisfactory   NA = This step is not counted

PROCEDURE STEPS	SELF	PARTNER	INSTRUCTOR
1. Pull patient's ledger card and place on current daysheet aligned with the first available line.	☐	☐	☐
2. Post the amount to be written off in the adjustment column in brackets indicating it is a debit, not a credit, adjustment.	☐	☐	☐
3. Subtract the adjustment from the outstanding/previous balance, and record in the current balance column.	☐	☐	☐
4. Return the ledger card to appropriate storage.	☐	☐	☐

CALCULATION

Total Possible Points: _____
Total Points Earned: _____ Multiplied by 100 = _____ Divided by Total Possible Points = _____%

Pass   **Fail**
☐   ☐   Comments:

Student's signature _____ Date _____
Partner's signature _____ Date _____
Instructor's signature _____ Date _____

Name _____   Date _____   Time _____

Procedure 12-6:	**POST COLLECTION AGENCY PAYMENTS**

EQUIPMENT/SUPPLIES: Pen, pegboard, calculator, daysheet, patient's ledger card

STANDARDS: Given the needed equipment and a place to work the student will perform this skill with _____% accuracy in a total of _____ minutes. (*Your instructor will tell you what the percentage and time limits will be before you begin.*)

KEY: 4 = Satisfactory   0 = Unsatisfactory   NA = This step is not counted

PROCEDURE STEPS	SELF	PARTNER	INSTRUCTOR
1. Review check stub or report from the collection agency explaining the amounts to be applied to the accounts.	☐	☐	☐
2. Pull the patients' ledger cards.	☐	☐	☐
3. Post the amount to be applied in the payment column for each patient.	☐	☐	☐
4. Adjust off the amount representing the percentage of the payment charged by the collection agency.	☐	☐	☐

CALCULATION

Total Possible Points: _____
Total Points Earned: _____ Multiplied by 100 = _____ Divided by Total Possible Points = _____%

Pass   **Fail**
☐   ☐   Comments:

Student's signature _____ Date _____
Partner's signature _____ Date _____
Instructor's signature _____ Date _____

Name _____ Date _____ Time _____

POST NSF CHECKS

EQUIPMENT/SUPPLIES: Pen, pegboard, calculator, daysheet, patient's ledger card

STANDARDS: Given the needed equipment and a place to work the student will perform this skill with _____% accuracy in a total of _____ minutes. (*Your instructor will tell you what the percentage and time limits will be before you begin.*)

KEY: 4 = Satisfactory   0 = Unsatisfactory   NA = This step is not counted

PROCEDURE STEPS	SELF	PARTNER	INSTRUCTOR
1. Pull patient's ledger card and place on current daysheet aligned with the first available line.	☐	☐	☐
2. Write the amount of the check in the payment column in brackets indicating it is a debit, not a credit, adjustment.	☐	☐	☐
3. Write "Check Returned For Nonsufficient Funds" in the description column.	☐	☐	☐
4. Post a returned check charge with an appropriate explanation in the charge column.	☐	☐	☐
5. Write "Bank Fee for Returned Check" in the description column.	☐	☐	☐
6. Call the patient to advise him of the returned check and the fee.	☐	☐	☐
7. Construct a proper letter of explanation and a copy of the ledger card and mail to patient.	☐	☐	☐
8. Place a copy of the letter and the check in the patient's file.	☐	☐	☐
9. Make arrangements for the patient to pay cash.	☐	☐	☐
10. Flag the patient's account as a credit risk for future transactions.	☐	☐	☐
11. Return the patient's ledger card to its storage area.	☐	☐	☐

CALCULATION

Total Possible Points: _____
Total Points Earned: _____ Multiplied by 100 = _____ Divided by Total Possible Points = _____%

Pass   **Fail**
☐   ☐   Comments:

Student's signature _____ Date _____
Partner's signature _____ Date _____
Instructor's signature _____ Date _____

Name _____ Date _____ Time _____

| Procedure 12-8: | **BALANCE A DAYSHEET** |

EQUIPMENT/SUPPLIES: Daysheet with totals brought forward, simulated exercise, calculator, pen

STANDARDS: Given the needed equipment and a place to work the student will perform this skill with _____% accuracy in a total of _____ minutes. (*Your instructor will tell you what the percentage and time limits will be before you begin.*)

KEY: 4 = Satisfactory   0 = Unsatisfactory   NA = This step is not counted

PROCEDURE STEPS	SELF	PARTNER	INSTRUCTOR
1. Be sure the totals from the previous daysheet are recorded in the column for previous totals.	☐	☐	☐
2. Total the charge column and place that number in the proper blank.	☐	☐	☐
3. Total the payment column and place that number in the proper blank.	☐	☐	☐
4. Total the adjustment column and place that number in the proper blank.	☐	☐	☐
5. Total the current balance column and place that number in the proper blank.	☐	☐	☐
6. Total the previous balance column and place that number in the proper blank.	☐	☐	☐
7. Add today's totals to the previous totals.	☐	☐	☐
8. Take the grand total of the previous balances, add the grand total of the charges, and subtract the grand total of the payments and adjustments. This number must equal the grand total of the current balance.	☐	☐	☐
9. If the numbers do not match, calculate your totals again, and continue looking for errors until the numbers match. This will prove that the daysheet is balanced, and there are no errors.	☐	☐	☐
10. Record the totals of the columns in the proper space on the next daysheet. You will be prepared for balancing the new daysheet.	☐	☐	☐

CALCULATION

Total Possible Points: _____
Total Points Earned: _____ Multiplied by 100 = _____ Divided by Total Possible Points = _____%

Pass   **Fail**
☐   ☐   Comments:

Student's signature _____ Date _____
Partner's signature _____ Date _____
Instructor's signature _____ Date _____

Name _____ Date _____ Time _____

Procedure 12-9:	COMPLETE A BANK DEPOSIT SLIP AND MAKE A DEPOSIT

EQUIPMENT/SUPPLIES: Calculator with tape, currency, coins, checks for deposit, deposit slip, endorsement stamp, deposit envelope

STANDARDS: Given the needed equipment and a place to work the student will perform this skill with _____% accuracy in a total of _____ minutes. (*Your instructor will tell you what the percentage and time limits will be before you begin.*)

KEY:　　4 = Satisfactory　　　0 = Unsatisfactory　　　NA = This step is not counted

PROCEDURE STEPS	SELF	PARTNER	INSTRUCTOR
1. Arrange bills face up and sort with the largest denomination on top.	☐	☐	☐
2. Record the total in the cash block on the deposit slip.	☐	☐	☐
3. Endorse the back of each check with "For Deposit Only."	☐	☐	☐
4. Record the amount of each check beside an identifying number on the deposit slip.	☐	☐	☐
5. Total and record the amounts of checks in the total of checks line on the deposit slip.	☐	☐	☐
6. Total and record the amount of cash and the amount of checks.	☐	☐	☐
7. Record the total amount of the deposit in the office checkbook register.	☐	☐	☐
8. Make a copy of both sides of the deposit slip for office records.	☐	☐	☐
9. Place the cash, checks, and the completed deposit slip in an envelope or bank bag for transporting to the bank for deposit.	☐	☐	☐

CALCULATION

Total Possible Points: _____
Total Points Earned: _____ Multiplied by 100 = _____ Divided by Total Possible Points = _____%

Pass　　**Fail**
☐　　　☐　　　Comments:

Student's signature _____ Date _____
Partner's signature _____ Date _____
Instructor's signature _____ Date _____

Name _____ Date _____ Time _____

Procedure 12-10:   RECONCILE A BANK STATEMENT

EQUIPMENT/SUPPLIES: Simulated bank statement, reconciliation worksheet, calculator, pen

STANDARDS: Given the needed equipment and a place to work the student will perform this skill with _____% accuracy in a total of _____ minutes. (*Your instructor will tell you what the percentage and time limits will be before you begin.*)

KEY: 4 = Satisfactory   0 = Unsatisfactory   NA = This step is not counted

PROCEDURE STEPS	SELF	PARTNER	INSTRUCTOR
1. Compare the opening balance on the new statement with the closing balance on the previous statement.	☐	☐	☐
2. List the bank balance in the appropriate space on the reconciliation worksheet.	☐	☐	☐
3. Compare the check entries on the statement with the entries in the check register.	☐	☐	☐
4. Determine if there are any outstanding checks.	☐	☐	☐
5. Total outstanding checks.	☐	☐	☐
6. Subtract from the checkbook balance items such as withdrawals, automatic payments, or service charges that appeared on the statement but not in the checkbook.	☐	☐	☐
7. Add to the bank statement balance any deposits not shown on the bank statement.	☐	☐	☐
8. Make sure balance in the checkbook and the bank statement agree.	☐	☐	☐

CALCULATION

Total Possible Points: _____
Total Points Earned: _____ Multiplied by 100 = _____ Divided by Total Possible Points = _____%

Pass **Fail**
☐   ☐

Comments:

Student's signature _____ Date _____
Partner's signature _____ Date _____
Instructor's signature _____ Date _____

Name _____ Date _____ Time _____

Procedure 12-11:	**MAINTAIN A PETTY CASH ACCOUNT**

EQUIPMENT/SUPPLIES: Cash box, play money, checkbook, simulated receipts, and/or vouchers representing expenditures

STANDARDS: Given the needed equipment and a place to work the student will perform this skill with _____% accuracy in a total of _____ minutes. (*Your instructor will tell you what the percentage and time limits will be before you begin.*)

KEY: 4 = Satisfactory   0 = Unsatisfactory   NA = This step is not counted

PROCEDURE STEPS	SELF	PARTNER	INSTRUCTOR
1. Count the money remaining in the box.	☐	☐	☐
2. Total the amounts of all vouchers in the petty cash box and determine the amount of expenditures.	☐	☐	☐
3. Subtract the amount of receipts from the original amount in petty cash, to equal the amount of cash remaining in the box.	☐	☐	☐
4. Balance the cash against the receipts.	☐	☐	☐
5. Write a check only for the amount that was used.	☐	☐	☐
6. Record totals on memo line of check stub.	☐	☐	☐
7. Sort and record all vouchers to the appropriate accounts.	☐	☐	☐
8. File the list of vouchers and attached receipts.	☐	☐	☐
9. Place cash in petty cash fund.	☐	☐	☐

CALCULATION

Total Possible Points: _____
Total Points Earned: _____ Multiplied by 100 = _____ Divided by Total Possible Points = _____%

Pass   **Fail**
☐   ☐   Comments:

Student's signature _____ Date _____
Partner's signature _____ Date _____
Instructor's signature _____ Date _____

Name _____ Date _____ Time _____

Procedure 12-12:	ORDERING SUPPLIES

EQUIPMENT/SUPPLIES: 5×7 index cards, file box with divider cards, computer with Internet (optional), medical supply catalogues

STANDARDS: Given the needed equipment and a place to work the student will perform this skill with _____% accuracy in a total of _____ minutes. (*Your instructor will tell you what the percentage and time limits will be before you begin.*)

KEY: 4 = Satisfactory 0 = Unsatisfactory NA = This step is not counted

PROCEDURE STEPS	SELF	PARTNER	INSTRUCTOR
1. Create a list of supplies to be ordered that is based on inventory done by employees.	☐	☐	☐
2. Create an index card for each supply on the list including the name of the supply in the top left corner, the name and contact information of vendor(s), and product identification number.	☐	☐	☐
3. File the index cards in the file box with divider cards alphabetically or by product type.	☐	☐	☐
4. Record the current price of the item and how the item is supplied.	☐	☐	☐
5. Record the reorder point.	☐	☐	☐

CALCULATION

Total Possible Points: _____
Total Points Earned: _____ Multiplied by 100 = _____ Divided by Total Possible Points = _____%

Pass **Fail**
☐ ☐ Comments:

Student's signature _____ Date _____
Partner's signature _____ Date _____
Instructor's signature _____ Date _____

Name _____ Date _____ Time _____

Procedure 12-13:   **WRITE A CHECK**

EQUIPMENT/SUPPLIES: Simulated page of checks from checkbook, scenario giving amount of check, check register

STANDARDS: Given the needed equipment and a place to work the student will perform this skill with _____% accuracy in a total of _____ minutes. (*Your instructor will tell you what the percentage and time limits will be before you begin.*)

KEY: 4 = Satisfactory   0 = Unsatisfactory   NA = This step is not counted

PROCEDURE STEPS	SELF	PARTNER	INSTRUCTOR

1. Fill out the check register with the following information:
   a. check number
   b. date
   c. payee information
   d. amount
   e. previous balance
   f. new balance
	☐	☐	☐

2. Enter date on check.	☐	☐	☐
3. Enter payee on check.	☐	☐	☐
4. Enter the amount of check using numerals.	☐	☐	☐
5. Write out the amount of the check beginning as far left as possible and make a straight line to fill in space between dollars and cents.	☐	☐	☐
6. Record cents as a fraction with 100 as the denominator.	☐	☐	☐
7. Obtain appropriate signature(s).	☐	☐	☐
8. Proofread for accuracy.	☐	☐	☐

CALCULATION

Total Possible Points: _____
Total Points Earned: _____ Multiplied by 100 = _____ Divided by Total Possible Points = _____%

Pass   **Fail**
☐   ☐   Comments:

Student's signature _____ Date _____
Partner's signature _____ Date _____
Instructor's signature _____ Date _____

Perform an inventory of supplies.

When you are working in a medical office, you may need to keep an inventory of all supplies. The inventory will help you decide when to order new supplies. It will also help you calculate how much money you will need to spend on supplies. Supplies are those items that are consumed quickly and need to be reordered on a regular basis.

If you are currently working in a medical office, use the form below to take an inventory of the supplies in the office. If you do not have access to a medical office, complete an inventory of the supplies in your kitchen or bathroom at home.

**Third Street
Physician's Office, Inc.**
123 Main Street
Baltimore, MD 21201
410-895-6214

Supply Inventory

Item Description	Item Number or Code	Number Needed in Stock	Number Currently in Stock	Date Ordered	Number Ordered	Unit Price	Total	Actual Delivery Date

Work Product 2

Perform an inventory of equipment.

When you are working in a medical office, you may need to keep an inventory of all equipment. The inventory will help you decide when to order new equipment. It will also help you calculate how much money you will need to spend on new equipment. Equipment includes items that can be used over and over and generally last many years.

If you are currently working in a medical office, use the form below to take an inventory of the equipment in the office. If you do not have access to a medical office, complete an inventory of the equipment in your kitchen or bathroom at home.

**Third Street
Physician's Office, Inc.**
123 Main Street
Baltimore, MD 21201
410-895-6214

Equipment Inventory

Item Description	Item Number or Code	Purchase Date	Condition	Comments	Expected New Purchase Date	Cost if Purchased This Year

Work Product 3

Post entries on a day sheet.

You will need to keep track of charges, payments, and adjustments throughout the day. One way to keep track is by using a day sheet. Fill out the day sheet with the transactions described below.

- Marco Rodriguez arrived at 8:00 AM complaining of a sharp pain in his knee. Mr. Rodriguez was examined by the physician and then x-rayed. Mr. Rodriguez has MedCo Insurance, with a co-pay of $35, which he paid using a credit card.
- Dominica Johnson had a general physical examination at 8:30 AM. In addition to normal examination, she received a tetanus booster shot. Ms. Johnson does not have health insurance. She paid in full by check.
- At 9:30 AM, John Ericksen came in with a sore throat. After examination, he was given a throat culture. Mr. Ericksen has HealthEez insurance. He has a co-pay of $20, which he was unable to pay today.

Physician Fees
  Sick visit: $55
  General physical: $125
  X-ray: $225
  Throat culture: $45
  Immunization – tetanus: $30
  Adjustments for MedCo Insurance: 20%
  Adjustments for HeathEez insurance: 25%

Day Sheet

Date	Description	Charges	Payments	Adjustments	Current Balance	Previous Balance	Name

Totals This Page

Totals Previous Page

Month-To-Date Totals

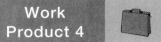

Work Product 4

Process a credit balance.

Mr. Rodriguez has switched to a different insurance company. His co-pay with his old carrier was $35 per visit. His new co-pay is $20 per visit. However, there was a billing oversight and Mr. Rodriguez paid his old co-pay. Process Mr. Rodriguez's credit balance on his ledger card.

DATE	DESCRIPTION	CHARGES	CREDITS PYMNTS.	ADJ.	BALANCE
	BALANCE FORWARD ➡				

FORM MR 10   PLEASE PAY LAST AMOUNT IN BALANCE COLUMN ⬐

Work Product 5

Process a refund.

Mr. Rodriguez has a credit balance of $15 on his account. You need to mail him a refund check. Fill out the patient's ledger card and write a short letter of explanation to Mr. Rodriguez. Print the letter and attach it to this page.

DATE	DESCRIPTION	CHARGES	CREDITS PYMNTS.	ADJ.	BALANCE
	BALANCE FORWARD ➡				

FORM MR 10   PLEASE PAY LAST AMOUNT IN BALANCE COLUMN ⬐

Work Product 6

Post adjustments.

Mr. Rodriguez visits your office for an x-ray of his knee. Your office normally charges $225 for a knee x-ray. However, Mr. Rodriguez's insurance carrier pays your office only $175 for a knee x-ray. Post the proper adjustment on the day sheet.

Day Sheet

Date	Description	Charges	Payments	Adjustments	Current Balance	Previous Balance	Name

Totals This Page				
Totals Previous Page				
Month-To-Date Totals				

Work Product 7

Post NSF checks.

You have just received a check that was returned for nonsufficient funds. The check was written by Martha Montgomery for $750. Post the proper information in the ledger card.

DATE	DESCRIPTION	CHARGES	CREDITS PYMNTS.	ADJ.	BALANCE
	BALANCE FORWARD →				

FORM MR 10   PLEASE PAY LAST AMOUNT IN BALANCE COLUMN ⟶

Work Product 8

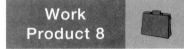

Post collection agency payments.

You receive a check for $787.50 and the following statement from your collection agency.

Jones & Jones Collections
Account: D. Larsen, MD

Debtor	Amount Collected	Fee	Balance
Martha Montgomery	$750.00	$187.50	$562.50
Johan Johansen	$300.00	$75.00	$225.00
		Total	$787.50

Post the payments to the day sheet.

Day Sheet

Date	Description	Charges	Payments	Adjustments	Current Balance	Previous Balance	Name

	Charges	Payments	Adjustments	Current Balance	Previous Balance
Totals This Page					
Totals Previous Page					
Month-To-Date Totals					

Work Product 9

Prepare a bank deposit.

Prepare a bank deposit for the following:

- check for $750 from Martin Montgomery
- check for $35 from Rita Gonzalez
- $125 cash

Newtown Bank, N.A.	DEPOSIT	ITEMS DEPOSITED	DOLLARS	CENTS
		Currency		.
		Coin		.
Name and account number will be verified when presented.		Checks 1		.
Name — Date		2		.
Address		3		.
		4		.
		Sub Total		.
Signature Sign here only if cash is received from deposit		Less Cash		.
Store Number (Commercial Accounts Only) — Account Number (For CAP Accounts, use 10-digit number.)	$	Total Deposit		.

Chapter Self-Assessment Quiz

1. The best place to put petty cash is:

   a. in the same drawer as the other cash and checks.

   b. in a separate, secured drawer.

   c. in an envelope stored in the staff room.

   d. in the physician's office.

   e. in a locked supply cabinet.

2. Which of the following information is found on a patient's ledger card?

   a. Date of birth

   b. Social Security number

   c. Blood type

   d. Insurance information

   e. Marital status

3. The purpose of the posting proofs section is to:

   a. enter the day's totals and balance the day sheet.

   b. update and maintain a patient's financial record.

   c. make note of any credit the patient has on file.

   d. make note of any debit the patient has on file.

   e. allow for any adjustments that need to be made.

4. Which of the following might you purchase using petty cash?

   a. Cotton swabs

   b. Thermometer covers

   c. Office supplies

   d. Non-latex gloves

   e. New x-ray machine

Scenario: A new patient comes in and gives you his insurance card. The patient's insurance allows $60 for a routine checkup. Of this, insurance will pay 75% of his bill. The actual price of the checkup is $60.

5. How much will the patient need to pay?

   a. $0

   b. $15

   c. $30

   d. $45

   e. $60

6. How much of a difference will remain?

   a. $0

   b. $5

   c. $10

   d. $15

   e. $60

End Scenario

7. A check register is used to:

   a. hold checks until they are ready for deposit.

   b. create a checklist of daily office duties.

   c. make a list of payments the office is still owed.

   d. record all checks that go in and out of the office.

   e. remind patients when their payment is due.

8. Ideally, if you are using a pegboard accounting system, what is the best way to organize your ledgers?

   a. File all ledgers alphabetically in a single tray.

   b. Alphabetically file paid ledgers in one tray, and ledgers with outstanding balances in another.

   c. Numerically file paid ledgers in the front of the tray, and ledgers with outstanding balances in the back.

   d. Alphabetically file paid ledgers into patients' folders, and ledgers with outstanding balances in a tray.

   e. File all ledgers into patients' folders.

9. Accounts receivable is:

   a. a record of all monies due to the practice.

   b. the people the practice owes money to.

   c. the transactions transferred from a different office.

   d. any outstanding inventory bills.

   e. a list of patients who have paid in the last month.

10. It is unsafe to use credit card account numbers on purchases made:

   a. over the phone.

   b. by fax.

   c. through e-mail.

   d. from a catalog.

   e. in person.

11. When you have a deposit that includes cash, what is the only way you should get it to the bank?

    a. Deliver it by hand.

    b. Deliver it into a depository.

    c. Send it by mail with enough postage.

    d. Deliver checks by mail and cash by hand.

    e. Do not accept cash as payment.

12. Which of the following is a benefit of paying bills by computer?

    a. You do not need to keep a record of paying your bills.

    b. Entering data into the computer is quick and easy.

    c. Information can be "memorized" and stored.

    d. You can divide columns into groups of expenses (rent, paychecks, etc.).

    e. You can easily correct any errors.

13. Most medical offices generally use:

    a. standard business checks.

    b. certified checks.

    c. traveler's checks.

    d. money orders.

    e. cash deposits.

14. What is a quick way to find order numbers when making a purchase?

    a. Check the packing slip of a previous order.

    b. Find a previous bill for any item numbers.

    c. Check past purchase orders for their order numbers.

    d. Call the supplier for a list of item numbers.

    e. Look at the supplier's website.

15. Summation reports are:

    a. lists of all the clients who entered the office.

    b. reports that track all expenses and income.

    c. computer reports that compile all daily totals.

    d. lists that analyze an office's activities.

    e. reports the IRS sends an office being audited.

16. Why is the adjustment column so important?

    a. It assists you in deciding the discount percentage.

    b. It records all transactions a patient has made in your office.

    c. It allows you to add discounts and credit to change the total.

    d. It keeps track of any changes a patient has in health care.

    e. It keeps track of bounced checks.

17. Which of the following is the correct order in which you use a ledger?

    a. Place ledger over day sheet and charge slip; file ledger in ledger tray; make entry on ledger card; give patient a copy of ledger as a receipt.

    b. Make entry on ledger card; give patient copy of ledger as receipt; place ledger over day sheet and charge slip; file ledger in ledger tray.

    c. Make entry on ledger card; place ledger over day sheet and charge slip; file ledger in ledger tray; give patient copy of ledger as receipt.

    d. Give patient copy of ledger as receipt; place ledger over day sheet and charge slip; make entry on ledger card; file ledger in ledger tray.

    e. Place ledger over day sheet and charge slip; make entry on ledger card; give patient copy of ledger as receipt; file ledger in ledger tray.

18. In a bookkeeping system, things of value relating to the practice are called:

    a. assets.

    b. liabilities.

    c. debits.

    d. credits.

    e. audits.

19. The amount of capital the physician has invested in the practice is referred to as:

    a. assets.

    b. credits.

    c. equity.

    d. liabilities.

    e. invoices.

20. Overpayments under $5 are generally:

    a. sent back to the patient.

    b. placed in petty cash.

    c. left on the account as a credit.

    d. deposited in a special overpayment account.

    e. mailed to the insurance company.

Health Insurance

☐ Read textbook chapter and take notes within the Chapter Notes outline. Answer the Learning Objectives as you reach them in the content, and then check them off.

☐ Work the Content Review questions—both Foundational Knowledge and Application.

☐ Perform the Active Learning exercise(s).

☐ Complete Professional Journal entries.

☐ Complete Skill Practice Activity(s) using Competency Evaluation Forms and Work Products, when appropriate.

☐ Take the Chapter Self-Assessment Quiz.

☐ Insert all appropriate pages into your Portfolio.

1. Spell and define the key terms.

2. Describe group, individual, and government-sponsored (public) health benefits and explain the differences between them.

3. Explain the differences between Medicare and Medicaid.

4. Explain how managed care programs work.

5. Explain the differences between health maintenance organizations, preferred provider organizations, and physician hospital organizations.

6. List the information required on a medical claim form and explain why each piece of information is needed.

7. Name two legal issues affecting claims submissions.

Note: Bold-faced headings are the major headings in the text chapter; headings in regular font are lower-level headings (i.e., the content is subordinate to, or falls "under," the major headings). Make sure you understand the key terms used in the chapter, as well as the concepts presented as Key Points.

TEXT SUBHEADINGS

NOTES

Introduction _____

_____

Key Term: health insurance
Key Point:
• You must keep abreast of changes as you are notified.

☐ **LEARNING OBJECTIVE 1:** Spell and define the key terms.

Health Benefits Plans _____

_____

Group Health Benefits _____

_____

Key Terms: employee; group member; eligibility; insured; claims; third-party administrator; dependent; claims administrator

Key Points:
- Group health benefits are sponsored by an organization, such as an employer, a union, or an association.
- To confirm a patient's eligibility, check the back of the patient's identification (ID) card (Fig. 13-2) for a web address or phone number to contact the **claims administrator** for the health benefits plan.

Health Care Savings Accounts _____

_____

Key Term: Health Care Savings Accounts (HSAs)

Individual Health Benefits _____

_____

Government-Sponsored (Public) Health Benefits _____

_____

Medicare _____

_____

Key Terms: deductible; crossover claim

Key Point:
- Medicare Part B pays for physician fees, both inpatient and outpatient; diagnostic testing; certain immunizations (influenza and pneumonia); and specific screening tests (PSA, mammograms, Pap smears, bone density testing, colorectal screening).

Medicaid _____

_____

Key Point:
- Medicaid is governed by both federal and state statutes and rules, and then implemented on a state and local level.

TRICARE/CHAMPVA

Key Point:
- Once admitted to the CHAMPVA program, patients select their own physician; this allows them the same benefits as private insurance.

☐ **LEARNING OBJECTIVE 2:** Describe group, individual, and government-sponsored (public) health benefits and explain the differences between them.

☐ **LEARNING OBJECTIVE 3:** Explain the differences between Medicare and Medicaid.

Managed Care

Key Terms: managed care; peer review organization; health maintenance organization (HMO); balance billing
Key Points:
- The contract usually establishes what prices will be charged for each service and the conditions under which a service would be covered.
- Failure to comply with the precertification requirements results in a financial penalty for the patient and possibly also for the physician and the hospital.

☐ **LEARNING OBJECTIVE 4:** Explain how managed care programs work.

Health Maintenance Organizations

Key Terms: deductible; coinsurance; fee-for-service; capitation; independent practice association (IPA); fee schedule
Key Points:
- In this respect, the HMO acts as both an insurer and a provider of service.
- Often, a portion of any reimbursement is withheld by the HMO and paid only if the HMO's total medical expense is within budget; this encourages the physician to be cost conscious in caring for patients.

Preferred Provider Organizations _____

Key Term: preferred provider organization (PPO)
Key Points:
- Whereas HMOs promise to provide services and have a financial risk in their relationships with subscribers, a **preferred provider organization (PPO)** is a type of health benefit program whose purpose is simply to contract with providers, then lease this network of contracted providers to health care plans.
- The physician agrees to accept the reimbursement by the claims administrator as payment in full, and agrees not to bill the patient for any difference between the physician's usual charge and the PPO-negotiated charge for the service.

Physician Hospital Organizations _____

Other Managed Care Programs _____

Key Point:
- The physician must complete and submit a referral form or call the claims administrator for approval of the referral. (See Box 13-2.)

☐ **LEARNING OBJECTIVE 5:** Explain the differences between health maintenance organizations, preferred provider organizations, and physician hospital organizations.

Workers' Compensation _____

Key Point:
- Workers' compensation benefits were developed to cover the expenses resulting from a work-related illness or injury.

Filing Claims _____

Key Terms: coordination of benefits; birthday rule; pre-existing condition
Key Point:
- The patient's ID card is a source of information necessary for complete and accurate claims submission.

☐ **LEARNING OBJECTIVE 6:** List the information required on a medical claim form and explain why each piece of information is needed.

Electronic Claims Submission _____

Key Point:
• Remember, HIPAA requires covered entities to submit electronic information safely and confidentially.

☐ **LEARNING OBJECTIVE 7:** Name two legal issues affecting claims submissions.

Explanation of Benefits _____

Key Point:
• You must check the EOB to be sure that all payments made to the physician are for the appropriate procedures and in the correct amounts.

Policies in the Practice _____

Key Terms: usual, customary, and reasonable (UCR); plan maximum
Key Point:
• Managed care plans require physicians to accept assignment, although many physicians do not accept assignment for non–managed care patients.

Content Review

FOUNDATIONAL KNOWLEDGE

The ABCs of Health Care

1. Elaine is 22 years old and is still eligible as a dependent. What could be a possible reason for this?

_____

_____

2. Read each person's health insurance scenario and then match it with the correct type of health insurance plan.

Scenario

a. Sandra was recently let go from her job and is unemployed. _____

b. Thomas has a plan that has less generous coverage and may limit or eliminate benefits for certain illnesses or injuries. _____

c. Mario just started a new job and signed up for health insurance at work. _____

Health Insurance Plan

1. Group

2. Individual

3. Government

3. Jim works for a company that offers an employee benefit whereby money is taken out of his paycheck and put toward medical care expenses. What is the name of this practice?

_____

_____

Name That Health Coverage

4. Determine which of the following are characteristics of Medicare or Medicaid. Place a check mark in the appropriate column below.

	Medicare	Medicaid
a. Provides coverage for low-income or indigent persons of all ages		
b. In a crossover claim, this is the primary coverage		
c. Implemented on a state or local level		
d. Physician reimbursement is considerably less than other insurances		
e. Patients receive a new ID card each month		
f. Program is broken down into part A and part B		
g. Provides coverage for persons suffering from end-stage renal disease		

5. Circle the services and procedures below that Medicaid may provide coverage for.

Dentistry

Inpatient hospital care

Cosmetic surgery

Outpatient treatment and services

Diagnostic services

Family planning

Mammograms

Wellness center fees

Alternative medicine

6. Which is true about how a managed care system is different from a traditional insurance coverage system?

    a. They usually are less costly.

    b. They cost more but have more benefits.

    c. They cost the same but have more benefits.

    d. You can only use network physicians.

7. Why do managed care programs require approved referrals?

_____

_____

8. Circle the type of insurance each characteristic matches.

    a. Tom can visit any provider he chooses, but some will be more expensive than others depending on if they are "in" or "out" of network.

HMO   **PPO**   **PHO**

b. This plan provides covered services rather than pays for them.

HMO	PPO	PHO

c. This plan does not typically use deductibles or co-insurance.

HMO	PPO	PHO

d. Participating providers, in some cases, assume responsibility for the overall medical budget and in others do not.

HMO	PPO	PHO

e. The purpose of this plan is to contract with providers.

HMO	PPO	PHO

f. This plan uses predetermined co-payments.

HMO	PPO	PHO

g. This plan includes a coalition of physicians and a hospital contracting with large employers, insurance carriers, etc.

HMO	PPO	PHO

9. What does a gatekeeper physician do?

_____

_____

10. A new patient comes to your office, and he hands you his insurance card. What information can you find on the back of his identification card?

_____

_____

Filing Claims Trouble-Free

11. What form do you fill out to submit an insurance claim?

_____

_____

12. When is a physician required to file a patient's claim or to extend credit?

_____

_____

13. Claims are sometimes denied, and it is your responsibility to take corrective actions. Read the scenarios below, and briefly state what action you should take.

a. Services are not covered by the plan. _____

b. Coding is deemed inappropriate for services provided. _____

c. Data is incomplete. _____

d. Patient cannot be identified as a covered person. _____

e. The patient is no longer covered by the plan. _____

14. Kairi is a dependent, and both of her parents have health care plans. There are no specific instructions about which plan is primary, so how do you choose which plan to use?

_____

_____

15. Mandy's primary care physician is included under her health plan. However, she has recently been experiencing chest pains, and her physician refers her to a cardiologist. What steps must you take to determine whether or not the cardiologist's visit will be covered?

_____

_____

16. Describe the main characteristics of primary and secondary insurance below.

Primary Insurance	Secondary Insurance
•	•

17. Why is it important to check the Explanation of Benefits?

_____

_____

18. There are some legal issues that affect claims submissions. What is a preexisting condition and how does it affect claim submission?

_____

_____

19. Match the following key terms to their definitions.

Key Terms

a. assignment of benefits _____
b. balance billing _____
c. capitation _____
d. carrier _____
e. claims administrator _____
f. co-insurance _____
g. coordination of benefits _____
h. co-payments _____
i. crossover claim _____
j. deductible _____
k. dependent _____
l. eligibility _____
m. explanation of benefits (EOB) _____
n. fee-for-service _____
o. fee schedule _____
p. group member _____
q. Healthcare Savings Account _____
r. health maintenance organization (HMO) _____

Definitions

1. an individual who manages the third-party reimbursement policies for a medical practice
2. the part of the payment for a service that a patient must pay
3. the determination of an insured's right to receive benefits from a third-party payer based on criteria such as payment of premiums
4. spouse, children, and sometimes other individuals designated by the insured who are covered under a health care plan
5. the transfer of the patient's legal right to collect third-party benefits to the provider of the services
6. a company that assumes the risk of an insurance company
7. a group of physicians and specialists that conducts a review of a disputed case and makes a final recommendation
8. an organization that provides a wide range of services through a contract with a specified group at a predetermined payment
9. billing the patients for the difference between the physician's charges and the Medicare-approved charges
10. an organization of nongroup physicians developed to allow independent physicians to compete with prepaid group practices
11. a coalition of physicians and a hospital contracting with large employers, insurance carriers, and other benefits groups to provide discounted health services
12. an established set of fees charged for specific services and paid by the patient or insurance carrier

s. independent practice association (IPA) _____

t. managed care _____

u. Medicare _____

v. peer review organization _____

w. physician hospital organization _____

x. preferred provider organization (PPO) _____

y. usual, customary, and reasonable (UCR) _____

z. utilization review _____

13. the practice of third-party payers to control costs by requiring physicians to adhere to specific rules as a condition of payment

14. the method of designating the order in multiple-carriers pay benefits to avoid duplication of payment

15. a statement from an insurance carrier that outlines which services are being paid

16. a government-sponsored health benefits package that provides insurance for the elderly

17. a claim that moves over automatically from one coverage to another for payment

18. a policyholder who is covered by a group insurance carrier

19. a type of health benefit program whose purpose is to contract with providers, then lease this network of contracted providers to health care plans

20. an employee benefit that allows individuals to save money through payroll deduction to accounts that can be used only for medical care

21. a list of preestablished fee allowances set for specific services performed by a provider

22. a managed care plan that pays a certain amount to a provider over a specific time for caring for the patients in the plan, regardless of what or how many services are performed

23. the basis of a physician's fee schedule for the normal cost of the same service or procedure in a similar geographic area and under the same or similar circumstances

24. the agreed-upon amount paid to the provider by a policyholder

25. an analysis of individual cases by a committee to make sure services and procedures being billed to a third-party payer are medically necessary

26. the amount paid by the patient before the carrier begins paying

20. True or False? Determine if the statements below are true or false. If false, explain why.

a. Approximately 80% of Americans are enrolled in health benefits plans of one sort or another.

_____

_____

b. A network of providers that make up the PHO may have no financial obligation to subscribers.

_____

_____

c. In managed care, a patient is not usually required to use network providers to receive full coverage.

_____

_____

d. An HMO requires the patient to pay the provider directly, then reimburses the patient.

_____

_____

APPLICATION

Critical Thinking Practice

1. Explain how managed care programs work.

_____

_____

2. A patient may be covered by more than one health plan. For example, the patient may have coverage through an employer while being a dependent on a spouse's plan. Identify the primary plan in this situation and explain coordination of benefits.

_____

_____

Patient Education

1. Mrs. Smith is moving out of the area and is seeing Dr. Jones, her private-practice physician, for the last time. After the move, Mrs. Smith will have to choose a new physician. Mrs. Smith has the choice of an HMO or a PPO. Mrs. Smith asks you to explain the difference. How can you teach Mrs. Smith about the differences between an HMO and a PPO?

_____

_____

Documentation

1. Isabelle Windels brings her 18-month-old daughter to the physician's office for an ear infection. This is the child's fourth ear infection in 3 months and she is no longer responding to antibiotics. The physician refers the patient to an ear, nose, and throat specialist. Mrs. Windels belongs to an HMO. Document this encounter in her chart and then explain any other paperwork you must fill out.

_____

_____

1. Interview three people about their health insurance. Ask them what they like about their service. What do they dislike? Compile a list of their comments to discuss with the class.

2. Visit the website for Medicare at www.medicare.gov. Locate their Frequently Asked Questions page. Read over the questions, and choose five that you believe are the most likely to be asked in a medical office. Design a pamphlet for your office that addresses these five questions.

3. Although a large percentage of Americans have some sort of health insurance, there are still many people who go without. Research online and in medical journals to see what solutions the government and health care companies are devising to reduce the number of uninsured Americans, and to provide better, cheaper, and more widespread health care. Choose one solution, and write a letter to the editor of a local newspaper explaining your position.

Professional
Journal

REFLECT

(Prompts and Ideas: Do you currently have health insurance or have you had health insurance in the past? What did you like about it? What did you not like about it?)

_____

_____

_____

_____

PONDER AND SOLVE

1. A Medicare patient feels overwhelmed by the costs of the services. What information can you offer to help?

_____

_____

_____

_____

_____

_____

2. A patient started coverage under a new insurance company and did not tell the medical office that there was any change at her last appointment. When you submitted the paperwork to the old insurance company, you found out that she no longer had coverage. What can you do?

_____

_____

_____

EXPERIENCE

Skills related to this chapter include:

1. Completing a CMS-1500 Claim Form (Procedure 13-1).

Record any common mistakes, lessons learned, and/or tips you discovered during your experience of practicing and demonstrating these skills:

_____

_____

_____

_____

_____

_____

_____

Skill Practice

PERFORMANCE OBJECTIVES:

1. Complete a CMS-1500 claim form (Procedure 13-1).

Name _____   Date _____   Time _____

EQUIPMENT: Case scenario, completed encounter form, blank CMS-1500 Claim Form, pen

STANDARDS: Given the needed equipment and a place to work the student will perform this skill with _____% accuracy in a total of _____ minutes. (*Your instructor will tell you what the percentage and time limits will be before you begin.*)

KEY: 4 = Satisfactory   0 = Unsatisfactory   NA = This step is not counted

PROCEDURE STEPS	SELF	PARTNER	INSTRUCTOR
1. Using the information provided in the case scenario, complete the demographic information in lines 1 through 11d.	☐	☐	☐
2. Insert "SOF" (signature on file) on lines 12 and 13. Check to be sure there is a current signature on file in the chart and that it is specifically for the third-party payer being filed.	☐	☐	☐
3. If the services being filed are for a hospital stay, insert information in lines 16, 18, and 32.	☐	☐	☐
4. If the services are related to an injury, insert the date of the accident in line 14.	☐	☐	☐
5. Insert dates of service.	☐	☐	☐
6. Using the encounter form, place the CPT code listed for each service and procedure checked off in column D of lines 21-24 on the form.	☐	☐	☐
7. Place the diagnostic codes indicated on the encounter form in lines 21 (1-4). List the reason for the encounter on line 21.1 and any other diagnoses listed on the encounter form that relate to the services or procedures.	☐	☐	☐
8. Reference the codes placed in lines 21 (1-4) to each line listing a different CPT code by placing the corresponding one-digit in line 24, column E.	☐	☐	☐

Calculation

Total Possible Points: _____
Total Points Earned: _____ Multiplied by 100 = _____ Divided by Total Possible Points = _____%

Pass **Fail**
☐   ☐   Comments:

Student's signature _____ Date _____
Partner's signature _____ Date _____
Instructor's signature _____ Date _____

Complete insurance claim forms.

Jackson Dishman is a 58-year-old man who is seen in the office for acute abdominal pain. Complete the CMS-1500 form using the information provided below:

297-01-2222
Jackson W. Dishman   Group #68735
123 Smith Avenue
Winston-Salem NC 27103   Date of Birth: 06-01-49

He is charged for an office visit which carries the CPT code 99213 and costs $150.00. The doctor has the CMA do a Radiologic Examination, abdomen; complete acute abdomen series (the CPT code 774022); and the charge for the x-rays is $250.00. The x-rays are normal. He pays nothing today. The physician sends Mr. Dishman home with a diagnosis of acute abdominal pain which (IDC-9 code is 789.0). He is to return in 2 days unless the pain becomes unbearable.

PLEASE
DO NOT
STAPLE
IN THIS
AREA

HEALTH INSURANCE CLAIM FORM

PICA · · · · · · · PICA

| | PICA |

1. MEDICARE   MEDICAID   CHAMPUS   CHAMPVA   GROUP HEALTH PLAN   FECA BLK LUNG   OTHER   **1a. INSURED'S I.D. NUMBER**   (FOR PROGRAM IN ITEM 1)

(Medicare #)   (Medicaid #)   (Sponsor's SSN)   (VA File #)   (SSN or ID)   (SSN)   (ID)

2. PATIENT'S NAME (Last Name, First Name, Middle Initial)   **3. PATIENT'S BIRTH DATE** MM | DD | YY   SEX   M   F   **4. INSURED'S NAME (Last Name, First Name, Middle Initial)**

5. PATIENT'S ADDRESS (No., Street)   **6. PATIENT RELATIONSHIP TO INSURED**   Self   Spouse   Child   Other   **7. INSURED'S ADDRESS (No., Street)**

CITY   STATE   **8. PATIENT STATUS**   Single   Married   Other   CITY   STATE

ZIP CODE   TELEPHONE (Include Area Code)   (   )   Employed   Full-Time Student   Part-Time Student   ZIP CODE   TELEPHONE (INCLUDE AREA CODE)   (   )

9. OTHER INSURED'S NAME (Last Name, First Name, Middle Initial)   **10. IS PATIENT'S CONDITION RELATED TO:**   **11. INSURED'S POLICY GROUP OR FECA NUMBER**

a. OTHER INSURED'S POLICY OR GROUP NUMBER   **a. EMPLOYMENT? (CURRENT OR PREVIOUS)**   YES   NO   **a. INSURED'S DATE OF BIRTH** MM | DD | YY   SEX   M   F

b. OTHER INSURED'S DATE OF BIRTH MM | DD | YY   SEX   M   F   **b. AUTO ACCIDENT?**   PLACE (State)   YES   NO   **b. EMPLOYER'S NAME OR SCHOOL NAME**

c. EMPLOYER'S NAME OR SCHOOL NAME   **c. OTHER ACCIDENT?**   YES   NO   **c. INSURANCE PLAN NAME OR PROGRAM NAME**

d. INSURANCE PLAN NAME OR PROGRAM NAME   **10d. RESERVED FOR LOCAL USE**   **d. IS THERE ANOTHER HEALTH BENEFIT PLAN?**   YES   NO   *If yes*, return to and complete item 9 a-d.

READ BACK OF FORM BEFORE COMPLETING & SIGNING THIS FORM.
12. PATIENT'S OR AUTHORIZED PERSON'S SIGNATURE I authorize the release of any medical or other information necessary to process this claim. I also request payment of government benefits either to myself or to the party who accepts assignment below.

SIGNED _____ DATE _____

13. INSURED'S OR AUTHORIZED PERSON'S SIGNATURE I authorize payment of medical benefits to the undersigned physician or supplier for services described below.

SIGNED _____

14. DATE OF CURRENT: MM | DD | YY   ILLNESS (First symptom) OR INJURY (Accident) OR PREGNANCY(LMP)   **15. IF PATIENT HAS HAD SAME OR SIMILAR ILLNESS. GIVE FIRST DATE** MM | DD | YY   **16. DATES PATIENT UNABLE TO WORK IN CURRENT OCCUPATION** MM | DD | YY FROM TO MM | DD | YY

17. NAME OF REFERRING PHYSICIAN OR OTHER SOURCE   **17a. I.D. NUMBER OF REFERRING PHYSICIAN**   **18. HOSPITALIZATION DATES RELATED TO CURRENT SERVICES** MM | DD | YY FROM TO MM | DD | YY

19. RESERVED FOR LOCAL USE   **20. OUTSIDE LAB?**   YES   NO $ CHARGES

21. DIAGNOSIS OR NATURE OF ILLNESS OR INJURY. (RELATE ITEMS 1,2,3 OR 4 TO ITEM 24E BY LINE)

1. ___.___   3. ___.___
2. ___.___   4. ___.___

22. MEDICAID RESUBMISSION CODE   ORIGINAL REF. NO.

23. PRIOR AUTHORIZATION NUMBER

24. A DATE(S) OF SERVICE						B Place of Service	C Type of Service	D PROCEDURES, SERVICES, OR SUPPLIES (Explain Unusual Circumstances) CPT/HCPCS	MODIFIER	E DIAGNOSIS CODE	F $ CHARGES	G DAYS OR UNITS	H EPSDT Family Plan	I EMG	J COB	K RESERVED FOR LOCAL USE
From MM	DD	YY	To MM	DD	YY											
1																
2																
3																
4																
5																
6																

25. FEDERAL TAX I.D. NUMBER   SSN EIN   **26. PATIENT'S ACCOUNT NO.**   **27. ACCEPT ASSIGNMENT?** (For govt. claims, see back)   YES   NO   **28. TOTAL CHARGE** $ **29. AMOUNT PAID** $ **30. BALANCE DUE** $

31. SIGNATURE OF PHYSICIAN OR SUPPLIER INCLUDING DEGREES OR CREDENTIALS (I certify that the statements on the reverse apply to this bill and are made a part thereof.)

SIGNED _____ DATE _____

32. NAME AND ADDRESS OF FACILITY WHERE SERVICES WERE RENDERED (If other than home or office)

33. PHYSICIAN'S, SUPPLIER'S BILLING NAME, ADDRESS, ZIP CODE & PHONE #

PIN#   GRP#

(APPROVED BY AMA COUNCIL ON MEDICAL SERVICE 8/88)   ***PLEASE PRINT OR TYPE***   APPROVED OMB-0938-0008 FORM CMS-1500 (12-90), FORM RRB-1500,
APPROVED OMB-1215-0055 FORM OWCP-1500, APPROVED OMB-0720-0001 (CHAMPUS)

Chapter Self-Assessment Quiz

1. Which of the following is frequently not covered in group health benefits packages?

   a. Birth control

   b. Childhood immunizations

   c. Routine diagnostic care

   d. Treatment for substance abuse

   e. Regular physical examinations

2. Any payment for medical services that is not paid by the patient or physician is said to be paid by a(n)

   a. second-party payer.

   b. first-party payer.

   c. insurance party payer.

   d. third-party payer.

   e. health care party payer.

3. The criteria a patient must meet for a group benefit plan to provide coverage are called:

   a. eligibility requirements.

   b. patient requirements.

   c. benefit plan requirements.

   d. physical requirements.

   e. insurance requirements.

4. Eligibility for a dependent requires that he is:

   a. unmarried.

   b. employed.

   c. living with the employee.

   d. younger than 18.

   e. an excellent student.

5. Whom should you contact about the eligibility of a patient for the health benefits plan?

   a. Claims administrator

   b. Claims investigator

   c. Insurance salesperson

   d. Insurance reviewer

   e. Claims insurer

Scenario: Aziz pays premiums directly to the insurance company, and the insurance company reimburses him for eligible medical expenses.

6. What type of insurance does Aziz have?

   a. Individual health benefits

   b. Public health benefits

   c. Managed care

   d. Preferred Provider Organization

   e. Health Maintenance Organization

7. Which of the following is likely true of Aziz's insurance?

   a. The insurance is provided by his employer.

   b. Money can be put aside into accounts used for medical expenses.

   c. There are certain restrictions for some illnesses and injuries.

   d. All providers are under contract with the insurer.

   e. There are two levels of benefits in the health plan.

End Scenario

8. An optional health benefits program offered to persons signing up for Social Security benefits is:

   a. Medicare Part A.

   b. Medicare Part B.

   c. Medicaid.

   d. TRICARE/CHAMPVA.

   e. HMO.

9. After the deductible has been met, what percentage of the approved charges does Medicare reimburse to the physician?

   a. 0

   b. 20

   c. 75

   d. 80

   e. 100

10. Which benefits program bases eligibility on a patient's eligibility for other state programs, such as welfare assistance?

    a. Workers' Compensation

    b. Medicare

    c. Medicaid

    d. TRICARE/CHAMPVA

    e. Social Security

11. Which of the following is a medical expense that Medicaid provides 100% coverage for?

    a. Family planning

    b. Colorectal screening

    c. Bone density testing

    d. Pap smears

    e. Mammograms

12. In a traditional insurance plan:

    a. the covered patient may seek care from any provider.

    b. the insurer has no relationship with the provider.

    c. a patient can be admitted to a hospital only if that admission has been certified by the insurer.

    d. there is no third-party payer.

    e. the patient cannot be billed for the deductible.

13. Which of the following is a plan typically developed by hospitals and physicians to attract patients?

    a. HMO

    b. PPO

    c. HSA

    d. TPA

    e. UCR

14. Which of the following is true about both HMOs and PPOs?

    a. Both allow patients to see any physician of their choice and receive benefits.

    b. Both contract directly with participating providers, hospitals, and physicians.

    c. Both offer benefits at two levels, commonly referred to as in-network and out-network.

    d. Both are not risk bearing and do not have any financial involvement in the health plan.

    e. Both incorporate independent practice associations.

15. Which of the following is a government-sponsored health benefits plan?

    a. TRICARE/CHAMPVA

    b. HMO

    c. HSA

    d. PPO

    e. PHO

16. If a provider is unethical, you should:

    a. correct the issue yourself.

    b. immediately stop working for the provider.

    c. comply with all requests to misrepresent medical records but report the physician.

    d. do whatever the physician asks to avoid confrontation.

    e. explain that you are legally bound to truthful billing, and report the physician.

17. A patient's ID card:

    a. contains the information needed to file a claim on it.

    b. should be updated at least once every 2 years.

    c. must be cleared before an emergency can be treated.

    d. is updated and sent to Medicaid patients bi-monthly.

    e. is not useful for determining if the patient is a dependent.

18. What information is needed to fill out a CMS-1500 claim form?

    a. A copy of the patient's chart

    b. Location where patient will be recovering

    c. Diagnostic codes from encounter form

    d. Copies of hospitalization paperwork

    e. Physician's record and degree

19. Claims that are submitted electronically:

    a. violate HIPAA standards.

    b. contain fewer errors than those that are mailed.

    c. require approval from the patient.

    d. increase costs for Medicare patients.

    e. reduce the reimbursement cycle.

20. Normally, coverage has an amount below which services are not reimbursable. This is referred to as the:

    a. deductible.

    b. coinsurance.

    c. balance billing.

    d. benefits.

    e. claim.

Diagnostic Coding

☐ Read textbook chapter and take notes within the Chapter Notes outline. Answer the Learning Objectives as you reach them in the content, and then check them off.

☐ Work the Content Review questions—both Foundational Knowledge and Application.

☐ Perform the Active Learning exercise(s).

☐ Complete Professional Journal entries.

☐ Complete Skill Practice Activity(s) using Competency Evaluation Forms and Work Products, when appropriate.

☐ Take the Chapter Self-Assessment Quiz.

☐ Insert all appropriate pages into your Portfolio.

1. Spell and define the key terms.
2. Describe the relationship between coding and reimbursement.
3. Name and describe the coding system used to describe diseases, injuries, and other reasons for encounters with a medical provider.

4. Explain the format of the ICD-9-CM.
5. Give four examples of ways E-codes are used.
6. List the steps in locating a proper code.
7. Explain common diagnostic coding guidelines.

Note: Bold-faced headings are the major headings in the text chapter; headings in regular font are lower-level headings (i.e., the content is subordinate to, or falls "under," the major headings). Make sure you understand the key terms used in the chapter, as well as the concepts presented as Key Points.

TEXT SUBHEADINGS

NOTES

Introduction _____

_____

Key Terms: *International Classification of Diseases, Ninth Revision, Clinical Modification*; medical necessity; advance beneficiary notice

Key Point:
• Coding is a way to standardize medical information for purposes such as collecting health care statistics, performing a medical care review, and indexing medical records. It is also used for health insurance claims processing (see Chapter 13). Because coding is the basis for reimbursement, it is imperative that you code patient visits accurately and precisely.

☐ **LEARNING OBJECTIVE 1:** Spell and define the key terms.

☐ **LEARNING OBJECTIVE 2:** Describe the relationship between coding and reimbursement.

Diagnostic Coding _____

Key Term: *International Classification of Diseases, Ninth Revision, Clinical Modification*
Key Point:
• ***International Classification of Diseases, Ninth Revision, Clinical Modification*** (ICD-9-CM) is a statistical classification system based on the *International Classification of Diseases, Ninth Revision* (ICD-9), developed by the World Health Organization (WHO).

Inpatient Versus Outpatient Coding _____

Key Terms: service; outpatient; inpatient

☐ **LEARNING OBJECTIVE 3:** Name and describe the coding system used to describe diseases, injuries, and other reasons for encounters with a medical provider.

ICD-9-CM: The Code Book _____

Key Point:
• You must update codes on superbills (preprinted bills listing a variety of procedures) or any other forms you use.

Tabular List of Diseases _____

Key Term: etiology

☐ **LEARNING OBJECTIVE 4:** Explain the format of the ICD-9-CM.

Supplementary Classifications _____

Key Terms: V-codes; E-codes

☐ **LEARNING OBJECTIVE 5:** Give four examples of ways E-codes are used.

Volume 2: Alphabetic Index to Diseases _____

Key Terms: main terms; cross-reference
Key Points:
- Always check all indentations in the index under the condition to ensure that you have the one most appropriate to the diagnosis you intend to code.
- Never code directly from the alphabetic index.

Volume 3: Inpatient Coding _____

Locating the Appropriate Code _____

Using the ICD-9-CM Conventions _____

Key Term: conventions
Key Point:
- They direct and guide the coder to the appropriate code and should be strictly adhered to.

Main Term _____

Key Term: eponym
Key Point:
- Find the condition, not the location.

Fourth and Fifth Digits _____

Key Term: specificity

☐ **LEARNING OBJECTIVE 6:** List the steps in locating a proper code.

Primary Codes _____

Key Term: primary diagnosis

When More Than One Code Is Used _____

> **Key Point:**
> • When patients have more than one diagnosis, it is necessary to convey an accurate picture of the patient's total condition.

Late Effects _____

> **Key Term:** late effects

Coding Suspected Conditions _____

> **Key Point:**
> • In the inpatient setting, coders list conditions after the patient's testing is complete.

Documentation Requirements _____

> **Key Term:** audit

☐ **LEARNING OBJECTIVE 7:** Explain common diagnostic coding guidelines.

The Future of Diagnostic Coding: *International Classification of Diseases, Tenth Revision* _____

Content Review

FOUNDATIONAL KNOWLEDGE

Who's Who?

1. Many different organizations are involved in developing and maintaining the ICD-9-CM. Match the organization with its role in maintaining the ICD-9-CM. Note: Some organizations may have more than one correct answer.

Organizations

a. Center for Medicare & Medicaid Services _____

b. National Center for Health Statistics _____

c. World Health Organization _____

Tasks

1. Approves changes made to the ICD-9-CM before publication

2. Maintains Volume 1

3. Maintains Volume 2

4. Maintains Volume 3

A Matter of Medical Necessity

2. A reasonable and capable physician believes that a patient needs a chest x-ray to rule out pneumonia. Does the procedure meet the grounds for medical necessity? Why? Why not?

_____

_____

3. A patient comes in complaining of chest pain. When you enter the codes for this patient encounter, you code that the patient has "acute myocardial infarction." Why would it be better to code this encounter "chest pain rule out myocardial infarction"?

_____

_____

4. Review the list of circumstances below and place a check mark to indicate whether a patient would be forced, given the circumstance, to sign an ABN. All of the patients below are covered by Medicare.

Circumstance	ABN	No ABN
a. The patient wishes to receive an immunization not covered by Medicare.		
b. The patient is undergoing a regularly scheduled checkup.		
c. The patient demands to be tested for an illness that the physician considers an impossibility.		
d. The patient has a badly sprained ankle and wishes to be treated.		
e. The patient is undergoing x-ray imaging per order of a physician.		

Coding Cues

5. When it comes to coding, it makes a difference if the patient is seen in an inpatient or outpatient facility. Review the list of places below. Place an **I** next to those places that are considered "Inpatient" and an **O** next to those places that are considered "Outpatient."

    a. _____ Hospital clinic

    b. _____ Health care provider's office

    c. _____ Hospital for less than 24 hours

    d. _____ Hospital for 24 hours or more

    e. _____ Hospital emergency room

6. Why is the third volume of the ICD-9-CM not used at a hospital's emergency department?

_____

_____

7. What is the difference in information used to code in the outpatient and inpatient settings?

_____

_____

8. You are reading a patient's chart and notice that it is marked with an E-code. However, the patient has experienced no physical injuries. Why might an E-code be used in this situation?

_____

_____

9. You ask a veteran medical assistant for advice on coding, especially how to go about finding a diagnosis with more than one word. Her response is, "Find the condition, not the location." What does she mean by this?

_____

_____

Cracking the CMS-1500

10. What is listed first on the CMS-1500? What does it represent?

_____

_____

11. Which of these is an unethical act? Explain why.

    a. Coding multiple conditions on the same CMS-1500

    b. Coding an unsupported diagnosis in order to make a service appear medically necessary

    c. Using a V-code to better explain the reason for a patient's visit

    d. Using ICD-9-CM search software to more easily access the codes contained in the ICD-9-CM

_____

_____

Mind Your Es and Vs

12. If a construction worker falls from a ladder and suffers an ankle fracture, what supplemental code is used?

_____

_____

13. When would you use the V-code for laboratory examination?

_____

_____

Troubleshooting Common Coding Problems

14. What should you do after finding a seemingly appropriate code in the alphabetic listing of volume 1 of the ICD-9-CM?

_____

_____

15. If you do not know the medical terminology for a diagnosis for a common problem, what would be a good first plan of action?

_____

_____

16. Determine the main term for the following multiple-word diagnoses.

Diagnosis	Main Term
a. chronic fatigue syndrome	
b. severe acute respiratory syndrome	
c. hemmorhagic encephalitis	
d. acute fulminating multiple sclerosis	
e. fractured left tibia	
f. breast cyst	

17. What is the purpose of the fourth and fifth digits often appended to categories?

_____

_____

18. Circle the main terms where you will find obstetric conditions.

delivery	*fetus*	*pregnancy*	*labor*
baby	*obstetrics*	*puerperal*	*gestational*

19. Match the following key terms to their definitions.

Key Terms

a. advance beneficiary notice _____

b. audits _____

c. conventions _____

d. cross-reference _____

e. E-codes _____

f. eponym _____

g. etiology _____

h. inpatient _____

i. *International Classification of Diseases, Ninth Revision, Clinical Modification* _____

j. late effects _____

k. main terms _____

l. medical necessity _____

m. outpatient _____

n. primary diagnosis _____

o. service _____

p. specificity _____

q. V-codes _____

Definitions

1. codes indicating the external causes of injuries and poisoning

2. conditions that result from another condition

3. general notes, symbols, typeface, format, and punctuation that direct and guide a coder to the most accurate ICD-9 code

4. the condition or chief complaint that brings a person to a medical facility for treatment

5. a procedure or service that would have been performed by any reasonable physician under the same or similar circumstances

6. a document that informs covered patients that Medicare may not cover a certain service and the patient will be responsible for the bill

7. a word based on or derived from a person's name

8. codes assigned to patients who receive service but have no illness, injury, or disorder

9. the billable tasks performed by a physician

10. refers to a medical setting in which patients are admitted for diagnostic, radiographic, or treatment purposes

11. an investigation performed by government, managed health care companies, and health care organizations to determine compliance and to detect fraud

12. a system for transforming verbal descriptions of disease, injuries, conditions, and procedures to numeric codes

13. refers to the cause of disease

14. refers to a medical setting in which patients receive care but are not admitted

15. verification against another source

16. relating to a definite result

17. words in a multiple-word diagnosis that a coder should locate in the alphabetic listing

20. Code the following diagnoses:

1. sick sinus syndrome
2. congestive heart failure with malignant hypertension
3. bilateral stenosis of carotid artery
4. aspiration pneumonia
5. gynecomastia

6. nephrosis due to diabetes
7. hematemesis
8. portal thrombophlebitis
9. acute viral conjunctivitis with hemorrhage
10. *E. coli* intestinal infection

21. True or False? Determine whether the following statements are true or false. If false, explain why.

a. Only the first three numbers of a code are necessary. _____

b. One should never code directly from the alphabetic index. _____

c. The main term describes a condition, not an aspect of anatomy. _____

d. In the outpatient setting, coders list conditions after the patient's testing is complete. _____

APPLICATION

Critical Thinking Practice

1. A patient entered the office complaining of chest pains. After examination, the physician decided to send him to a specialist in order to rule out the possibility of angina pectoris. Which code should be placed on the CMA-1500 first as the primary diagnosis or reason for the visit? Why?

_____

_____

2. What might result from improper medical coding?

_____

_____

Patient Education

1. After looking at the CMS-1500 for her visit, a patient asks why there is an alphanumeric string instead of a diagnosis. Explain as you would to a patient what the code represents.

_____

_____

Documentation
1. The physician has informed you that the diagnosis for your patient is "atrial septal defect as current complication following acute myocardial infarction." How would you code this diagnosis?

_____

_____

Active Learning

1. Find the ICD-9-CM codes for the following diseases:
- Acute gastric ulcer with hemorrhage and perforation without obstruction

- Meningococcal pericarditis

- Impetigo

- Benign essential hypertension

2. Determine the diseases associated with the following ICD-9-CM codes:
- 431
- 558.3
- 758.0
- 299.11

3. Determine the E-codes for the following:
- Inhalation and ingestion of other object causing obstruction of respiratory tract or suffocation
- Insulins and antidiabetic agents causing adverse effects in therapeutic use
- Burning caused by conflagration in private dwelling

Professional Journal

REFLECT

(Prompts and Ideas: Digital editions of the ICD-9-CM have changed the way medical coders practice their craft. Reflect on the nature of this change and how digital tools can make your job as a medical coder easier.)

_____

_____

_____

_____

_____

_____

PONDER AND SOLVE

1. In the ICD-9-CM, burns are listed in the range 940–949, a subset of 800–999 — Injury and Poisoning. However, if you look for the code for sunburn, you will not find it there. Find the code for sunburn and explain why it does not belong in the range 940–949. You do not need to know exactly why, but consider the diagnoses that appear in 940–949 and how sunburn compares with them.

_____

_____

_____

_____

_____

2. A patient is concerned that her insurance provider will not cover her visit because the diagnosis is for a very minor ailment. She requests that you mark her CMA-1500 with a more severe disorder that demands similar treatment. How would you deal with this situation? What would you tell the patient? How might you involve the physician?

_____

_____

_____

_____

_____

_____

EXPERIENCE

Skills related to this chapter include:

1. Locating a Diagnostic Code (Procedure 14-1).

Record any common mistakes, lessons learned, and/or tips you discovered during your experience of practicing and demonstrating these skills:

_____

_____

_____

_____

_____

_____

_____

_____

Skill Practice

PERFORMANCE OBJECTIVE:

1. Locate an appropriate ICD-9-CM code (Procedure 14-1).

Name _____ Date _____ Time _____

LOCATING A DIAGNOSTIC CODE

EQUIPMENT: Diagnosis, ICD-9-CM, Volumes 1 and 2 code book, medical dictionary

STANDARDS: Given the needed equipment and a place to work the student will perform this skill with _____% accuracy in a total of _____ minutes. (*Your instructor will tell you what the percentage and time limits will be before you begin.*)

KEY: 4 = Satisfactory   0 = Unsatisfactory   NA = This step is not counted

PROCEDURE STEPS	SELF	PARTNER	INSTRUCTOR
1. Using the diagnosis "chronic rheumatoid arthritis," choose the main term within the diagnostic statement. If necessary, look up the word(s) in your dictionary.	☐	☐	☐
2. Locate the main term in Volume 2.	☐	☐	☐
3. Refer to all notes and conventions under the main term.	☐	☐	☐
4. Find the appropriate indented subordinate term.	☐	☐	☐
5. Follow any relevant instructions, such as "see also."	☐	☐	☐
6. Confirm the selected code by cross-referencing to Volume 1. Make sure you have added any fourth or fifth digits necessary.	☐	☐	☐
7. Assign the code.	☐	☐	☐

CALCULATION

Total Possible Points: _____
Total Points Earned: _____ Multiplied by 100 = _____ Divided by Total Possible Points = _____%

Pass   **Fail**
☐   ☐   Comments:

Student's signature _____ Date _____
Partner's signature _____ Date _____
Instructor's signature _____ Date _____

Work Product

Perform diagnostic coding.

Kayla Tawes, age 38, has just completed a general physical. Her examination consisted of the following:

- an EKG to monitor a previously diagnosed arrhythmia
- urine collection to test for diabetes
- blood sampling to test cholesterol levels

Because Ms. Tawes is a breast cancer survivor, in addition to the routine examination, she was given a mammogram. Her physician prescribed a tetanus booster as well, because she has been renovating an old stable and has suffered several small skin punctures over the past few weeks.

Complete the CMS-1500 form with the proper diagnostic coding for the patient's visit. Create fictional personal patient information where necessary to fill in all essential details when completing the CMS-1500.

PLEASE
DO NOT
STAPLE
IN THIS
AREA

← CARRIER →

| | PICA | | | | | | **HEALTH INSURANCE CLAIM FORM** | PICA | | |

1. MEDICARE	MEDICAID	CHAMPUS	CHAMPVA	GROUP HEALTH PLAN	FECA BLK LUNG	OTHER	1a. INSURED'S I.D. NUMBER	(FOR PROGRAM IN ITEM 1)
(Medicare #)	(Medicaid #)	(Sponsor's SSN)	(VA File #)	(SSN or ID)	(SSN)	(ID)		

2. PATIENT'S NAME (Last Name, First Name, Middle Initial)

3. PATIENT'S BIRTH DATE MM DD YY   SEX M □ F □

4. INSURED'S NAME (Last Name, First Name, Middle Initial)

5. PATIENT'S ADDRESS (No., Street)

6. PATIENT RELATIONSHIP TO INSURED Self □ Spouse □ Child □ Other □

7. INSURED'S ADDRESS (No., Street)

CITY   STATE

8. PATIENT STATUS Single □ Married □ Other □

Employed □ Full-Time Student □ Part-Time Student □

CITY   STATE

ZIP CODE   TELEPHONE (Include Area Code) ( )

ZIP CODE   TELEPHONE (INCLUDE AREA CODE) ( )

9. OTHER INSURED'S NAME (Last Name, First Name, Middle Initial)

10. IS PATIENT'S CONDITION RELATED TO:

11. INSURED'S POLICY GROUP OR FECA NUMBER

a. OTHER INSURED'S POLICY OR GROUP NUMBER

a. EMPLOYMENT? (CURRENT OR PREVIOUS) □ YES □ NO

a. INSURED'S DATE OF BIRTH MM DD YY   SEX M □ F □

b. OTHER INSURED'S DATE OF BIRTH MM DD YY   SEX M □ F □

b. AUTO ACCIDENT? PLACE (State) □ YES □ NO

b. EMPLOYER'S NAME OR SCHOOL NAME

c. EMPLOYER'S NAME OR SCHOOL NAME

c. OTHER ACCIDENT? □ YES □ NO

c. INSURANCE PLAN NAME OR PROGRAM NAME

d. INSURANCE PLAN NAME OR PROGRAM NAME

10d. RESERVED FOR LOCAL USE

d. IS THERE ANOTHER HEALTH BENEFIT PLAN? □ YES □ NO *If yes*, return to and complete item 9 a-d.

READ BACK OF FORM BEFORE COMPLETING & SIGNING THIS FORM.
12. PATIENT'S OR AUTHORIZED PERSON'S SIGNATURE I authorize the release of any medical or other information necessary to process this claim. I also request payment of government benefits either to myself or to the party who accepts assignment below.

SIGNED _____ DATE _____

13. INSURED'S OR AUTHORIZED PERSON'S SIGNATURE I authorize payment of medical benefits to the undersigned physician or supplier for services described below.

SIGNED _____

14. DATE OF CURRENT: MM DD YY ► ILLNESS (First symptom) OR INJURY (Accident) OR PREGNANCY(LMP)

15. IF PATIENT HAS HAD SAME OR SIMILAR ILLNESS. GIVE FIRST DATE MM DD YY

16. DATES PATIENT UNABLE TO WORK IN CURRENT OCCUPATION FROM MM DD YY TO MM DD YY

17. NAME OF REFERRING PHYSICIAN OR OTHER SOURCE

17a. I.D. NUMBER OF REFERRING PHYSICIAN

18. HOSPITALIZATION DATES RELATED TO CURRENT SERVICES FROM MM DD YY TO MM DD YY

19. RESERVED FOR LOCAL USE

20. OUTSIDE LAB? □ YES □ NO $ CHARGES

21. DIAGNOSIS OR NATURE OF ILLNESS OR INJURY. (RELATE ITEMS 1,2,3 OR 4 TO ITEM 24E BY LINE)

1. |___.__| 3. |___.__|

2. |___.__| 4. |___.__|

22. MEDICAID RESUBMISSION CODE   ORIGINAL REF. NO.

23. PRIOR AUTHORIZATION NUMBER

24. A DATE(S) OF SERVICE						B Place of Service	C Type of Service	D PROCEDURES, SERVICES, OR SUPPLIES (Explain Unusual Circumstances) CPT/HCPCS	MODIFIER	E DIAGNOSIS CODE	F $ CHARGES	G DAYS OR UNITS	H EPSDT Family Plan	I EMG	J COB	K RESERVED FOR LOCAL USE
From MM	DD	YY	To MM	DD	YY											
1																
2																
3																
4																
5																
6																

25. FEDERAL TAX I.D. NUMBER SSN □ EIN □

26. PATIENT'S ACCOUNT NO.

27. ACCEPT ASSIGNMENT? (For govt. claims, see back) □ YES □ NO

28. TOTAL CHARGE $

29. AMOUNT PAID $

30. BALANCE DUE $

31. SIGNATURE OF PHYSICIAN OR SUPPLIER INCLUDING DEGREES OR CREDENTIALS (I certify that the statements on the reverse apply to this bill and are made a part thereof.)

SIGNED _____ DATE _____

32. NAME AND ADDRESS OF FACILITY WHERE SERVICES WERE RENDERED (If other than home or office)

33. PHYSICIAN'S, SUPPLIER'S BILLING NAME, ADDRESS, ZIP CODE & PHONE #

PIN#   GRP#

(APPROVED BY AMA COUNCIL ON MEDICAL SERVICE 8/88) ***PLEASE PRINT OR TYPE*** APPROVED OMB-0938-0008 FORM CMS-1500 (12-90), FORM RRB-1500,
APPROVED OMB-1215-0055 FORM OWCP-1500, APPROVED OMB-0720-0001 (CHAMPUS)

PATIENT AND INSURED INFORMATION →

PHYSICIAN OR SUPPLIER INFORMATION →

1. Which most accurately states the purpose of coding?

   a. Coding assists patients in accessing insurance databases.

   b. Coding determines the reimbursement of medical fees.

   c. Coding is used to track a physician's payments.

   d. Coding is used to index patients' claims forms.

   e. Coding identifies patients in a database.

2. A patient signs an advance beneficiary notice (ABN) to:

   a. consent to medically necessary procedures.

   b. assign payment to Medicare.

   c. accept responsibility for payment.

   d. assign responsibility for payment to a beneficiary.

   e. consent to a medically unnecessary procedure.

3. The content of the ICD-9-CM is a(n):

   a. classification of diseases and list of procedures.

   b. statistical grouping of trends in diseases.

   c. clinical modification of codes used by hospitals.

   d. ninth volume in an index of diseases.

   e. international document for monitoring coding.

4. Which is true of Volume 3 of the ICD-9-CM?

   a. It is organized by location on the patient's body.

   b. It is used to code mostly outpatient procedures.

   c. It is an alphabetical listing of diseases.

   d. It is used by hospitals to report procedures and services.

   e. It is an index of Volumes 1 and 2.

5. Physician's services are reported:

   a. on the UB-92.

   b. on the CMS-1500.

   c. on the uniform bill.

   d. on the advance beneficiary notice.

   e. on bills from health institutions.

6. Which of these would be considered inpatient coding?

   a. Hospital same-day surgery

   b. Hour-long testing in a hospital CAT scan

   c. Treatment in the emergency room

   d. Observation status in a hospital

   e. Meals and testing during a hospital stay

7. In Volume 1 of the ICD-9-CM, chapters are grouped:

   a. by alphabetic ordering of diseases and injuries.

   b. alphabetically by eponym.

   c. by location in the body.

   d. by etiology and anatomic system.

   e. by surgical specialty.

8. The fourth and fifth digits in a code indicate the:

   a. anatomical location where a procedure was performed.

   b. number of times a test was executed.

   c. higher definitions of a code.

   d. code for the patient's general disease.

   e. traumatic origins of a disease (i.e., injury, deliberate violence).

9. A V-code might indicate a(n):

   a. immunization.

   b. poisoning.

   c. accident.

   d. diagnosis.

   e. treatment.

10. V-codes are used:

    a. for outpatient coding.

    b. when reimbursement is not needed.

    c. when a patient is not sick.

    d. to indicate testing for HIV.

    e. for infectious diseases.

11. What is the purpose of E-codes?

    a. They code for immunizations and other preventive procedures.

    b. They are used to code medical testing before a diagnosis.

    c. They assist insurance companies in making reimbursements.

    d. They indicate why a patient has an injury or poisoning.

    e. They indicate if a procedure was inpatient or outpatient.

12. Which of the following agencies are *least* interested in E-codes?

   a. Insurance underwriters

   b. Insurance claim providers

   c. National safety programs

   d. Public health agencies

   e. Workers' compensation lawyers

13. How is Volume 2 of the ICD-9-CM different from Volume 1?

   a. Volume 2 contains diagnostic terms that are not used in Volume 1.

   b. Volume 2 is organized into 17 chapters rather than 3 sections.

   c. Volume 2 does not contain E-codes, but Volume 1 does.

   d. Volume 2 contains hospital coding to cross-reference with Volume 1.

   e. Volume 2 provides information about the fourth and fifth digits of a code.

14. After finding a code in Volume 2, you should:

   a. record the code on the CMS-1500.

   b. consult Volume 3 for subordinate terms.

   c. cross-reference the code with Volume 1.

   d. indicate if the code is inpatient or outpatient.

   e. record the code on the UB-92.

15. Volume 3 of the ICD-9-CM is organized:

   a. by disease.

   b. by anatomy.

   c. into 17 chapters.

   d. into three sections.

   e. by surgical specialty.

16. One example of an eponym is:

   a. Crohn disease.

   b. bacterial meningitis.

   c. influenza virus.

   d. pruritus.

   e. pneumonia.

17. What is the first step to locating a diagnostic code?

   a. Determine where the diagnosis occurs in the body.

   b. Choose the main term within the diagnostic statement.

   c. Begin looking up the diagnosis in Volume 1 of the ICD-9-CM.

   d. Consult the CMS-1500 for reimbursement codes.

   e. Use Volume 3 of the ICD-9-CM to find the disease.

18. Which code is listed first on a CMS-1500?

   a. A reasonable second opinion

   b. Relevant laboratory work

   c. Diagnostic tests

   d. The symptoms of an illness

   e. The primary diagnosis

19. How do you code for late effects?

   a. Code for the treatment of the disease that causes late effects.

   b. Code for the disease that is causing the current condition.

   c. First code for the current condition, and then list the cause.

   d. Only code for the current condition.

   e. Only code for the cause of the current condition.

20. You should not code for a brain tumor:

   a. when the patient comes in for an MRI.

   b. after the tumor is confirmed on an MRI.

   c. when the diagnosed patient comes in for treatment.

   d. any time after the patient has been diagnosed.

   e. when the patient seeks specialist care.

Outpatient Procedural Coding

Chapter Checklist

☐ Read textbook chapter and take notes within the Chapter Notes outline. Answer the Learning Objectives as you reach them in the content, and then check them off.

☐ Work the Content Review questions—both Foundational Knowledge and Application.

☐ Perform the Active Learning exercise(s).

☐ Complete Professional Journal entries.

☐ Complete Skill Practice Activity(s) using Competency Evaluation Forms and Work Products, when appropriate.

☐ Take the Chapter Self-Assessment Quiz.

☐ Insert all appropriate pages into your Portfolio.

Learning Objectives

1. Spell and define the key terms.
2. Explain the Healthcare Common Procedure Coding System (HCPCS), levels I and II.
3. Explain the format of level I, Current Procedural Terminology (CPT-4) and its use.
4. Explain what diagnostic related groups (DRGs) are and how they are used to determine Medicare payments.
5. Discuss the goals of resource-based relative value system (RBRVS).
6. Describe the relationship between coding and reimbursement.

Chapter Notes

Note: Bold-faced headings are the major headings in the text chapter; headings in regular font are lower-level headings (i.e., the content is subordinate to, or falls "under," the major headings). Make sure you understand the key terms used in the chapter, as well as the concepts presented as Key Points.

TEXT SUBHEADINGS **NOTES**

Introduction _____

_____

☐ **LEARNING OBJECTIVE 1:** Spell and define the key terms.

Health Care Procedural Coding System _____

Key Term: Healthcare Common Procedure Coding System

☐ **LEARNING OBJECTIVE 2:** Explain the Healthcare Common Procedure Coding System (HCPCS), levels I and II.

Physician's Current Procedural Terminology (CPT) _____

Key Term: Current Procedural Terminology
Key Point:
• HCPCS level I codes or the Physician's **Current Procedural Terminology (CPT)** is a comprehensive listing of medical terms and codes for the uniform coding of procedures and services provided by physicians.

Performing Procedural Coding _____

Key Term: procedure

The Layout of CPT-4 _____

The Alphabetic Index _____

Reading Descriptors _____

Key Term: descriptor

Place of Service _____

Section Guidelines _____

Unlisted Procedures and Special Reports _____

_____

☐ **LEARNING OBJECTIVE 3:** Explain the format of level I, Current Procedural Terminology (CPT-4) and its use.

Evaluation and Management Codes _____

_____

Key Point:
- E/M codes describe various patient histories, examinations, and decisions physicians must make in evaluating and treating patients in various settings (e.g., office, outpatient, hospital).

Key Components _____

_____

Key Term: key components
Key Point:
- History, physical examination, and medical decision making are three **key components** for a visit.

History _____

_____

_____

Examination _____

_____

_____

Medical Decision Making _____

_____

_____

Time _____

_____

Key Point:
- When time spent with the patient is more than 50% of the typical time for the visit, time becomes the deciding factor in choosing an E/M code.

Other Categories of Evaluation and Management Codes _____

_____

_____

Anesthesia Section _____

_____

Key Term: modifiers

Surgery Section _____

_____

Content of the Surgery Section _____

_____

Radiology Section _____

_____

Pathology and Laboratory Section _____

_____

Medicine Section _____

_____

CPT-4 Modifiers _____

_____

Key Point:
• Failure to use an appropriate modifier causes database and reimbursement errors.

Reimbursement _____

_____

Diagnostic Related Groups _____

_____

Key Terms: diagnostic related groups; outlier
Key Point:
• **Diagnostic related groups** (DRGs) are categories into which inpatients are placed according to the similarity of their diagnoses, treatment, and length of hospital stay.

☐ **LEARNING OBJECTIVE 4:** Explain what diagnostic related groups (DRGs) are and how they are used to determine Medicare payments.

Resource-Based Relative Value Scale _____

Key Term: resource-based relative value scale
Key Point:
- The goal of RBRVS is to reduce Medicare Part B costs and to establish national standards for payment based on CPT-4 codes.

☐ **LEARNING OBJECTIVE 5:** Discuss the goals of resource-based relative value system (RBRVS).

Fraud and Coding _____

Key Term: upcoding

☐ **LEARNING OBJECTIVE 6:** Describe the relationship between coding and reimbursement.

Content Review

FOUNDATIONAL KNOWLEDGE

Understanding the CPT-4

1. Fill in the chart below to show the difference between Level I HPCS and Level II.

Level I	Level II

2. What are the six major sections of the CPT-4?

a. _____

b. _____

c. _____

d. _____

e. _____

f. _____

3. How is the CPT alphabetic index used in the medical office?

_____

_____

Understanding E/M Codes

4. Define the seven components of the E/M codes.

Component	Definition
a. history	
b. physician examination	
c. medical decision making	
d. counseling	
e. coordination of care	
f. nature of presenting problem	
g. time	

5. How many numbers do E/M codes have?

    a. Two

    b. Five

    c. Seven

    d. Ten

6. Read the scenario below. Then, highlight or underline the medical decision making section.

Anikka was seen today for a follow-up on her broken wrist. The cast was removed 2 weeks ago, and she said she is still unable to achieve full range of movement in her wrist without pain. On exam, her wrist appeared swollen, and she mentioned tenderness. X-ray revealed slight fracture in carpals. Dr. Levy splinted the wrist, and referred her to an orthopedic surgeon for possible surgery. I spoke with Anikka, instructing her to avoid exerting her wrist and to keep it splinted until she has seen the surgeon. Dr. Levy suggested aspirin for pain.

7. Now, read the same scenario again. Then, highlight or underline the history section.

Anikka was seen today for a follow-up on her broken wrist. The cast was removed 2 weeks ago, and she said she is still unable to achieve full range of movement in her wrist without pain. On exam, her wrist appeared swollen, and she mentioned tenderness. X-ray revealed slight fracture in carpals. Dr. Levy splinted the wrist, and referred her to an orthopedic surgeon for possible surgery. I spoke with Anikka, instructing her to avoid exerting her wrist and to keep it splinted until she has seen the surgeon. Dr. Levy suggested aspirin for pain.

8. Read the scenario below.

Mr. Ekko presents today for removal of stitches from calf wound. Upon inspection, wound seems to have healed well, but scar tissue is still slightly inflamed. I prescribed antibacterial cream for him to apply twice a day, and instructed him to still keep the area bandaged. I told him to let us know if the swelling has not gone down within a week, and to come in if it gets any worse.

Circle the correct level of medical decision making involved.

Straightforward   Low complexity

Moderate complexity   High complexity

9. Why is it important to check the constitution of a surgery package with a third-party payer?

_____

_____

10. A patient experiences complications after an appendectomy and has to be hospitalized for several days. Will the time spent in the hospital be coded as part of a surgery package or separately?

_____

_____

11. Fill in the medical terminology chart below about the CPT subcategory on repair, revision, or reconstruction.

Suffix	Meaning
-pexy	
	surgical repair
-rrhaphy	

12. Name four factors that go into radiology coding.

a. _____

b. _____

c. _____

d. _____

13. What role do modifiers play in coding?

_____

_____

14. When would you use 99 as the first numbers in your modifier?

_____

_____

Reimbursement

15. What is the goal of the resource-based relative value scale (RBRVS)?

_____

_____

16. How does coding play a part in reimbursement?

_____

_____

17. What are DRGs, and how are they used to determine Medicare payments?

_____

_____

18. Medicare is often a target for upcoding and fraud. What can Medicare do to protect itself from this?

_____

_____

19. Match the following key terms to their definitions.

Key Terms	Definitions
a. Current Procedural Terminology _____	1. a patient whose hospital stay is longer than amount allowed by the DRG
b. descriptor _____	2. categories used to determine hospital and physician reimbursement for Medicare patients' inpatient services

c. Diagnostic Related Group _____

d. Health Care Common Procedure Coding System _____

e. key component _____

f. modifiers _____

g. outlier _____

h. procedure _____

i. Resource-Based Relative Value Scale _____

j. upcoding _____

3. a value scale designed to decrease Medicare Part B costs and establish national standards for coding and payment

4. billing more than the proper fee for a service by selecting a code that is higher on the coding scale

5. description of a service listed with its code number

6. numbers or letters added to a code to clarify the service or procedure provided

7. a comprehensive listing of medical terms and codes for the uniform coding of procedures and services that are provided by physicians

8. a medical service or test that is coded for reimbursement

9. a standardized coding system that is used primarily to identify products, supplies, and services

10. the criteria or factors on which the selection of CPT-4 evaluation and management is based

20. Assign the appropriate CPT code for the following:

a. occult blood in stool, two simultaneous guaiac tests

b. blood ethanol levels

c. transurethral resection of prostate

d. flexible sigmoidoscopy for biopsy

e. radiation therapy requiring general anesthesia

f. hair transplant, 21 punch grafts

g. breast reduction, left

h. open repair of left Dupuytren's contracture

i. partial removal left turbinate

j. newborn clamp circumcision

21. True or False? Determine whether the following statements are true or false. If false, explain why.

a. It is permissible to leave out modifiers if a note is made on the patient's sheet.

_____

_____

b. When time spent with a patient is more than 50% of the typical time for the visit, time becomes the deciding factor in choosing a code.

_____

_____

c. The number of tests you perform is the final number in the coding.

_____

_____

d. The amount of time a physician spends with a patient has no effect on the coding for that exam.

_____

_____

APPLICATION

Critical Thinking Practice

1. A patient undergoes surgery to remove her gallbladder, and she needs to stay in the hospital overnight. Her insurance company labels this sort of operation as an outpatient surgery. What can you do to code this information on the claim form?

_____

_____

2. What are some ways to reduce the likelihood of a Medicare audit of your office?

_____

_____

Patient Education

1. A patient has a recurring skin rash, and the physician suggests that she see a dermatologist. The patient doesn't understand the difference between a referral and a consultation. How would you explain this to her?

_____

_____

Documentation

1. An 18-year-old patient visits a gynecologist for the first time. She needs a Pap smear and a breast examination, as well as consultation regarding contraceptives. Write a detailed note in her chart that can be used for coding purposes.

_____

_____

Active Learning

1. Read the scenario below.

A young teen comes in for a routine check. He is weighed and measured, and blood is drawn for diagnosis. The physician comes in and spends approximately 15 minutes of a 25-minute visit discussing how the teen recently became a vegetarian. The physician offers advice on ways to supplement his diet to keep him healthy. Blood tests come back with a low iron count, so the physician prescribes iron tablets.

Look online or go through a HCPCS book to find the correct coding for the teen's chart. Be sure to get all the information on his chart, but avoid upcoding and adding modifiers for services not mentioned.

2. Create five different medical scenarios that would require coding, and write them down on a sheet of paper. Then, after you have coded each scenario on a separate piece of paper, switch with a partner. When you are both done, compare notes. Check for any discrepancies between your answers by going through an HCPCS book.

3. It is important to familiarize yourself with the code book so that when you are coding for billing, you know how and where to search for a specific code. Using a copy of both the CPT-4 book and the ICD-9-CM book, flip through and find codes for common office procedures such as taking blood samples, testing reflexes, counseling, and testing blood pressure. Then, look through and make a list of codes for a less common task, like mole removal or splinting a fractured ankle. Be sure to list the steps you took to find your code (e.g., looking up *splint, fractures, ankle*). Also make a note of what types of codes you would use from the ICD-9 book, and jot down a few codes you might be likely to use.

Professional Journal

REFLECT

(Prompts and Ideas: Sometimes upcoding is accidental; however, many times this is not the case. What would motivate someone to upcode deliberately? How can it happen accidentally?)

_____

_____

_____

PONDER AND SOLVE

1. For 20 minutes of a 30-minute exam, the physician was talking with the patient. Most of this time was spent talking about getting more exercise and keeping in shape; however, almost ten minutes of the time was spent discussing non-health-related issues. The physician marked the patient's chart as having talked for 20 minutes. How would you code this? Do you still write in 20 minutes, because they were talking, or do you code it as 10 minutes, which is the amount of time they talked about health-related things? Why?

_____

_____

_____

_____

_____

_____

2. A patient complains that she is getting charged too much, and you check over her chart. You find that the physician has been up-coding regularly on this patient's chart. How do you react to this situation? How do you deal with the patient, and how would you confront the physician?

_____

_____

_____

_____

_____

_____

_____

EXPERIENCE

Skills related to this chapter include:

1. Locating a CPT Code (Procedure 15-1).

   Record any common mistakes, lessons learned, and/or tips you discovered during your experience of practicing and demonstrating these skills:

_____

_____

_____

_____

_____

_____

_____

Skill Practice

PERFORMANCE OBJECTIVES:

1. Perform procedural coding (Procedure 15-1).

Name _____ Date _____ Time _____

Procedure 15-1:	**LOCATING A CPT CODE**

EQUIPMENT: CPT-4 code book, patient chart, scenario

STANDARDS: Given the needed equipment and a place to work the student will perform this skill with _____% accuracy in a total of _____ minutes. (*Your instructor will tell you what the percentage and time limits will be before you begin.*)

KEY: 4 = Satisfactory   0 = Unsatisfactory   NA = This step is not counted

PROCEDURE STEPS	SELF	PARTNER	INSTRUCTOR
1. Identify the exact procedure performed.	☐	☐	☐
2. Obtain the documentation of the procedure in the patient's chart.	☐	☐	☐
3. Choose the proper code book.	☐	☐	☐
4. Using the alphabetic index, locate the procedure.	☐	☐	☐
5. Locate the code or range of codes given in the tabular section.	☐	☐	☐
6. Read the descriptors to find the one that most closely describes the procedure.	☐	☐	☐
7. Check the section guidelines for any special circumstances.	☐	☐	☐
8. Review the documentation to be sure it justifies the code.	☐	☐	☐
9. Determine if any modifiers are needed.	☐	☐	☐
10. Select the code and place it in the appropriate field of the CMS-1500 form.	☐	☐	☐

CALCULATION

Total Possible Points: _____
Total Points Earned: _____ Multiplied by 100 = _____ Divided by Total Possible Points = _____%

Pass   **Fail**
☐   ☐   Comments:

Student's signature _____ Date _____
Partner's signature _____ Date _____
Instructor's signature _____ Date _____

Work Product 1

Perform procedural coding.

Kayla Tawes, age 38, has just completed a general physical. Her examination consisted of the following:

- an EKG to monitor a previously diagnosed arrhythmia
- urine collection to test for diabetes
- blood sampling to test cholesterol levels

Because Ms. Tawes is a breast cancer survivor, in addition to the routine examination, she was given a mammogram. Her physician prescribed a tetanus booster as well, because she has been renovating an old stable and has suffered several small skin punctures over the past few weeks.

Complete the CMS-1500 form with the proper procedural coding for the patient's visit. Use the same personal patient information you used for Work Product 1 in Chapter 14 to fill in all essential details when completing the CMS-1500.

PLEASE
DO NOT
STAPLE
IN THIS
AREA

CARRIER →

| | PICA | | **HEALTH INSURANCE CLAIM FORM** | PICA | |

1. MEDICARE   MEDICAID   CHAMPUS   CHAMPVA   GROUP HEALTH PLAN   FECA BLK LUNG   OTHER
   (Medicare #)   (Medicaid #)   (Sponsor's SSN)   (VA File #)   (SSN or ID)   (SSN)   (ID)

1a. INSURED'S I.D. NUMBER   (FOR PROGRAM IN ITEM 1)

2. PATIENT'S NAME (Last Name, First Name, Middle Initial)

3. PATIENT'S BIRTH DATE   MM   DD   YY   **SEX**   M   F

4. INSURED'S NAME (Last Name, First Name, Middle Initial)

5. PATIENT'S ADDRESS (No., Street)

6. PATIENT RELATIONSHIP TO INSURED   Self   Spouse   Child   Other

7. INSURED'S ADDRESS (No., Street)

CITY   STATE

8. PATIENT STATUS   Single   Married   Other

CITY   STATE

ZIP CODE   TELEPHONE (Include Area Code)   ( )

Employed   Full-Time Student   Part-Time Student

ZIP CODE   TELEPHONE (INCLUDE AREA CODE)   ( )

9. OTHER INSURED'S NAME (Last Name, First Name, Middle Initial)

10. IS PATIENT'S CONDITION RELATED TO:

11. INSURED'S POLICY GROUP OR FECA NUMBER

a. OTHER INSURED'S POLICY OR GROUP NUMBER

a. EMPLOYMENT? (CURRENT OR PREVIOUS)   YES   NO

a. INSURED'S DATE OF BIRTH   MM   DD   YY   **SEX**   M   F

b. OTHER INSURED'S DATE OF BIRTH   MM   DD   YY   **SEX**   M   F

b. AUTO ACCIDENT?   PLACE (State)   YES   NO

b. EMPLOYER'S NAME OR SCHOOL NAME

c. EMPLOYER'S NAME OR SCHOOL NAME

c. OTHER ACCIDENT?   YES   NO

c. INSURANCE PLAN NAME OR PROGRAM NAME

d. INSURANCE PLAN NAME OR PROGRAM NAME

10d. RESERVED FOR LOCAL USE

d. IS THERE ANOTHER HEALTH BENEFIT PLAN?   YES   NO   *If yes*, return to and complete item 9 a-d.

READ BACK OF FORM BEFORE COMPLETING & SIGNING THIS FORM.
12. PATIENT'S OR AUTHORIZED PERSON'S SIGNATURE I authorize the release of any medical or other information necessary to process this claim. I also request payment of government benefits either to myself or to the party who accepts assignment below.

SIGNED _____ DATE _____

13. INSURED'S OR AUTHORIZED PERSON'S SIGNATURE I authorize payment of medical benefits to the undersigned physician or supplier for services described below.

SIGNED _____

14. DATE OF CURRENT: MM DD YY   ILLNESS (First symptom) OR INJURY (Accident) OR PREGNANCY(LMP)

15. IF PATIENT HAS HAD SAME OR SIMILAR ILLNESS. GIVE FIRST DATE MM DD YY

16. DATES PATIENT UNABLE TO WORK IN CURRENT OCCUPATION FROM MM DD YY TO MM DD YY

17. NAME OF REFERRING PHYSICIAN OR OTHER SOURCE

17a. I.D. NUMBER OF REFERRING PHYSICIAN

18. HOSPITALIZATION DATES RELATED TO CURRENT SERVICES FROM MM DD YY TO MM DD YY

19. RESERVED FOR LOCAL USE

20. OUTSIDE LAB?   YES   NO $ CHARGES

21. DIAGNOSIS OR NATURE OF ILLNESS OR INJURY. (RELATE ITEMS 1,2,3 OR 4 TO ITEM 24E BY LINE)

1. ____.____   3. ____.____
2. ____.____   4. ____.____

22. MEDICAID RESUBMISSION CODE   ORIGINAL REF. NO.

23. PRIOR AUTHORIZATION NUMBER

24. A DATE(S) OF SERVICE						B Place of Service	C Type of Service	D PROCEDURES, SERVICES, OR SUPPLIES (Explain Unusual Circumstances) CPT/HCPCS MODIFIER	E DIAGNOSIS CODE	F $ CHARGES	G DAYS OR UNITS	H EPSDT Family Plan	I EMG	J COB	K RESERVED FOR LOCAL USE
From MM	DD	YY	To MM	DD	YY										
1															
2															
3															
4															
5															
6															

25. FEDERAL TAX I.D. NUMBER   SSN EIN

26. PATIENT'S ACCOUNT NO.

27. ACCEPT ASSIGNMENT? (For govt. claims, see back)   YES   NO

28. TOTAL CHARGE $

29. AMOUNT PAID $

30. BALANCE DUE $

31. SIGNATURE OF PHYSICIAN OR SUPPLIER INCLUDING DEGREES OR CREDENTIALS (I certify that the statements on the reverse apply to this bill and are made a part thereof.)

SIGNED _____ DATE _____

32. NAME AND ADDRESS OF FACILITY WHERE SERVICES WERE RENDERED (If other than home or office)

33. PHYSICIAN'S, SUPPLIER'S BILLING NAME, ADDRESS, ZIP CODE & PHONE #

PIN#   GRP#

PATIENT AND INSURED INFORMATION

PHYSICIAN OR SUPPLIER INFORMATION

(APPROVED BY AMA COUNCIL ON MEDICAL SERVICE 8/88)   **PLEASE PRINT OR TYPE**   APPROVED OMB-0938-0008 FORM CMS-1500 (12-90), FORM RRB-1500, APPROVED OMB-1215-0055 FORM OWCP-1500, APPROVED OMB-0720-0001 (CHAMPUS)

1. In the case of an unlisted code, the medical assistant should:

   a. notify the AMA so that a new code is issued.

   b. submit a copy of the procedure report with the claim.

   c. obtain authorization from the AMA to proceed with the procedure.

   d. include the code that fits the most and add a note to explain the differences.

   e. not charge the patient for the procedure.

2. Which kind of information appears in a special report?

   a. Type of medicine prescribed

   b. Patient history

   c. Allergic reactions

   d. Possible procedural risks

   e. Equipment necessary for the treatment

3. On a medical record, the key components contained in E/M codes indicate:

   a. the scope and result of a medical visit.

   b. the duties of a physician toward his patients.

   c. the definition and description of a performed procedure.

   d. the services that a medical assistant may perform.

   e. the charges that are owed to the insurance company.

4. Time becomes a key component in a medical record when:

   a. the visit lasts more than one hour.

   b. more than half of the visit is spent counseling.

   c. the physician decides for a series of regular visits.

   d. the visit lasts longer than it was initially established.

   e. the patient is constantly late for his or her appointments.

5. When assigning a level of medical decision making, you should consider the:

   a. medication the patient is on.

   b. available coding for the procedure.

   c. patient's symptoms during the visit.

   d. insurance coverage allowed to the patient.

   e. patient's medical history.

6. In the anesthesia section, the physical status modifier indicates the patient's:

   a. medical history.

   b. conditions after surgery.

   c. good health before surgery.

   d. reactions to past anesthesia.

   e. condition prior to the administration of anesthesia.

7. Which of the following is included in a surgical package?

   a. General anesthesia

   b. Hospitalization time

   c. Complications related to the surgery

   d. Prescriptions given after the operation

   e. Uncomplicated follow-up care

8. How are procedures organized in the subsections of the surgery section of the CPT-4?

   a. By invasiveness

   b. By location and type

   c. In alphabetical order

   d. In order of difficulty of procedure

   e. By average recurrence of procedure

9. Which is the first digit that appears on radiology codes?

   a. 1

   b. 6

   c. 7

   d. 8

   e. 9

10. Diagnostic related groups (DRGs) are a group of:

   a. codes pertaining to one particular treatment.

   b. inpatients sharing a similar medical history.

   c. modifiers attached to a single procedural form.

   d. physicians agreeing on a procedure for a particular medical condition.

   e. inpatients sharing similar diagnoses, treatment, and length of hospital stay.

11. The resource-based relative value scale (RBRVS) gives information on the:

    a. difficulty level of a particular surgical operation.

    b. maximum fee that physicians can charge for a procedure.

    c. reimbursement given to physicians for Medicare services.

    d. average fee asked by physicians for emergency procedures.

    e. mminimum amount of time the physician should spend with a patient.

12. The Medicare allowed charge is calculated by:

    a. adding the RVU and the national conversion factor.

    b. dividing the RVU by the national conversion factor.

    c. multiplying the RVU by the national conversion factor.

    d. subtracting the RVU from the national conversion factor.

    e. finding the average between the RVU and the national conversion factor.

13. Upcoding is:

    a. billing more than the proper fee for a service.

    b. correcting an erroneous code in medical records.

    c. auditing claims retroactively for suspected fraud.

    d. comparing the documentation in the record with the codes received.

    e. researching new codes online.

14. Who has jurisdiction over a fraudulent medical practice?

    a. CMS

    b. AMA

    c. Medicare

    d. U.S. Attorney General

    e. State's supreme court

15. The purpose of the Level II HCPCS codes is to:

    a. decode different types of code modifiers.

    b. attribute a code to every step of a medical procedure.

    c. list the practices eligible for reimbursement by Medicare.

    d. identify services, supplies, and equipment not identified by CPT codes.

    e. provide coding information for various types of anesthesia.

16. Which of these sections is included in the HCPCS Level I code listing?

    a. Orthotics

    b. Injections

    c. Vision care

    d. Dental services

    e. Pathology and laboratory

17. How is a consultation different from a referral?

    a. A consultation is needed when the patient wants to change physicians.

    b. A consultation is needed when the physician asks for the opinion of another provider.

    c. A consultation is needed when the patient is transferred to another physician for treatment.

    d. A consultation is needed when the physician needs a team of doctors to carry out a procedure.

    e. A consultation is needed before the physician can submit insurance claims.

18. Which of the following is contained in Appendix B in the CPT-4?

    a. Legislation against medical fraud

    b. Detailed explanation of the modifiers

    c. Revisions made since the last editions

    d. Explanation on how to file for reimbursement

    e. Examples concerning the Evaluation and Management sections

19. Drug screening is considered quantitative when checking:

    a. for the amount of illegal drugs in the blood.

    b. for the presence of illegal drugs in the blood.

    c. for the proper level of therapeutic drug in the blood.

    d. that the therapeutic drug is not interacting with other medications.

    e. that the drug is not causing an allergic reaction.

20. Which place requires the use of an emergency department service code?

    a. Private clinic

    b. Nursing home

    c. Physician's office

    d. 24-hour pharmacy

    e. Mental health center

PART

III

Career
Strategies

Competing in the Job Market

Making the Transition: Student to Employee

Chapter Checklist

- ☐ Read textbook chapter and take notes within the Chapter Notes outline. Answer the Learning Objectives as you reach them in the content, and then check them off.
- ☐ Work the Content Review questions—both Foundational Knowledge and Application.
- ☐ Perform the Active Learning exercise(s).

- ☐ Complete Professional Journal entries.
- ☐ Complete Skill Practice Activity(s) using Competency Evaluation Forms and Work Products, when appropriate.
- ☐ Take the Chapter Self-Assessment Quiz.
- ☐ Insert all appropriate pages into your Portfolio.

Learning Objectives

1. Spell and define the key terms.
2. Explain the purpose of the externship experience.
3. List your professional responsibilities during externship.
4. List personal and professional attributes necessary to ensure a successful externship.
5. Understand the importance of the evaluation process.
6. Determine your best career direction based on your skills and strengths.
7. Identify the steps necessary to apply for the right position and be able to accomplish those steps.

8. Draft an appropriate cover letter.
9. List the steps and guidelines in completing an employment application.
10. List guidelines for an effective interview that will lead to employment.
11. Identify the steps that you need to take to ensure proper career advancement.
12. Explain the process for recertification of a medical assisting credential.
13. Describe the importance of membership in a professional organization.

Chapter Notes

Note: Bold-faced headings are the major headings in the text chapter; headings in regular font are lower-level headings (i.e., the content is subordinate to, or falls "under," the major headings). Make sure you understand the key terms used in the chapter, as well as the concepts presented as Key Points.

TEXT SUBHEADINGS   **NOTES**

Introduction _____

_____

☐ **LEARNING OBJECTIVE 1:** Spell and define the key terms.

Externships _____

_____

Key Term: externship
Key Point:
- An **externship** is a training program that gives you the experience of working in a professional medical office under the supervision of a preceptor or supervisor who will help you to apply the theories and procedures you learned during classroom training.

☐ **LEARNING OBJECTIVE 2:** Explain the purpose of the externship experience.

Types of Facilities _____

_____

Key Point:
- As a medical assisting student, you will experience an extensive scope of procedures during an externship in a general or family practice clinic or office.

Extern Sites _____

_____

Key Term: preceptor
Key Point:
- An ideal site should provide a variety of experiences, both in administrative (front office) and clinical (back office) procedures.

Externship Benefits _____

_____

Benefits to the Student _____

_____

_____

Benefits to the Medical Assisting Program _____

_____

Key Point:
• Medical assisting programs also rely on the medical profession to aid in updating and revising the curriculum and course content to ensure that the methods and procedures presented to the students from year to year are current.

Benefits to the Externship Site _____

_____

Externship Responsibilities _____

_____

_____

Responsibilities of the Student _____

_____

Key Points:
• You must be dependable.
• You must act in a professional manner.
• You must be well groomed and meet the program's dress code.

☐ **LEARNING OBJECTIVE 3:** List your professional responsibilities during externship.

Responsibilities of the Medical Assisting Program _____

_____

_____

Responsibilities of the Externship Site _____

_____

_____

Guidelines for a Successful Externship _____

_____

_____

Procedural Performance _____

_____

Key Point:
• You will be judged on your ability to measure up to the standard of care for an entry-level medical assistant.

Preparedness _____

_____

_____

Attendance _____

_____

Key Point:
- If at any time you will be late or will not be able to attend the site for any reason, you must notify both the externship coordinator and the site preceptor.

Appearance _____

_____

Key Point:
- You have only one opportunity to make a first impression.

Attitude _____

_____

Key Points:
- Much attitude is determined by how well you handle change and direction and how adaptable and flexible you are during difficult assignments.
- Your attitude determines your altitude.

☐ **LEARNING OBJECTIVE 4:** List personal and professional attributes necessary to ensure a successful externship.

Externship Documentation _____

_____

Key Point:
- Most programs use a time sheet or record of some sort to document your hours in the externship.

Externship Evaluations _____

_____

_____

Graduate Surveys _____

_____

_____

Employer Surveys _____

_____

☐ **LEARNING OBJECTIVE 5:** Understand the importance of the evaluation process.

Establish the Job for You _____

Setting Employment Goals _____

Key Points:
- The best way to set a goal and eventually get what you want is to study your strengths and weaknesses and from that self-knowledge design the best job for you.
- To win the position you want, you have to learn to sell yourself.

Self-Analysis _____

☐ **LEARNING OBJECTIVE 6:** Determine your best career direction based on your skills and strengths.

Finding the Right Job _____

Key Term: networking
Key Point:
- Many studies show that most positions are never advertised in the media.

☐ **LEARNING OBJECTIVE 7:** Identify the steps necessary to apply for the right position and be able to accomplish those steps.

Applying for the Job _____

Answering Newspaper Advertisements _____

Preparing Your Résumé _____

Key Term: résumé
Key Point:
- When you have chosen the people you want to use as references, be sure to ask their permission.

Preparing Your Cover Letter _____

☐ **LEARNING OBJECTIVE 8:** Draft an appropriate cover letter.

Completing an Employment Application _____

☐ **LEARNING OBJECTIVE 9:** List the steps and guidelines in completing an employment application.

The Interview _____

Preparing for the Interview _____

Key Term: portfolio

Crucial Interview Questions _____

Follow-Up _____

☐ **LEARNING OBJECTIVE 10:** List guidelines for an effective interview that will lead to employment.

Leaving a Job _____

Be a Lifelong Learner _____

☐ **LEARNING OBJECTIVE 11:** Identify the steps that you need to take to ensure proper career advancement.

Recertification _____

☐ **LEARNING OBJECTIVE 12:** Explain the process for recertification of a medical assisting credential.

Professionalism _____

_____

☐ **LEARNING OBJECTIVE 13:** Describe the importance of membership in a professional organization.

Content Review

FOUNDATIONAL KNOWLEDGE

Externship Basics

1. What is the purpose of an externship?

_____

_____

2. Fill in the table to show the difference between primary care providers and general practice facilities.

Primary Care Provider	General Practice Facility

3. How will the site preceptor assist you in your externship?

_____

_____

4. List three responsibilities you will have during an externship.

a. _____

b. _____

c. _____

5. Your externship preceptor has said that you cannot receive permission to draw blood and perform other phlebotomy procedures. However, you know this is an area that you need to learn more about in a practical setting. How can you learn more about these procedures at your externship site if you cannot perform them yourself?

_____

_____

6. Preparation is Key

Personal preparation for your externship will save you many headaches once your experience is underway. What are the four main ways you can prepare yourself for your externship?

a. _____

b. _____

c. _____

d. _____

7. Appearance Matters

Review the descriptions below to see what three students wore on the first day of their medical assisting externships. Then decide if the student is dressed appropriately or inappropriately. If the student is dressed inappropriately, explain what changes you would recommend.

a. Marsha wore burgundy and navy scrubs along with a set of bangle bracelets, her favorite gemstone rings, and a pair of comfortable flip-flops.

_____

b. Lloyd also wore the required scrubs with a pair of clean white sneakers. His long dreadlocks were brushed away from his face and placed in a neat ponytail above his shoulders.

_____

c. Barry wore the required uniform and a pair of dark walking shoes. He even had his hairstylist color the tips of his spiked mohawk hair burgundy to match.

_____

Evaluating Externships

8. Your school will likely request that you fill out an evaluation form to determine if your externship site was effective for training. This helps the school decide if it's a good site for future externships. Review the list of questions below and place a check in the "Yes" or "No" column to show if it is a question that you should consider when filling out your site evaluation form on your externship.

	Yes	No
a. Was the overall experience positive or negative?		
b. Was my preceptor fun to be around?		
c. Did the office have a good cafeteria or break room?		
d. Were opportunities for learning abundant and freely offered or hard to obtain?		
e. Was my preceptor flexible about taking personal time during the day for phone calls and breaks?		
f. Were staff personnel open and caring or unwelcoming?		
g. Was the preceptor available and easily approachable or preoccupied and distant?		

9. During your externship, you realize that you really enjoy and are passionate about caring for sick children. You also know that you would like to explore medical careers that require further training beyond your medical assisting program. As you seek employment, what factors would you consider based on these two facts about yourself? What long-term goals would you set? What steps would you take once on the job? What other factors would you consider as you plan for your future?

_____

_____

Landing the Job

10. List five traditional sources of information for job openings.

a. _____

b. _____

c. _____

d. _____

e. _____

11. Circle the items that should be included on a résumé.

contact information	race	relevant volunteer work	birth date
experience	picture of yourself	list of professional goals	education

Ready, Set, Action!

12. Choose a more accurate action word from the box to replace the words in bold.

Action Words

generates	ensures	implement and maintain	interviews	records	articulates
draw and collect	prepares	selects	measures	assists	composes

a. **Helps** in examination and treatment of patients under the direction of a physician. _____

b. **Talks to** patients, **takes** vital signs (i.e., pulse rate, temperature, blood pressure, weight, and height), and **writes** information on patients' charts. _____

c. **Get** blood samples from patients and prepare specimens for laboratory analysis. _____

d. **Set up** treatment rooms for examination of patients. _____

Acing the Interview

13. Fill in the chart to explain what information you should include in the first, second, and third paragraphs of your cover letter.

a. First Paragraph	
b. Second Paragraph	
c. Third Paragraph	

14. Read each of the following tips for completing a job application. Place a check mark in the "Good Idea" column if the statement is a good idea, or rule, to follow when completing an application. Place a check mark in the "Bad Idea" column if the statement is not a good idea.

Best Practices for Completing an Application	Good Idea	Bad Idea
a. Read through application completely before beginning.		
b. Follow the instructions exactly.		
c. In the line for wage or salary desired, write highest pay possible.		
d. Answer every question. If the question does not apply to you, draw a line or write "N/A" so that the interviewer will know that you did not overlook the question.		
e. Use your best cursive writing.		
f. Highlight important information in red ink.		
g. Ask for two applications. Use the first one for practice.		

If you checked "Bad Idea" for any of the above, write the number and explain why.

_____

_____

15. Read the questions in the box. If you should ask them during an interview, place a check in the "Yes" column; if not, place a check in the "No" column.

Questions to Ask	Yes	No
a. What are the responsibilities of the position offered?		
b. What is the benefit package? Is there access to a 401(k) plan or other retirement plan? Health insurance? Life insurance?		
c. Is it acceptable to take three weeks off during the holiday season?		
d. How does the facility feel about continuing education? Is time off offered to employees to upgrade their skills? Does the facility subsidize the expense?		
e. Do I have to work with physicians who have bad attitudes?		
f. How many potlucks and happy hours does this office usually have?		
g. Is there a job performance or evaluation process?		

16. Explain what it means to be a lifelong learner.

_____

_____

17. How can you prepare for the process of recertification?

_____

_____

18. List two professional organizations to research and join while you are a student.

a. _____

b. _____

19. Match the following key terms to their definitions.

Key Terms	Definitions
a. externship _____	**1.** a teacher; one who gives direction, as in a technical matter
b. networking _____	**2.** an educational course that allows the student to obtain hands-on experience
c. portfolio _____	**3.** a system of personal and professional relationships through which to share information
d. preceptor _____	**4.** a document summarizing an individual's work experience or professional qualifications
e. résumé _____	**5.** a portable case containing documents

20. True or False? Determine whether the following statements are true or false. If false, explain why.

a. When you see dangerous practices, it is usually best to confront the employees first.

_____

_____

b. An Internet search is the best way to search for a job.

_____

_____

c. Include hobbies and personal interests on your résumé.

_____

_____

d. Write a long and detailed cover letter.

_____

_____

APPLICATION

Critical Thinking Practice

1. During an interview, you are asked to explain why your grades were low last semester. How would you answer this question honestly while still speaking about yourself fairly and objectively?

_____

_____

2. There are multiple gaps in your work history and your interviewer asks you to explain. One of the gaps is from relocation and other gaps are from taking time off to evaluate what you wanted to be doing. How would you explain this to your interviewer?

_____

_____

Patient Education

1. While working as an extern at a family care provider, you encounter an elderly patient who is uncomfortable with the fact that you as a student are participating in her care. What would you say to help her feel more comfortable?

_____

_____

Documentation

1. Your school would like to update its form to evaluate the externship experience for students. Make a list of 10 questions that should be included in this evaluation form to determine if it is a strong placement.

_____

_____

Active Learning

1. Write a list of your strengths and weaknesses as discussed in the chapter. Critically evaluate what you are able to contribute to the job and address your weaknesses. How can you work with these weaknesses to make them strengths? Now evaluate what kind of medical assisting job would best work with what you are already good at and how you would like to continue to grow in your professional development. Identify for yourself what type of job would be ideal for you.

2. Look for your ideal job in the newspaper, through an employment office, temping service, etc. Search carefully throughout your field noting what is available and what the current job market is like. Now write a résumé that is tailored to your ideal job. Write a cover letter and assemble your portfolio. Apply for this job when you are ready!

3. Practice interviewing with a fellow student. Make sure that you take turns asking questions so that you can both get to experience being on each side of the interview.

Professional Journal

REFLECT

(Prompts and Ideas: Are you nervous about job interviews? How can you calm yourself and gain the confidence that you need to answer the questions? What are you most looking forward to in your health care career?)

_____

_____

_____

_____

_____

_____

_____

PONDER AND SOLVE

1. You happen to know that dozens of other people have interviewed for the same position as you. You are nervous because this job is very important to you. Your interview has been going amazingly well despite your inner nervousness, and your interviewer asks you why she should hire you for this job. She asks why you would be the best person. You take a couple of seconds to consider these questions and then respond. What do you say?

_____

_____

_____

_____

_____

_____

_____

2. You have been completing an externship at an obstetric clinic. You have really enjoyed all of the new experience and knowledge that you have acquired with this externship. However, you also feel that there were some inner workings at the office that required better management and more professionalism. When, where, and how would you communicate these observations?

_____

_____

_____

_____

_____

_____

_____

EXPERIENCE

1. Writing a Résumé (Procedure 16-1).

Record any common mistakes, lessons learned, and/or tips you discovered during your experience of practicing and demonstrating these skills:

_____

_____

_____

_____

_____

_____

_____

Skill Practice

PERFORMANCE OBJECTIVES:

1. Write a résumé to properly communicate skills and strengths (Procedure 16-1).

Name _____ Date _____ Time _____

Procedure 16-1: WRITING A RÉSUMÉ

EQUIPMENT/SUPPLIES: Word processor, paper, personal information

STANDARDS: Given the needed equipment and a place to work, the student will perform this skill with _____% accuracy in a total of _____ minutes. *(Your instructor will tell you what the percentage and time limits will be before you begin practicing.)*

KEY: 4 = Satisfactory   0 = Unsatisfactory   NA = This step is not counted

PROCEDURE STEPS	SELF	PARTNER	INSTRUCTOR
1. At the top of the page, center your name, address, and phone numbers.	☐	☐	☐
2. List your education starting with the most current and working back. List graduation dates and areas of study. It is not necessary to go all the way back to elementary school.	☐	☐	☐
3. Using the chronological format, list your prior related work experience with dates, responsibilities, company, and supervisor's name.	☐	☐	☐
4. List any volunteer work with dates and places.	☐	☐	☐
5. List skills you possess including those acquired in your program and on your externship.	☐	☐	☐
6. List any certifications or awards received.	☐	☐	☐
7. List any information relevant to a certain position. Example: competence in spreadsheet applications for a job in a patient billing department.	☐	☐	☐
8. After obtaining permission and/or notifying the people, prepare a list of references with their addresses and phone contact information.	☐	☐	☐
9. Carefully proofread the resume for accuracy and typographical errors.	☐	☐	☐
10. Have someone else proofread the résumé for errors other than content.	☐	☐	☐
11. Print the résumé on high-quality paper.	☐	☐	☐

CALCULATION

Total Possible Points: _____
Total Points Earned: _____ Multiplied by 100 = _____ Divided by Total Possible Points = _____%

Pass   **Fail**
☐   ☐   Comments:

Student signature _____ Date _____
Partner signature _____ Date _____
Instructor signature _____ Date _____

1. Most externships range from:

  a. 160–240 hours a semester.

  b. 80–160 hours a semester.

  c. 200–240 hours a semester.

  d. 240–300 hours a semester.

  e. 260–300 hours a semester.

2. Preceptors are typically:

  a. physicians.

  b. nurses.

  c. graduate medical assistants.

  d. academic instructors.

  e. other students.

3. When responding to a newspaper advertisement, you should:

  a. mail your résumé and a portfolio.

  b. send your résumé by e-mail.

  c. phone right away to inquire about the job.

  d. follow the instructions in the advertisement.

  e. call to schedule an interview.

4. A CMA wishing to recertify must either retake the examination or complete:

  a. 60 hours of continuing education credits.

  b. 50 hours of continuing education credits.

  c. 100 hours of continuing education credits.

  d. 30 hours of continuing education credits.

  e. 75 hours of continuing education credits.

5. Two standard ways of listing experience on a résumé are:

  a. functional and chronological.

  b. functional and alphabetical.

  c. alphabetical and chronological.

  d. chronological and referential.

  e. referential and alphabetical.

6. During your externship, it is a good practice to arrive:

  a. a few minutes early.

  b. half an hour early.

  c. right on time.

  d. with enough time to beat traffic.

  e. as early as you can.

7. What is the appropriate length of a résumé?

  a. One page

  b. Two pages

  c. Three pages

  d. As long as it needs to be

  e. Check with the potential employer first

8. In addition to providing proof of general immunizations, what other vaccinations may be required before you begin your externship?

  a. Vaccination for strep throat

  b. Vaccination for cancer

  c. Vaccination for hepatitis B

  d. Vaccination for hepatitis C

  e. Vaccination for HIV

9. During your externship, you are expected to perform as:

  a. the student that you are; your preceptor will teach you the same skills as in the classroom.

  b. an experienced professional; your preceptor will expect you to perform every task perfectly.

  c. an entry-level employee; your preceptor will expect you to perform at the level of a new employee in the field.

  d. a patient; you have to see what it feels like to be on the receiving end of treatment.

  e. independently as possible; your preceptor will not have time to answer many questions.

10. Checking for telephone messages and arranging the day's appointments should be done:

  a. during your lunch break.

  b. at the close of the business day.

  c. after the office has opened.

  d. before the scheduled opening.

  e. between patients.

11. Fingernails should be kept short and clean to avoid:

  a. making your supervisor upset.

  b. accidentally scratching or harming a patient.

  c. transferring pathogens or ripping gloves.

  d. getting nail polish chips in lab samples.

  e. infecting sterile materials or surfaces.

12. Which document provides proof that tasks are performed and learning is taking place?

  a. Timesheet

  b. Journal

  c. Survey

  d. Evaluation

  e. Personal interview

13. Which document is used to improve performance and services offered to students?

  a. Timesheet

  b. Journal

  c. Survey

  d. Evaluation

  e. Personal interview

14. Membership in your professional allied health organization proves:

  a. that you are an allied health student.

  b. your level of professionalism and seriousness of purpose.

  c. that you will become a medical professional in two years.

  d. your willingness to network with other professionals.

  e. your interest in the medical field.

15. Which question should you avoid asking during an interview?

  a. Is there access to a 401(k) plan?

  b. Is tuition reimbursement available?

  c. How many weeks of vacation are available the first year?

  d. Are uniforms or lab coats worn?

  e. What are the responsibilities of this position?

16. If you decide to leave your job, it is a good idea to:

  a. tell your employer the day before you plan to leave.

  b. make sure your new job will pay more.

  c. get contact information for all of the new friends you made.

  d. finish all duties and tie up any loose ends.

  e. criticize employees during an exit interview.

17. If you are having a problem performing your assigned job duties, it is best to:

  a. volunteer for extra hours.

  b. inform your preceptor and instructor.

  c. ask for less challenging work.

  d. ask for a different externship site.

  e. switch your course of studies.

18. When anticipating calls from prospective employers, avoid:

  a. leaving silly or cute messages on your answering machine.

  b. telling family members or roommates that you are expecting important telephone calls.

  c. keeping a pen near the telephone at all times.

  d. checking messages on a regular basis.

  e. calling them every day after submitting your resume.

19. If bilingual applicants are encouraged to apply for a position you want, you should:

  a. learn simple greetings and act as if you can speak several languages.

  b. learn simple greetings and admit that you know a few words but are not fluent.

  c. do nothing; being bilingual is not important.

  d. avoid applying since you do not fluently speak another language.

  e. learn how to answer possible interview questions in two different languages.

20. Being a lifelong learner is a must for all medical professionals because:

  a. medical professionals have to recertify every five years.

  b. medical professionals are widely respected.

  c. changes in procedures, medical technologies, and legal issues occur frequently.

  d. changes in medical technologies are decreasing the need for medical professionals.

  e. medical professionals are required to change legal statutes once a year.